DON'T GIVE UP THE DAY JOB

DON'T GIVE UP THE DAY JOB

DES McKEOWN
WITH BILL LECKIE

MAINSTREAM
PUBLISHING

EDINBURGH AND LONDON

First published in Great Britain in 2001 by
MAINSTREAM PUBLISHING COMPANY (EDINBURGH) LTD
7 Albany Street
Edinburgh EH1 3UG

ISBN 1 84018 455 8

A catalogue record for this book is available
from the British Library

Typeset in Billboard and Times
Printed and bound in Great Britain by
Mackays of Chatham

FOREWORD

by Billy McNeill MBE

I'M ONE OF THE LUCKY ONES. I dreamed of playing football for a living and the dream came true. Better still, I got to play for my boyhood heroes – and, beyond my wildest fantasies, was captain the night we won the European Cup. I played for my country, travelled the world, met the rich and the famous. Football was good to me.

But I also know the flip side.

As a player, you dread being told you're not good enough. Again, I was lucky. I made it through the apprenticeship. But I saw others I'd grown up with cast aside and it wasn't nice.

As a manager, I had to do the casting aside. And *that* was horrible. I've had tough boys from hard backgrounds break down and cry in front of me. You could see the devastation in their eyes because, like me, they wanted nothing more out of life than to spend it kicking a ball around and getting paid for it. You could feel the panic as they realised that they hadn't prepared for this moment and saw a void open up in front of them.

So many try and fail to make it and are left with nothing. They haven't studied, haven't learned a trade. They never doubted their ability for a moment. Then again, so many who *did* make it would one day also be left staring into that same chasm, their golden days behind them and only dark ones ahead. Making fortunes from the game is a recent phenomenon – and, even then, it's only for the chosen few. The game eats them up and spits them out, leaves them with no useful skills and often no nest egg. It can be a wonderful profession, but it is also a cruel one.

Once upon a time I had to make the decision that Des McKeown wasn't good enough. But it turned out he was also one of the lucky ones.

I remember Des as a solid, quick defender with a good left foot, but also as a boy with more upstairs than most. Even when his dream came true and he signed for Celtic, he refused to get carried away. He was a student and wanted to finish his degree, no matter how it affected his football. And it did. It's hard enough to make it at a place like Parkhead if you're training every day without doing it part-time.

I think he probably always knew the day would come when we would let him go. There was no way he could have progressed at the rate we needed him to with the workload he had. But who knows, maybe even if he'd been full-time we'd have let him go. It happens to so many youngsters. Some get the breaks, are in the right place at the right time – others don't.

Des knew the odds were against him. So he stacked them back in his own favour by getting an alternative career. It takes a special person to analyse himself that deeply – especially when he's 17 and has a head full of dreams. Des deserves so much credit for mapping his life out so far ahead. And when I see him now, a successful salesman who has found his level as a footballer, I realise that more should think like him. So few make it to the very top, so many are left with nothing, that the idea of having the best of both worlds is a sensible one.

Of course, years ago most clubs were part-time, with famous players coming off shifts in factories or down pits to entertain thousands on a Saturday. It never did those guys any harm – so, who knows, maybe the game will go full circle. Maybe more players at middle-of-the-roads clubs will go back to day jobs and play football as a hobby.

I know for a fact Des McKeown is happy he did, and I'm delighted that he's still making it up and down touchlines all over Scotland.

At least he knows his life will be a happy one long after he's hung up his boots.

May 2001

ONE

Saturday, 10 June 2000. Somewhere over the Atlantic Ocean.

I STARTED AT THE TOP in football and worked my way down.

It was November 1987, a couple of months into Celtic's centenary season, in which they would win the Double. It was also the year they asked a skinny left-back called Des McKeown to sign for them.

I'd played one reserve game for them already, against junior side Vale of Clyde, but now here I was on a cloudy Wednesday afternoon, running out of the tunnel at Dens Park. Doing it for real. The starting eleven? I could name them all, but in truth only two guys really affected my day – keeper Allen McKnight and legendary left-sided midfielder Tommy Burns. One kept giving me the ball, the other kept taking it. My 90 minutes went:

> Collect from Allen, look up, give it to Tommy.
> Collect from Allen, look up, give it to Tommy.
> Collect from Allen, look up, give it to Tommy.
> Collect from Allen, look up, give it to Tommy.
> Collect from Allen, look up, give it to Tommy.
> Collect from Allen, look up, give it to Tommy.

Afterwards, Tommy was brilliant with me, but then again he's a brilliant guy.

'So,' he said in the dressing-room, 'who else is interested in you, Des?'

I told him there was Hearts, Dundee United, Motherwell, Coventry, St Johnstone, Airdrie, Dumbarton and a few more. He smiled and patted my shoulder.

'Aye, but there's only one you *really* want to sign for, isn't there?'

And he was right. Like thousands of boys, I'd always dreamed of playing for Celtic. But unlike 99.9 per cent of them, my dream had become reality. If they told me now I wasn't good enough I could always say I'd worn the Hoops.

But things were about to get even better.

In they came – manager Billy McNeill, maybe the greatest Celtic player of them all, his number two Tommy Craig, coach Bobby Lennox and chief scout John Kelman, on whose recommendation I was being tried out. Big Billy shook my hand and I still remember every word he said to me.

'You did well, son. Very well. We were very impressed and we'd like to offer you terms.'

'There's only one problem with this one,' Lennox chipped in. 'He wants to play too much football.'

Tommy Burns shook his head and patted my shoulder again.

'Don't you listen, son, you can never play too much football.'

And that was me hooked. I wanted to be part of all this, part of these guys. To be a footballer. There was only one snag. I'd already made the decision that would ensure I never made it all the way to the top even if I had the ability.

I wanted to stay part-time.

I was at Jordanhill College, in the first year of a Sports Management degree, and as I was bright enough to know I might not be good enough to make a living out of football alone I'd vowed to see it through.

Big Billy knew this, but in that dressing-room in Dundee he made one last effort to change my mind.

'You sure we can't offer you full-time terms, son?'

'Yes, I'm sure,' I heard myself say and part of me hated myself for it.

But it was the best decision of my life. Even as a teenager I was always confident it was the right thing to do. And now, as I move into my thirties and see how many other journeymen players didn't make the same choice, I give thanks for having at least a tiny bit of sense in my head.

Part-time footballer. Part-time football. The two phrases have a stigma attached to them. To most people, a part-time footballer sounds like one who's not as good as a full-time footballer. Part-time football sounds . . . well, *grim*.

'Oh, things are bad there – the talk is they're going part-time.'

They make it sound like a disease. Yet if only people would think logically about the game today they'd realise there's nothing grim or second-rate about being part-time. In fact, when I look around me it seems the only sensible way for so many players and clubs to go. Clubs are finding it harder and harder to keep going, yet they insist on keeping their squads on full-time wages simply to save face. They don't want to catch the disease. Going – they can hardly bring themselves to spit the words out – *part-time* would be like admitting defeat.

And going bust wouldn't be?

What would be so wrong with middle-of-the-road clubs without great ambitions of making the top flight, without great crowds or great potential, putting players on part-time contracts? After all, it worked for decades – because, despite what the New Footy Fan might believe, full-time football is a relatively new concept for many clubs. For years, right up until maybe the mid-70s, most players in Scotland had day jobs. And, mark my words, before too long most will have day jobs again.

It pains me when I see guys my age or older desperate for another year's full-time contract, stretching out the only career they've ever known to the very last, patching up injuries to keep themselves chugging along for another campaign. All they're really doing is putting off the inevitable. They're putting off joining the real world.

I look at my wee pal Allan Moore, gone 36 and making £350 a week at Partick Thistle if he's lucky, and know for a fact he knows nothing outside of the game. You can't blame him for plugging on, taking full-time money wherever he can get it, but you can blame the game as a whole for letting it happen.

Too many boys with stars in their eyes are sucked into a world which closets them from reality, which chews them up and spits them out with nothing to show for maybe 20 years of being kicked black and blue. At 17, they're bouncing with enthusiasm and visions of cup finals. At 35, they're hobbling with arthritis and facing the dole. No money behind them, no new career in front of them. When the dressing-room door shuts behind them for the last time, it's as if half their lives never actually happened.

That's why I never, ever look back on my decision to sign for Celtic as a part-timer with any regrets, any bitterness, any if-onlys.

Tell a lie, there was one time. There did come a point when I was coming to crunch time at Parkhead, to new-contract time, when I wondered if I should pack in college and give football a go full-time. I wondered if maybe, even if I wasn't going to be the greatest full-back in the world, it might just be worth the adventure. But by then, the decision had already been made for me. The club felt that without two years of full-time training under my belt I hadn't developed like some of the other boys and they were letting me go.

I was gutted. Shattered. Call it what you will, I felt like it. And worse. OK, so I'd made my own choice to stay part-time, but a little bit of me still had this fantasy that I might be able to combine the two, to be a success in business and a superstar in the Premier League.

I was kidding myself and no one else.

By the time my college course was complete, I was an Airdrie player and heading slowly towards finding my own level.

Of course, my experience might be the very argument some are looking for *against* part-time football. They'll say that players don't develop as well without day-in, day-out coaching. It's an argument I might agree with if full-timers *were* coached day-in, day-out.

They're not, though.

They might *run* day-in, day-out. They might practise set-pieces day-in, day-out. They might have a laugh and joke through the eight-a-sides day-in, day-out. But do they learn? Has 20 years in full-time football made Allan Moore a better footballer? I doubt it.

We don't coach players in this country. Look at Celtic and Rangers – as I'm writing this, neither of them even have a decent training ground or anywhere for their youngsters to learn the basics of the game. So what chance is there of Partick Thistle players progressing?

I could see an argument for more full-time footballers if football at that level was actually a full-time job. But you won't find a part-timer who trains any less in a week than someone who earns his money exclusively from the game. Thistle's part-timers are in Sunday mornings, Wednesday nights and Thursday nights. The full-timers do one session more, but I also do a gym circuit twice a week and a set of stomach exercises every single night.

Even then, it's not all about fitness. It's about knowledge of the game, understanding the game, understanding your own body. How many full-timers are brought back in after training each day to watch videos of Barcelona or Real Madrid in action? To find out about how players in other countries work? To learn about diet and lifestyle? I'll bet you could count the clubs who do this on the fingers of one hand.

Remember the outcry when Paul Sturrock wanted St Johnstone's players to work 9–5? People laughed at him, said he was off his head. But why was he? If a player is taking a full-time wage from a club, surely the club is entitled to a full week's work? And maybe if full-timers actually worked full-time, maybe if they did more than just keep reasonably fit and bond in the dressing-room, more of them would be ready for what comes after the boots get hung up.

Whenever I get the chance I still go along to watch Celtic and sometimes bump into someone who has already left football behind for the real world.

David Elliot also started out at Parkhead, before moving on to Thistle, St Mirren, Falkirk, Hibs and back to Thistle again. He started as a winger, moved to full-back and I'd have killed for his pace, if not his situation. Despite a fairly successful career, by the time Davie was in his late twenties the economic reality of being a journeyman footballer hit home. It was time to find a proper job. And so there he was, back at Parkhead as one of Strathclyde Police's finest.

For Davie, for Moorie, for scores more, the time comes when they have to find something new to pay the mortgage. When that time is depends on injury, a manager's whim or, if they're lucky, their own decision to quit. Popular opinion is that every footballer is paid bucketloads of dosh, but guys like Moorie would laugh at the myth. Sure, most guys earn well enough at full-time level – an OK basic, appearance money and win bonuses can add up to a good middle-management wage – but it doesn't last long. A footballer is packing it in just when most of his neighbours are blossoming in their own careers. The average footballer doesn't earn enough in his career to be able to put money away to look after the bills once it's over.

Then there are guys like me. The – *ptoo!* – part-timers. The money we make from football doesn't dictate what size of house we live in, how many cars we have, what type of holiday we take. Sure, the money helps, but it doesn't affect our lifestyle in the same way. I live in a lovely detached house in Cumbernauld, about 20 minutes from Glasgow city centre. By day, I'm sales director for stationery company OyezStraker Scotland. I've spent ten years working 7.30 a.m. to 5.30 p.m. five days a week to get there and the reward is a salary ten times what football pays me. My wife Carolyn has her own career in community education and we have two beautiful daughters, seven-year-old Danielle and three-year-old Taylor. If football stopped tomorrow, we'd still have our home and our two cars and the kids would go without nothing.

It all makes me wonder why more guys who *know* they'll never become footballing millionaires don't go part-time earlier and build a career which they could be settled into by the time they retire from the game. And I keep going back to the reason I mentioned right at the start. Snobbery. Few full-timers fancy the comedown of going part-time. Some don't feel there's the same prestige, others simply don't hold part-timers in the same esteem as 'real' players. And, nagging at the back of many minds, there's also the fear that they won't be able to adjust and will therefore be exposed as failures.

Full-time football cocoons men. Clubs look after everything for them, tell them what to wear, when to be where they need to be, what role to play, where to run, when to change jobs. Then the cocoon breaks open. Suddenly, at 35 going on 18, there is no more turning up in a tracksuit at 9.30 and being home again by lunchtime. No more massages when you feel stiff. No more six or seven weeks off every summer. And, very probably, no more fun. Just necessity.

I'm lucky. I love my day job and it's a huge part of my life. Hopefully, Davie Elliot will get the same satisfaction from his new career and so will others who take the plunge into a career outside football. The rest? Sadly, clubs themselves will eventually take the decision out of their hands, just as Celtic took it out of mine.

I can see, in the not-too-distant future, a day when every club outside of the SPL is part-time. And you know what? I don't think it'll harm the game half as badly as the majority seem to think. The sooner clubs operate within their means, the sooner players will get a realistic perspective of what comes next in their lives.

You know, I almost make it sound like I've got it all sussed out. So how come I'm thinking about all this when I should be relaxed and without a care in the world? I'll tell you why. It's because this part-time, pocket-money job of mine, this hobby, this bit of fun which doesn't affect my tax bracket by one cent, obsesses me. My day job brings 90 per cent of my money. The hobby should take up 10 per cent of my time. But ask Carolyn and she'll tell you that's nonsense. Fact is, football dictates 90 per cent of my life; when I sleep, when I eat, what I eat, when I go out, when my family sees me, when and where we go on holiday. All of it is down to football, all of it and more.

Right now we're flying back from a fortnight in Florida and it's been a brilliant break for all of us. But Carolyn and the girls had no option about when we were going. It was now or never. And already, even before the captain's started our descent into Glasgow, I know my summer is over. I know another season's coming. I know Carolyn knows it too.

My wife puts up with a lot – and I mean 'puts up with'. She's no mouse in the corner, happily letting hubby get on with men's stuff. She tells me I'm off my head, tells me I'm daft to let football rule so much of my life, all our lives. And she's right, of course. But once you're in football, there's no way out. No one ever wants to stop playing. No one even really wants to be a manager; it's just a way of staying involved. The guys who write about it would rather be playing. The fans want to be out there too. I'm one of the tiny minority who ever get to play it for a living, to live out everyone else's fantasies, and that means so much that you can't put it into words.

The cost? Not seeing the kids before they go to bed for ten months of the year, not getting a game of golf on days off. Not getting days off, full stop. Going from being a responsible executive all week to be shouted at non-stop from the dugout on a Saturday. Being told you're useless by some fat, wheezing drunk on the terraces.

It's all worth it. Most of the time. Usually. Sometimes.

Do I need it? Financially, no – but inside me? God, yes. Even if inside me right now I'm churning like a tumble dryer – and not because of the turbulence outside! No, it's the thought of a game that happened more than a month ago that's doing it.

TWO

EMBARRASSMENT. That was the only word to sum up my feelings as I sat alone in the away dressing-room at Gayfield Park today. Through the wall, I could hear the muffled excitement of the game going on, a game I'd once been part of. Well, sort of been part of. Let's say I'd been out there, standing around for 67 minutes. I got three headers, two kicks and four throw-ins and that was about it for my input. I probably did more for Arbroath's cause than for ours. In the end, being subbed was a relief. It was the gaffer putting me out of my misery. I was hurting at the inadequacy of my performance. And as I trudged to the touchline, I found myself doing something I'd never done in my career.

I kept going.

Past the bench, past the mocking home fans, down the tunnel, along the little brickwork corridor, past the boardroom, past the ever-smiling tea-ladies Margaret and Karen without so much as a nod and into the away dressing-room.

I've been lucky. In 400-odd senior games over 13 seasons I've rarely had the hook. I tend to see the job through, dogged if not inspired. But what that means is when the board *does* go up and it's 'Come in, No. 3', you really feel it. And I really, *really* felt it today.

All we'd had to do was draw and fourth place in the Second Division was ours – not exactly winning the Champions League, I'll grant you, but more significant than usual. See, the top three – Clyde, Ross County and Alloa – had already gone up to make it ten in the First Division after St Mirren and Dunfermline moved up to the SPL. Got it so far? But Airdrie were in dire financial straits and possibly only a few days away from liquidation. If they went under, they'd lose their league status and have to apply to re-join the league at Third Division level. And the fourth-placed team in the Second would go up. See now why an end-of-season trip to windy Arbroath meant so much to everyone at Partick Thistle? It might just have been our ticket back to the big time. Well, the bigger time.

All we'd needed was a crappy, scrappy draw. A scrambled nil-nil, all goal-line clearances and missed sitters by the other lot. A dramatic comeback from two down with minutes left, maybe even the other way round, going 2–0 up then collapsing and hanging on. But no, none of these scenarios happened. We lost 3–2, with my three headers, two kicks and four throw-ins doing damn little to change things. And when my number came up, all I wanted to do was get away from the misery and be alone with my thoughts. I hadn't felt this way since . . . since, OK, I'll tell you. Since Sunday, 2 November 1997, to be exact. The date's tattooed on my brain because it was the occasion of my biggest professional game so far. The Scottish League Challenge Cup final, Queen of the South v Falkirk at Fir Park, Motherwell.

They got nearly 11,000 in that day, all there to see two sets of players who were unlikely ever to play in a cup final again. This was the journeyman's cup final, the diddy team fan's cup final, the cup most journalists would run a mile from rather than cover. A cup final my Queens team-mates and me lost 1–0 to a David Hagen goal.

As a team, we were beaten but not disgraced. Our fans even demanded – and got – a lap of honour, complete with silly hats, flags, scarves and blue-and-white wigs. We milked the ovation for all it was worth, then trudged back to the dressing-room and the reality of defeat. Everyone was mentally and physically shattered, but most of the lads were delighted with their efforts. Me? I sat in a corner, pulled my silly hat over my silly face and shed a tear. A tear for having let myself down, a tear for being anonymous in the biggest game of my life, a tear because my mother Isabel and father William were in the stand. It had been my mother's first game and ill health would make it my father's last. The tears kept coming because I couldn't do anything to change the course of the game for the thousands who'd come to support us, and because it *hurt*!

My performance that day at Fir Park was later described by Kilmarnock manager Bobby Williamson as the worst he'd ever seen by a professional footballer. It certainly felt like it at the time. And now here I was in the away dressing-room at Gayfield Park, two and a half years later, weighing that day up against this. The jury in my mind took no time to decide that, yes, this performance had been even worse. Thank goodness Bobby Williamson hadn't been there.

Difference is, back in November '97 I got the chance to put things right a few days later in our next league game. Not this time. This time it was over, finito, end of season, see you in July. When *would* I get the chance to put things right this time? Would I get that chance at all? If I did, would it be in a Thistle shirt or for Auchtermuchty Stanklifters Reserves?

As I sat there, sweat drying on tightening muscles, I knew my summer had already been ruined by those 67 horrible minutes. If only I'd got more involved. If only I'd gone on a couple of runs, slung in a few crosses, got in a crunching tackle early doors. If only, if only, if only. The bad footballer's best friend. If-onlys don't count though, results do. And this result, a result not helped by my three headers, two kicks and four throw-ins, would leave me insecure all summer long.

May is a hard enough time for the professional footballer: who will the manager sign? Will there still be a place for me? How will my last performance of the old season affect my chances in the new? If it all went pear-shaped, where would I go? Would I have a choice of new clubs, of a new start? Or would I sit by the phone for an offer that would never come?

Would this miserable, windy, nothing performance be my last in senior football?

It had been a long, hard season. I'd played 38 games and scored twice, not bad for someone who usually plays left-back in a team that hadn't scored bucketloads. Now that it was all over, I should have been looking forward to Orlando with Carolyn and the kids. Instead, I was already beyond that, focusing on 1 July when pre-season training would begin and how I needed to go back in super-fit condition.

It could be the biggest day of my career, presuming I still had one.

I decided to have two to three weeks' complete rest, then build up my training programme so that after Orlando I'd be ready for three weeks' hard work on my own in the gym before pre-season. Who the hell invented the phrase 'part-time football'?

Come quarter to five, the boys trooped in to join me. Nobody was saying much, not even our normally raucous manager John Lambie or his equally-noisy number two Gerry Collins – and it's not often that happens after a defeat. I think everyone was a bit numb.

It was only on the bus home that I began my recovery, what clever people would call a catharsis. As ever, the boys were babbling away, but I stared out of the window, thinking about everything and nothing, drifting in and out of the conversation around me. Then the crack got onto music and my ears pricked up. Someone mentioned Phil Collins, our big centre-back Alan Archibald said something about his hit 'In the Air Tonight' and I started thinking about an episode of *Miami Vice* when that song plays as a depressed Don Johnson cruises the city with his Ferrari stereo pumping. Call me 'Mr '80s', but right there and then I couldn't think of a better release. So when the bus dropped me at a hotel just outside Glasgow and I picked up my car, I drove to Asda in Cumbernauld, bought a Phil Collins CD and pumped it out.

On a hilltop high above the town, above the lights, the noise, the smells, above everyone else's worries, I parked up and sat back and 'In the Air Tonight' started to ease the pain of a rotten day. The embarrassment will never be erased. But for a few corny minutes it was at least forgotten.

THREE

TOUCHDOWN. Cabin doors to manual, McKeown's mind to automatic pilot. Summer's over, football's back. See you in May, girls. No more holidays, no autumn superbreak to a European city, no midwinter retreat to the Canaries or the pistes.

It's at times like these you wonder exactly why you sacrifice your family life, why you put yourself through so much for so little financial gain, in the name of a hobby. Year after year you find your daily, weekly, monthly timetables suffer because everything has to revolve around football. It governs when you eat, when you sleep, who you sleep with, what pastimes you have, how often you see your wife and family, when you get away from it all, when you can have a sociable drink, when you go to church, when you go to the dentist – everything, basically, which Joe and Josephine Public do without a second thought.

Why, why, why, why? Any professional footballer will give you his own personal reasons – but it all boils down to one fact. They have to do it if they want to remain professional footballers. Sacrificing everything to play the game is simply *what you do* – not that the public ever notices this side of our job. Come to think of it, most of the public don't even see it as a job. They see the glam lifestyles, the bundles of cash, the beautiful wives/girlfriends/mistresses/boyfriends, the media exposure and the endless material trappings of success. But it's only a tiny percentage who get their mitts on all that stuff – and far too often they're the ones who *don't* sacrifice the unhealthy things in life for the sake of their careers.

So what about the other 95 per cent? Why do we sacrifice everything for none of the rewards – apart from the beautiful partner bit? (I've managed that much, just in case Carolyn reads this and does my head in.) The motivation for each individual player may be different – money, enjoyment, the feeling of belonging to a group, natural talent, will to win, wanting to be the best, social status, entertainment, sheer old-fashioned love of the game. I can only answer for me. I sacrifice everything because of a passion for football that just cannot truly be defined. A former manager of mine once said: 'The only people who don't understand how important football is are women and men who sit down to take a piss.' OK, so it's not a very PC way to put it across, but you get the point. You either know what a passion for football is about or you don't.

Mine comes from wanting to play at the highest level my ability allows me to for as long as I can. From wanting to be part of a team, to succeed. And because it's now such an integral part of my life that I couldn't possibly imagine life without it. Sad? Maybe, but true. And I'm not alone. The majority of football people I've met in my life are exactly the same, people who live it, breathe it, love it. And just to prove it, we're home just in time for the start of Euro 2000, so I can now let TV dictate the bits of my next three weeks that are not spent in the gym. Heaven.

Sunday, 11 June 2000

My first gym session. Felt OK on the treadmill and the body circuit I've done daily for donkey's years goes like clockwork as usual. It consists of 600 sit-ups, 180 press-ups, dozens of squats and plenty of stretching. I do it no matter where I am or how busy I am.

Spent the rest of the day catching up on paperwork, opening mail and answering e-mails. Back to work tomorrow with a day in the office at Clydebank.

I then ring round various friends in the game to catch up with lower-division signings – it's easier than trying to follow them through the papers, the majority of which couldn't really give a monkey's.

Thursday, 22 June 2000

A funny old game? Oh yes, bloody hilarious. The Scottish League fixtures are out today and guess where Thistle go on day one? A chocolate biscuit to the man at the back who said 'Arbroath'.

No sooner has the pain of 6 May started to subside into the mists of time than it all comes flooding back again.

My first thought is that it's the perfect chance to exorcise the ghost of a truly awful performance. My second is that I'm not there yet. We're not even at pre-season and I've got to come through that before I even think about re-establishing myself in the team. I don't even know if I'll turn up for training and find a new signing there to threaten my place. For 13 years it's been the same, yet for 13 years I've never missed the first kick of the first game of any season through any reason but injury. Rivals have come and gone, but I've survived so far.

I'm not about to give up now without plenty kicking and scratching.

Friday, 23 June 2000

Did I say pre-training training was going like clockwork? Forget it.

I've been doing my cardiovascular programme every second day since 11 June, with a body circuit each day in between and I'm really happy with my fitness level. With one week until I go back to Thistle, I've enough time to step up the workrate and be in perfect shape.

But that was before tonight when I collapsed in the street.

I came round to find blood oozing from a wound at the back of my head. Carolyn's brother Gary is visiting and between them they got me back to the house and told me that when I fell, I gave my napper a right old batter off the road. Within 20 minutes I was in casualty at Stobhill Hospital and feeling none-too-clever. The think-bubbles as we drove there would have read something like:

> *Carolyn*: 'Why did he conk out like that? Was it something to do with that head injury against Stirling Albion last season when he was rushed to hospital with acute concussion? My God, he ended up back there twice within a week because it was so bad!'
> *Des*: 'When will I train again? Will I miss any pre-season? Will this affect my season?'

The Stobhill people x-rayed me and carry out all sorts of tests. The doc suggested I see a neurologist for a more accurate diagnosis. Carolyn's questions were left unanswered. More worryingly, so were mine.

The family's reaction was predictable – I need to slow down, I'm doing too much, I can't keep putting all these physical and mental demands on my body. I know they said it all for the right reasons but I didn't want to hear it. I just wanted someone to say I was OK to play football.

Monday, 26 June 2000

My appointment with Dr Richard Metcalf at Ross Hall Hospital is fixed for 4 July. Thistle's doc tells me to rest and see how I feel when pre-season starts on Saturday, but when I tell him I'm still feeling dodgy and my head's sore he says maybe I shouldn't do anything until I see Dr Metcalf.

I'll give it until Saturday. I've got a hobby to protect.

FOUR

Saturday, 1 July 2000

WOKE TODAY LIKE A KID on Christmas morning. The old excitement was there as I scampered to get out of the house and over to Firhill. It took a few seconds to remember my head problem. But, yes, it felt fine. Excellent.

I can't wait to get to training and see the ones who've been retained, the ones who were out-of-contract but have re-signed – Alan Archibald and Danny Lennon – and the new boys. So far there are three. Jamie Smith, a young central defender, has come from Stranraer for around £20,000, a lot of dosh considering our perilous financial position and the fact that there are so many boys available for free. Then there's David McCallum – not the Invisible Man, we hope – who's come on a free from Stirling Albion, plus highly experienced midfielder Ian Cameron, who's been at Firhill before. Others will turn up by invitation of JL and GC, who want to look at them and them at us.

After a slice of toast and a cup of tea, I head for work and find JL on his throne, puffing away on a ciggie and already showing the stress of the job. Walter Cannon, the club physio – or, as some call him, vet – is calibrating the treatment room scales to make sure our weights are recorded accurately.

As the new bodies filter in I'm asked by chief executive, Alan Dick, to introduce them to the squad. At every club I've been at for the past ten years I've invariably been spokesperson, boot-deal organiser, transfer go-between and social convenor. Maybe I've just got that sort of face.

I introduce Stephen Craigan (centre-back, ex-Motherwell), Michael Brown (keeper, ex-Rangers and Motherwell), an Albanian goalkeeper (mysteriously only known to us as Julian) plus Jamie and David to the rest.

In no time everyone is mixing well, telling summer holiday stories and cracking gags. At this level there's very little problem with players being above themselves – anyone even slightly aloof is soon brought down to earth with a bump. The Second Division is no place for prima donnas and as a result the crack in most dressing-rooms is great. This is one of the main things I'll miss when the inevitable happens and the boots get hung up.

Dressing-room humour's never as funny when relayed to friends outside football, yet within the walls it cracks you up. Even before the first lung-bursting run of a new pre-season, the place is electric already. The wind-ups have begun. And, cor blimey, here comes another not-so-strange face – Tommy 'Tid' Callaghan, recently promoted from permanent fifteenth man to Under-18 coach. His boys are changing down a little flight of stairs in the away dressing-room, but the magnetism of the banter with the grown-ups is too much for his ever-more-rotund physique. As he walks in, the boys he's played alongside for two seasons let rip.

'Fuck off, Tid! You're one of them now!'

'Say nothing, Tid's here!'

'Oi, Tubby Scoffalot, away and make JL his tea!'

Tid takes it well. Even if his playing contribution this last while has been disappointing, his ability to make the boys and management smile was truly top-drawer. He's endeared himself to many, though the decision to give him the U18 job was widely criticised. I'm sure he'll repay JL's faith many times over and I hope the fans give him a chance to prove himself. At least he knows in his heart we wouldn't turn on him. Well, not yet, anyway . . .

The vet weighs us – at 11st. 12 lb, I'm exactly the same as at the last session of last season – then we take cars over the Kingston Bridge to Strathclyde Police's sports ground at Lochinch for our first session.

Training today lasted two and a half hours and basically consisted of:

> Warm-up, taken by yours truly.
> Three sets of five 100-yard sprints in a set timescale.
> Three sets of six 100-yard runs with the ball.
> A final, increasingly demanding run, called The Coffin.

By the end of a particularly knackering first day, certain players were looking well. Others were struggling. The majority did enough to suggest they have looked after themselves during the close season.

JL finished the session with our sit-ups routine – known as stomachs – and this is where the men were separated from the boys. You know the ones who're struggling because they don't stop telling you. I feel fine and I thank my discipline in doing these exercises all year round for 13 seasons.

Having been through the torture of 13 professional first pre-season days under maybe ten managers, there's only one constant – the weather! As usual, Day One is conducted in blazing sunshine and blistering heat. My balding skull is frazzled – and thinking of baldness, it dawned that I was the oldest member of the squad here today. Ian Cameron is even more geriatric than my 30 years, but he was still on holiday, as were Martin Hardie, Danny Lennon and Stephen Docherty.

After a shower, I headed home for lunch and some precious family time.

Sunday, 2 July 2000

No matter how well you prepare for Day One, it never stops you waking on Day Two as stiff as Gyproc. My hamstrings are tighter than two Aberdonians on a flag day and my calves are throbbing. I worry for the guys who were struggling yesterday.

Spent the day preparing for tomorrow's sales meeting at Clydebank, then marvelled at the Euro 2000 final. The effort, application and fitness of Italy and France were a lesson to every footballer as they ran themselves into the ground days after gruelling semi-finals. Every man was a credit to the profession and I was fairly happy that France won. They were probably the best team over the piece and it was interesting to hear the comments of the so-called experts on the TV panels. I know none of these experts personally, though I've been in Ally McCoist's company a couple of times, but in my opinion the job is money for old rope. TV pundits are there to analyse, yet very few do. Instead, they merely describe a goal/move/save/cross/tackle we've all just seen in their own words as opposed to explaining why or how the situation has arisen.

I tend to analyse football more than most of my friends and I think I take more out of games this way. I look at formations, tactics, movement, set-pieces, while the majority of guys I watch will follow the ball and very little else. Am I sub-consciously preparing myself for coaching or management? Or is it conscious?

The day ended with my usual routine of 600 stomachs, a half-hour soak in the bath and a half-hour leg massage from Carolyn. Lights out at midnight and there the diary also closes . . .

Monday, 3 July 2000

Leave for Clydebank at 6.45 a.m. to have everything organised for our monthly sales meeting. As sales director, I work with a six-man team and my managing director, Reg McAtee.

There's a huge football interest amongst the team. Reg is a Celtic man through and through, as is Stephen McCall, who covers Edinburgh. Craig Williams – known as Elvis thanks to his awful karaoke efforts – covers the West Coast and is a Rangers fan. Graham 'Car Wash' Connell does Central Scotland, plays in midfield for Queens Park after being freed from Thistle by JL and supports Rangers. So too Ray Hardie, our Aberdeen man. Peter Davidson is a new employee and I haven't worked him out yet, although as he was chairman of Ally McCoist's testimonial committee, an educated guess suggests Rangers. Duncan Brown is our relief business manager – covering for holidays and illness – and believe it or not he's a Thistle diehard.

As the guys arrive at Clydebank, they are each given the bad news. Reg, in his holiday-bound euphoria, has left his office locked and as Stephen is in the States with his family we have six salesmen with nowhere to meet. I call Thistle and find commercial girl Mandy Stark already in the office at 8.10 a.m., give her the sob story, and after breakfast in Clydebank we're in the Firhill boardroom by 9.30 a.m. The office girls keep the tea and coffee coming and I treat the guys to lunch at Di Maggio's in the West End. A lovely bowl of pasta sets me up for tonight's training session.

My legs are still tight. God knows what they would have been like if Carolyn hadn't given me a massage. All the boys are saying the same, although most are busier complaining that their stomachs are sore from sit-ups. We're at Lochinch again and it's interesting to see Queens Park – Car Wash and all – going through their paces on the other side of the fields.

After training I go over to Tid's to let him use the Internet on my laptop. He's heard he's taken abuse on the fanzine website, but there's actually more support than nasty comments. We have a chuckle at some of the stuff, the best of which was from a boy who'd played for our Under-16s last season and had met Tid on various occasions. He told how Tid was a decent guy, funny and full of encouragement for the youngsters. But Tid nearly fell off the couch when the testimonial ended: 'What greater motivation could a young player need but the fact that if Tom Callaghan had made it, so could they?'

Home for 10.45 p.m., beans on toast and bed for by 11.30 p.m.

Tuesday, 4 July 2000

Long lie this morning – didn't leave home until seven. Concluded negotiations on two contracts, one for a large firm of solicitors I've been chasing for two and a half years. They begin buying today. The other is a new educational facility on the south side of the Clyde and, after a month of talks, could prove very lucrative. There are similarities between these negotiations and football – sometimes a manager needs two or three years to get the player he wants. Sometimes the deal is no problem and is done in two or three days.

Later, I'm at Ross Hall Hospital to see Dr Metcalf about my head problem. He gives me the all-clear, but although everyone else is delighted with his diagnosis, I still have some concerns over occasional blurred vision and dizzy spells.

Home at eight to play father and husband. Spend some time with Danielle and Taylor, finish off some paperwork, plant some shrubs for Carolyn, do my stomachs and finally sit down to a bowl of pasta at 11.15 p.m.

Wednesday, 5 July 2000

Got to Firhill early and had a long chat with JL about signing targets. I'm the middleman in negotiations with a mate of mine from Queen of the South, Stevie Mallan. Stevie's been a great servant, but their new manager John Connolly wants to bring in his own players. JL likes Stevie, a tough, hard-working, brave and quick striker. He's good for 15-20 goals a season – and as our top scorer last season got a heady seven, we could do with that.

Some of the other deals JL wants to do are complex – mainly because most of his targets want to stay full-time. JL's got no problem with that, but the money on offer's barely £15,000 a year before bonuses. Few outside the game would believe it's as low as that.

One of JL's targets, much-travelled striker Paul 'Mowgli' McGrillen, is in the dressing-room when I get there. He was in with the full-timers yesterday and is close to agreeing terms. Reaction from our fans to the prospect of Mowgli signing has not been good, mainly because he's usually been responsible for the odd penalty against us. I hope he wins them over.

Stephen Docherty, Danny Lennon and Martin Hardie are back from holiday and join in another joyfully testing session.

Off at 6.45 a.m. to meet Ray Hardie for a day's calls in Kirkcaldy and Cupar, after which I take him in to Stark's Park to meet an old pal, Raith Rovers manager Peter Hetherston. We wait in the tearoom for the squad to return from training and I see other familiar faces such as Paul Tosh, Kevin Gaughan, Peter's number two Kenny Black, Craig McEwan and my old Celtic team-mate Gerry Creaney.

Gerry was the only other part-timer when I signed and the differences in our careers since then highlight exactly why I made the decision I did. Sure, he went on to bigger and better things as a full-timer while I went off to Airdrie. He made the first team, earned a big-money move to Portsmouth and then a £1 million switch to Manchester City, but since then his career's been pretty much on hold. OK – more accurately, it's been spiralling out of control. Each move since City has taken him down, down, down and you can only hope he's put away the money he's made to look after himself when it finally comes to an end.

How fickle football is – one minute you're a £1m player making national headlines, the next you're trying to prove yourself in pre-season training with a skint Scottish First Division side. I wish him all the best.

Peter – Silky to his mates – appears and takes Ray and myself into the cupboard that doubles as an office for him and Kenny. He organises soup and toast and tells us his plans. As we discuss players, agents, nights out and opposition, Ray sits slack-jawed at the breadth and pace of the conversation and at just how down-to-earth Silky is. He has no airs or graces, he's just a Coatbridge boy done good – and a funny, funny guy.

After about an hour, sides sore with laughing, we head off to Cupar to finish our business. I'm back in Glasgow at six and heading for training.

There's another new, but familiar, face tonight – Mark McNally, another member of that Celtic reserve squad of '88. He played more than 100 times in the Hoops before hopping around Southend, Stoke City, Dundee United and most recently Ayr United. He's now clubless and JL has invited him in for a look.

For the second time in a day, I'm left thinking back to the day I said no to full-time football and concentrated on a career. Even on my worst days, I'm still sure it was the right choice. My ability was always limited – only attitude and desire has got me anywhere – but I'm OK financially, with a fairly secure job. Who knows where I'd be if I'd gone full-time? Clubless and hawking myself around the Second Division? Hitting 30 with no nest egg, fearing the thought of a real job in the real world? One thing's for sure, it's a harder lifestyle change for Gerry and Mark at 30 than it was for me at 19.

On the way home, another old QoS pal, Ginger George Rowe, phones to tell me he's signing for Arbroath and that Stevie Mallan will probably join him. I alert JL, but basically we can't look at the package. So there you have it, even more spice for that first game of the season.

Bed at midnight.

Friday, 7 July 2000

Today I negotiate a boot deal for Thistle with Sandy Greaves of Greaves Sports in Glasgow. We go back years – I don't quite remember how it started, but basically every club I have been involved with has, at some point, benefited from our friendship. Sandy's a timebomb, a highly stressed individual who prefers to be on the shop floor rather than in his office. He lives and breathes sports retailing.

My timing could not be worse. His assistant Maxine alerts me that this is the first day of their sale, but I take the bull by the horns – I have many problems, but shyness is not one – and collar Sandy to see what deal he can do me. He starts by confirming that my timing is indeed shite. However, 30 minutes later I'm leaving the shop with a pair of Valsport boots that look good and feel great. I'll show them to the boys at training tomorrow and if they like them I'll put a price to the club.

Sandy gives me the boots free for my use and promises some other Valsport kit – he's great that way, he even had me trying the Adidas Predator boot for him years ago, to give him feedback before they were officially launched. So let it be known that the only players who had these slices of hush-hush prototype were:

> John Collins (Celtic and Scotland)
> Paul Ince (Manchester United and England)
> Des McKeown (Albion Rovers and Oyez)

My feedback was that I thought the unique design could mean I'd be able to swerve wingers off the pitch and back on.

The day ends like every Friday night during the season – clear of paperwork by 7.30 p.m., a phone-in curry, then an episode of *Friends* with my three favourite ladies.

Saturday, 8 July 2000

While for footballers it's the running season, others prefer to march. And it is because of these people that I'm late getting to Firhill.

I encounter two groups of Orangemen, one on Garscube Road and the other on Maryhill Road, and only the assistance of a local policeman gets me to the stadium in time to discuss the boot deal before training at ten.

JL and GC are impressed with Sandy's goods and like my suggestion that the club provides a pair of training boots and a pair of match boots in this style. Anyone who wants any other make has to buy his own and isn't due a refund. Usually the club would pay £35 towards a player's own boots, but I want Sandy to get a bulk order for his generous offer. Chief executive Alan Dick agrees the club will pay £75 for two pairs of boots. It's a good deal for Thistle, who get £160 of kit for their £75. I just hope Sandy's happy.

The boys like the demo boots and few mumble, though my sales training helps. I've given them the alternatives:

   a) Take the club boots for nothing.
   b) Buy your own with no compensation.

There's really no choice. GC takes down sizes and I'm armed for Monday's talks with Sandy.

Training is demanding, but very enjoyable. JL tells me to take the squad through picturesque Pollok Country Park on a 20-minute Fartlek run. Fartlek? Sounds noisy, missus – but it's actually fairly dull, as befits an exercise developed in Sweden, a run where the pace varies to help build up stamina over different distances.

Afterwards, we play a game with three sets of goalposts and now, at last, we start to see the benefits of all last week's hard work. Initially, the passing's slack and the movement lethargic. But after ten minutes the ball's zipping about one- or two-touch and everyone's on his toes.

After this there's some more running, some shooting then more running. During a final shooting exercise some of the boys are moaning that their legs feel tight, so muggins suggests to JL and GC they might scale things down and avoid unnecessary pulls and strains. To their credit, they listen and decide enough's enough. Last thing they need is a spate of injuries before a ball's kicked for real. The plan is to run with a first-team squad of 18-20 (sadly, not in age – I'm too old for Club 18-30 now) and no reserve team. Still, 20 players seem plenty when you only need 16 on a Saturday. Until you find that Doc's still nursing an ankle injury from last season and David McCallum's tweaked a hammy. Any more crocks and you're struggling.

After changing, JL calls his faithful together and sayeth: 'Verily, youse have done well, have the Sabbath off.'

Sunday, 9 July 2000

And so the Sabbath arrives and I take my day off.

As if.

Today is the only time of the week when I can spend any decent – and I hate this phrase, but it describes it well – quality time with the family.

First off, a trip round some relations, before I take Dani and Taylor five minutes up the road to Westerwood Country Club for an afternoon's swim. Their confidence in the water has increased dramatically since Orlando.

Carolyn hits the gym, stepping up her training for the Glasgow Half Marathon in August. As the kids splash about I hit the jacuzzi to soothe the legs and while I'm bubbling away, Taylor – who's three and a half – asks why I'm not wearing a bathing suit top. It's at moments like this you realise your kids are growing up fast – and that you've not been there to see it all happen. Their mum sees them far more than I do and therefore sees more day-to-day change. If I only spend proper time with them once a week, I sometimes see dramatic changes, even over seven days. But what can you do about comments like that one other than laugh and enjoy the time we *do* spend together? We hit McDonald's for McNuggets all round and BBQ sauce all over the place.

Back home, I spend a couple of hours snowed under with paperwork, do a body circuit then hit the road again. I'm on business up the East Coast tomorrow and an overnight stay in Edinburgh will set me up for an early kick-off.

Having checked into my hotel, I have a lovely bath and sweet dreams.

Monday, 10 July 2000

After a morning in Edinburgh I have a couple of appointments in Glasgow before finalising the boot deal with Sandy, who, as usual, is a man possessed. After I catch his attention and lasso him to slow down, he phones Valsport for a deal. They agree to £80 for two pairs. I phone

Alan Dick, he gives me the OK and I leave the shop with ten pairs of £85 football boots to distribute at training tonight.

To say I was aware of my sudden value as I walked along Gordon Street with both hands full of carrier bags is an understatement and I hotfoot it to the car before the cargo ends up being distributed around the boozers of Glasgow.

Over at Firhill, I commandeer the office to finish off some paperwork before JL corners me about the boots. I tell him everything's under control.

The squad's coming together now with the addition today of Mowgli McGrillen, defender Stephen Craigan from Motherwell and Derek 'Deeks' McWilliams who has re-signed after being here at the tail-end of last season. JL is on the phone trying to make another signing.

The boys are desperate to try their new boots for size. Everyone's delighted – if the title was won on style we'd have the trophy already.

Training tonight is more based around match situations and we're using the ball more and more – even if some of the guys still moan that we only get it to disguise yet more running. However, a quick shifty across the Lochinch pitches shows how lucky we are. Queens Park are being absolutely run into the ground by coach John McCormack – with, I'm surprised and delighted to report, my day job tea-boy Graham Connell leading the pack. Must be all the cars I get him to wash.

On the next pitch are our Under-18s, with Tid working them just as hard – he's got the stopwatch round his neck and the kids are slogging their little guts out. Not bad for a guy who hated pre-season training with a passion.

Our goalies have a new coach and they're working away on their own. What a strange breed they are, a race apart from all other footballers. Any outfield player will tell you the same. They say goalkeepers need to be daft, but that's about the nicest adjective you could use to describe most I've met. Not that they aren't nice guys – it's just that they must put some Mental Powder in their gloves or something, because the second they pull them on they flip. Without the gloves a keeper might be a loving, caring family man without a worry in the world, a bloke who's kind to puppies and who'd give you his last penny. A one-off, a diamond, a real 24-carat belter of a man. But with them? Moody, insecure, paranoid, super-serious and only comfortable in the company of similarly-gloved nutjobs. They moan about everything, especially when shooting practice begins. 'He was too close,' they'll howl, or 'Don't hit it so hard'. Yet in real games they'd dive in among hungry sharks to grab a toothbrush. Off their heads, every one of them. Not that I'm one for generalising.

Meanwhile, talking of insanity, former St Johnstone, Hearts, Dunfermline and Airdrie winger, Lee Evans lookalike and all-round bundle of energy Allan Moore, is also at training tonight. JL thinks he might do us a turn and I hope so. He's a good player, a great guy in the dressing-room and good friend of Tid and mine.

Tuesday, 11 July 2000

Graham and I take one of his clients, a buyer from Keystone Valves called George Henderson, for lunch at La Fiorentina near Ibrox.

George is a football man and pretty soon we're onto far more important conversation than business – he's a Hamilton Accies man and still feels aggrieved that they were relegated last season after being deducted a record 15 points for their players striking over unpaid wages. On April Fool's Day, the team failed to turn up for a Second Division game at Stenhousemuir – the first down-boots this century – and all hell broke loose. The Scottish League had several options. They could have fined the Accies, but as the club were too skint to pay the wages, what was the point? They could have taken the three points away, but then how many other cash-strapped clubs would have risked the same in return for a week of not squaring up its players? In the end, they ordered the game to be replayed – Accies, ironically, won – and stripped them of enough points to put them bottom of the league, but still with enough games left to get out of trouble of their own accord.

George and Graham agreed this was way over the top, so I spent most of the lunch arguing why I backed the league. First up, this wasn't the first time Accies players had not been paid. The players had threatened strike action several weeks before, but relented when the board 'found' the cash. Neither was this a new phenomenon in Scottish football. Both Clydebank and Morton players had been in a similar position in recent years and someone, somewhere had to show club owners it simply wasn't on. The Accies board gambled their players wouldn't have the bottle to strike. But I'm also sure they checked the rulebook, which stated that the Scottish League had the right to impose a three-point penalty and 'any other punishment deemed suitable' and gambled again that a wrist-slap fine would be the worst they'd get on top. *They called the bluff of their employees and the League and lost.* I asked George and Graham: 'If your gaffer didn't pay you, would you work on? No way!' They shrugged and hummed and hawed, but the fact is that while most of us would walk out if we weren't paid, there's a public perception of footballers and their bosses having some special relationship, some kind of 'show must go on' mentality.

A footballer has to live with certain anomalies in his career. I cannot walk away from Partick Thistle the way I can from OyezStraker – although the EU are working towards football being bound by the same rules of resignation and notice periods as everyone else enjoys. And sure, what the Hamilton players did on April Fool's Day rebounded on their club – but tough. The real long-term benefit of their strike action will be felt by their own profession. Directors will now really have to think hard before breaching their contracts with the players because they've now seen the consequences – and, before long, many other employment issues regarding my part-time job will have to be addressed.

Ask yourself: in what other profession can the employer treat their employee in the way some football managers treat their players? In what other profession can a line manager verbally abuse and – because this also happens – *physically* abuse their employees in the way some football managers do and not face losing their job or even criminal charges? In what other profession can the employer dictate at the shortest of notice when the employee attends their workplace, how often and for how long? And in what other profession would the employee feel *honoured* to be part of it all? Because twisted as this may sound, most footballers wouldn't have it any other way. They come into the game with their eyes wide open and expecting all the horrors I've set out above – and more. It's part of football, albeit a part which is more acceptable when you're getting paid in full and on time. Ask the Hamilton players how it feels when you don't and the story might be very different. But ask how many of them would rather not be a footballer at all and not one will put his hand up.

Wednesday, 12 July 2000

Before our first pre-season friendly, at home to Motherwell, my pal and best man Damian McKenna treats me to lunch – my usual matchday special of pasta.

That night we face a side peppered with well-known names like Ged Brannan, Derek Adams, John Davies, Paul Harvey, Stevie Woods and John Spencer. We have ex-Well man Stephen Craigan, Jamie Smith, Paul McGrillen and the newly signed Allan Moore making their debuts along with trialists Mark McNally and the mysterious Albanian keeper 'Julian'.

The game finishes 3–3 with our goals coming from the impressive Scott McLean, back from a close-season knee op, Martin Hardie and Derek Lyle. The small but fabulously gifted Spencer gets two for Well.

It's been a good exercise and has also given JL food for thought in terms of performance. I play the full 90 at left-back and my fitness feels good – shame about my distribution!

Thursday, 13 July 2000

A right good start to the day – six months of beavering away at a company in Cumbernauld ends with me securing their stationery contract.

After that I'm in Glasgow all day and after a stop-off to pick up the rest of the boots, I head for training – and now it's all about the ball and shaping the team. JL's very happy with the quality and effort and even allows the boys away without doing their stomachs. He must be getting soft. Pity I'd done mine *before* training.

For the third time this week, Dani and Taylor are already sound asleep when Daddy gets home. Mummy is in front of the TV with a beer, swooning over George Clooney.

Saturday, 15 July 2000

A closed-door game with Hamilton Accies at Lochinch today.

After picking up Moorie, then collecting his boots from Greaves, we make Firhill just in time to see Tid and his Under-18 squad leave for their first pre-season game.

JL, meanwhile, makes wholesale changes from Wednesday night. These games are all about fitness and therefore squad rotation is a foregone conclusion. But try telling that to a guy who finds himself on the bench for one. That is to say, me. Am I a sub because of my performance on Wednesday? What if my replacement has a blinder? Where do I stand in the great scheme of things? Where do I stand full stop?

My replacement is David McCallum, now over his hammy. Stopper Alan Archibald is also demoted to the bench to give Mark McNally another game. The mysterious Julian makes way for Kenny Arthur in goal and Robert Dunn comes in up front for Mowgli, who has a slight groin strain.

Joining myself, Archie and Julian on the bench are youngsters Willie Howie and Derek Lyle, as well as the very tanned Ian Cameron, back from holiday yesterday and familiar with most of the squad through having been a Jag before and having been around football so long.

JL tells us before the start what substitutions we'll make at half-time. I'll be going on for Deeks McWilliams wide left of a midfield four. Wide and tricky I am not, but I'd rather play there than not play at all.

We're 2–1 up at the break thanks to Dunnsy and Scott McLean and when JL switches things I know I must do better than Wednesday because David played well first half.

The fight for the jersey is on.

It's a poor second half by any standard. Our lack of communication, cohesion and creativity leaves JL fuming. As does the scoreline – somehow we snatch a 3–2 defeat from the jaws of victory and the gaffers make sure *everyone* knows where they stand.

Personally, the exercise has been beneficial from a fitness point of view and I'm happier with my distribution. I actually manage to find team-mates more often than I do the opposition.

JL senses tired legs and says there's no spark. Bizarrely, he gives everyone Monday off. The full-timers play a Rangers XI on Tuesday, the part-timers need not report until Wednesday – though most say they'll do some sort of workout on Monday to keep ticking over.

It's the first time in 14 pre-seasons I've been given a day off.

JL and GC go for talks with Mark McNally and his agent. Mark's been impressive in both outings so far and Carlisle also want a look, so JL might need to tie something up quickly.

Almost everyone has an agent now, every full-time player anyway. Fewer part-timers are represented, but that will change as more and more clubs cut costs and the number of guys like me increase. Me? I've never had an agent. My dad talked to all the clubs who were interested in me, the way most dads did back then, and since then I've negotiated all my deals personally. Why? For one, not too many agents would have been interested in representing me – there's not enough in it for them. And for another thing, few could have negotiated better deals than I've got for myself.

I know quite a few Scottish agents, guys like Frank Walker, Robert Connor, Alan McInally, Billy Dickson, Michael Oliver, Danny Crainie, Willie McKay and John Viola. How do I feel about them? They're basically earning on the back of how successful their players are. As a result, it may be to the agent's advantage for a client to actively try and re-negotiate his contract before it's up – or, indeed, for the agent himself to proactively manufacture transfer speculation. This can not only unsettle clubs, but the very players it is supposed to be benefiting. So yes, sometimes agents do more harm than good for all concerned in football. However, there's obviously a need for them in an era when some of the sums thrown around are too great for ordinary lads to get a grip of. I've just never felt that need – nor been lucky enough to be offered the kind of deals even the brightest player can't handle on his own.

Maybe I'd feel different if I was a better player.

Sunday, 16 July / Monday, 17 July 2000

Glasgow Fair weekend means Monday off from work and time for a real family-orientated weekend – the last time Carolyn, the kids and I will all be together until 12 August.

Thistle have a trip to Ireland next weekend and when I get back Carolyn will already be in Philadelphia on business, taking Dani with her and leaving Taylor and I to our own devices.

Sunday starts with a couple of hours in the Westerwood pool, followed by a barbecue in the garden – not often good weather and Bank Holidays go together, is it? – then an evening with neighbours Gerry and Elaine and all the kids in the street.

In between, I manage 25 minutes of skipping and a body circuit.

Monday's more of the same – a run in the car, a lovely lunch, then home to a couple of hours' paperwork followed by a workout at Westerwood to replace tonight's cancelled training session. After two weeks of pre-season I'm feeling much stronger on the treadmill.

Later Carolyn and I will watch *Angela's Ashes* on video, but first I take in the weekend papers, scouring the sports pages for titbits on the Scottish lower divisions. Like most Scotsmen, I read the papers from back to front. But tonight, it's only when I reach the front that my thoughts are truly provoked.

Today's tabloid tragedy is George Best, drunk again, 18 weeks after being told one more drink could kill him. He'd fallen out with his wife, so he went on a bender.

Poor Georgie.

He must be the only guy on the planet who argues with his wife, because if every marital barney means a husband being found paralytic on a park bench, all my friends have marriages made in heaven. Yet the nation is united in its sympathy for a legend! He's received messages of support from everyone who's anyone! Britain is agreed – it's a wee shame what's happened to Georgie Boy! Well, call me cold-hearted, cynical or downright cruel, but I have not one single molecule of sympathy for George Best.

George Best has milked football for decades without giving anything constructive in return. At every turn he and bitter old sidekicks like Rodney Marsh bleat on and on about how poor the game is nowadays. They tell us how much better the standard was when they played, how there are no characters any more, how players today couldn't lace their boots – or is it their drinks? – how players today are paid too damn much, but at the same time what incredible amounts they themselves would have been worth. Truth is, these guys are rolled out on telly and radio to do nothing but damn players who would have given their right arm to possess half the ability of George Best, yet continue to give their all long after Best himself had swanned out on the game. These are guys playing at the top of their profession, yet a man who wasted his talent ridicules them. Had George Best possessed *half* the commitment displayed by the majority of today's pros or even a *quarter* of the dedication of part-timers who work shifts first and train second, he might just have stayed at the top longer than the age of 26, and had a career *really* worth admiring.

Put a run-of-the-mill pro's attitude into Best and he might just have challenged the Peles, Eusebios, Puskases and Maradonas for the crown of the World's Greatest Footballer. Without that attitude, though, he has become what he is. Bestie nowadays? Bestie on 50K a week? Can you imagine what he would be up to with that money at his disposal? Even more failed clothes shops, even more wives, even more drink, even more nights on a park bench!

The only sadness I feel in all of this story is for those who dreamed of being George Best and have been let down by their hero. For those who adored the boy from Belfast and ended up disillusioned. For those whose careers were cut short by a cruel twist of fate and not because of self-abuse. For those like Alan Morgan, whose footballing dreams were shattered along with his knee while playing for Thistle last year. Today, he can only walk with the aid of a splint. Alan was never going to be the next George Best, but he could have made a worthwhile name for himself. That chance was taken away from him, he didn't choose to throw it away.

Isn't it strange, though, how the mega-talented usually have a vice which eventually crucifies them? Maradona, Baxter, Greaves, Best, Gazza and many more all gave into terrible temptations. I'm not saying footballers should be choirboys but, should their excesses come back to bite them, they shouldn't expect sympathy from lesser mortals who stuck at it with what they had.

As my anger at all this subsides and the day draws to a close, so a real tragedy emerges and a huge sadness wells inside us all. The body of eight-year-old Sarah Payne has been found after a long, heartbreaking wait for her family. Now let's talk about sympathy, sadness and life being unfair.

Tuesday, 18 July 2000

My gaffer Reg is back from the USA. I know this because my 7.30 a.m. alarm call has been reinstated. Usually the call is for him to bounce ideas off me or ask for information on our sales force's activity in the field. We also talk football a lot, usually Reg sounding off his concerns about his beloved Celtic. His knowledge of the lower divisions is better than most, but it's still pretty limited.

My mum's been watching the girls all day, so I nip over to Milton of Campsie and pick them up after work. Tuesday's the one night of the week when my dinner is always made and put on the table for me. God bless Saint Isabel.

I get home around seven, finish my paperwork, skip for 25 minutes then do my body circuit and finally manage a chat with Carolyn before bed at midnight.

Wednesday, 19 July 2000

Spent much of the day in Leonardo's restaurant in Glasgow's Bothwell Street, finalising invites to our company Golf Day in August and our Race Day at Ayr in September, drinking tea and eating their free tablet.

At Firhill, JL seems happy with the performance of the full-timers yesterday against Rangers, calling it probably the best performance he's likely to see this season. How's that for optimism? He also tells me he's quite happy that my performances have not been up to scratch, that he doesn't want me firing on full cylinders until 5 August. How's that for a morale boost?

Training tonight is again much more designed to game situations, with the squad split into three teams, the functions shorter and sharper and a real competitive edge. So competitive, in fact, it's not too long

before the first fall-out and handbags at dawn. Culprits are young
Dunnsy, who's given the ball away, and the more experienced Deeks
McWilliams, who's on the same team and gives him a bollocking.
Dunnsy chirps back and off they go. They square up, guys dive in, the
situation calms down and blood pressures are reduced. How often have
I seen this movie? How often has the red mist descended over players,
coaches and managers in these situations? One minute training's going
along dandy, the next a pass goes astray or a word is spoken out of turn
and suddenly guys who normally wouldn't say boo to a goose become
Hercules and want to take on the world. In the heat of the moment I have
seen devout Christians swear and fight, throwing punches at anybody
who got in the way; guys square up over where they sit in the dressing-
room; mild-mannered gentlemen with respectable, high-earning jobs
outside football grab people by the throats; doors kicked, walls punched,
teacups smashed.

Football must encourage a kind of schizophrenia. One minute Dr
Jekyll, the next Mr Hyde. Fans see some of it on the pitch at games or
via TV, but that's only the tip of the iceberg. What goes on within the
inner sanctum of football clubs and the privacy of training grounds
generally remains there. The dressing-room code of silence must not be
broken.

Dunnsy and Derek's altercation can be seen to be healthy. It shows
they care, that they don't want to be beaten, that they want to set higher
standards, to improve. Yet if all of these benefits can be gained from
every fall-out, why don't JL and GC want training games to be full of
skirmishes? It would certainly save them a lot of pep talks.

Away from training ground scraps, what is making their job more
difficult is the current injury situation. Walter 'The Vet' Cannon's
physiotherapy room is more like Emergency Ward 10. He's currently
treating:

*Doc – ankle aggravated during training.
*David McCallum – tweaked hamstring again yesterday versus
     Rangers.
*Moorie – blisters due to hard ground, a common pre-season
     problem.
*Derek Lyle – ripped tights.
*Scott McLean – sympathy for Del's ripped tights.

Others are complaining of sore legs and tiredness, mainly the full-time
boys. We part-timers are feeling like a million dollars. Sometimes I

wonder how these guys would – or could – adjust to having a 'real' job as well. Many have tried and failed. Their body clocks can't operate and they don't know when to eat before training, what to eat before training, even if they *should* eat before training. But more and more are going to have to adjust as the likelihood of more part-time clubs looms ever closer. Either that or they'll be lost to the game.

Thursday, 20 July 2000

Partick Thistle have a very large family, though sadly many of them don't visit often enough. It's this latent support which makes very few outsiders realise the club's potential – I certainly didn't until I signed in June 1998.

Working in Glasgow, I came across very few Queen of the South fans – the odd Dumfries expat would recognise me or my name, but we're talking extremely odd – yet as soon as I signed for Thistle, people were appearing out of cupboards, toilets, boardrooms and cars telling me how they never realised I 'played' football. For my part, I'd no idea how many people I knew, even within my client base, who were Thistle fans. It was astonishing and it's been a real positive from a business point of view.

Hopefully someday, all the armchair Thistle fans will actually come out and pay their money. But that day isn't likely to come before Thistle again make the top flight, where they last played six years ago. It needs SPL football, TV coverage, sponsorship opportunities and media exposure to bring some people to games. Whether I'll still be around the place by the time they get it remains to be seen. All I can do is work hard while I'm needed to try and get us on the right road.

At Firhill, there are concerns over the right-back slot. Doc isn't shaking that ankle knock and I think JL's contemplating a signing. He also confirms his delight at Dunnsy and Deeks' fall-out last night – as suspected, he sees it as a positive. He's happy with the way the players are coming together, both on the playing and personality sides.

Training again is short and sharp and JL throws in a couple of really enjoyable functions – trouble is, they're all designed for the right hand side of the park, so the pressure's on left-footed players like me, Archie and Ian Cameron to get our swingers into working order.

Later we have a game and JL and GC are delighted with the workrate. We finish relatively early and gangling midfield genital Martin Hardie, an Edinburgh electrician, says he may even have time for dinner tonight before packing for our trip to Ireland. Me? I'll pack tomorrow night. Tonight I'm off to Tesco before heading home to see the kids, who should still be up as we have finished earlier.

Oh, the glamour of it all . . .

Saturday, 22 July 2000

The season's first crisis – we've been let down by kitmakers SECCA and our club tracksuits haven't arrived in time for Ireland, so as Moorie's wife Kim drops us off at 8.15 a.m. we certainly don't appear part of a very professional club. Every player is dressed in his own tracky or shorts, each in different styles and colours of tops – and then there's Derek Lyle, looking a million dollars in head-to-toe denim. It's amateur hour and we look like Ragarse Rovers. The only uniformity comes from chairman Brown McMaster and director Allan Cowan, both resplendent in blazer, shirt and tie and cream chinos. I tell them they look like Jack Lemmon and Tony Curtis in *Some Like it Hot*. How they laugh.

We're taking two guest players with us. One is Sandy Stewart, 11 years at Airdrie yet recently made redundant, with a year of his contract remaining, by the financially challenged club's provisional liquidator KPMG. Sandy's a versatile player, but mainly a right-back who could just be the answer to JL's problem position. The other is Jered Stirling, who started here before going to Motherwell and who's been with us for most of pre-season. Young, fit and possessing a sweet left foot.

Who said 'ominous'?

It's a buoyant crew who set off from Firhill, a bit like boys on a school trip. Before Glasgow is behind us all the crisps and sweets are scoffed, we're talking nights out and complaining about how early we've had to turn up. Me? I'm delighted. I didn't have to be up until 7 a.m., so that was a 45-minute lie-in. Lovely.

The bus ride to Troon, from where we Seacat to Belfast, passes quickly – partly because of Scott McLean's chat but mostly because he produces a pack of cards. We play Chase the Ace for relatively small cash and the banter's fabulous. Scott – aka 'Trigger' after the failed Mensa candidate in *Only Fools and Horses* – is also sporting a drastically shaven head. The fact that he did it himself without any sign of decapitation proves quite a talking point.

The Seacat is delayed half an hour, so we have two hours in total at the terminal. It's at times like these that you find who the extroverts are, who the conversationalists are, who prefers his own company and who didn't get enough sleep last night.

A hard core of about 12 have congregated and are passing the time with general knowledge or football-orientated quizzes. The voices most commonly heard organising and suggesting options are Moorie, Danny Lennon and yours truly.

The hilarity and noise generated by the guys soon has the remainder of the terminal glancing our way and wondering what the joke is. As well as passing the time, the games also allow an insight into which players are quicker mentally than others, who has what musical taste and who will do anything to win. For one game where you have to name musical artistes in alphabetical order, Danny mentions Daniel O'Donnell and The Nolans, which suggests pretty dodgy taste. Trigger lives up to his name – for the letter 'I' he says Engelbert Humperdink.

The time flown in, we are soon powering our way to Belfast. A 20-minute transfer by coach takes us to our base for the next three days – The Hilton Hotel, Templepatrick. That's right. The *Hilton*! We reckon there must be some mistake. Maybe missed a zero off the room rate – or are we in the campsite out the back? No, we're inside right enough. There's even a red carpet rolled out at reception to meet the coach. Or is it for the Rolls-Royces carrying two wedding parties?

I'm sharing with new signing Jamie Smith. We settle in and within 15 minutes are sitting down to a meal before tonight's opening game against Derry City. Half an hour later, at 4.30 p.m., we're back on the coach to Derry. At their Brandywell ground, GC names the team: The Mysterious Julian, Sandy Stewart, Danny, Jamie, Stephen Craigan, Moorie, Ian Cameron, Trigger, Mowgli, Deeks and me. Everyone else is on the bench.

We kick off at 7.30 p.m. in blistering heat on a firm but well-kept pitch. There are maybe 300-400 there, including a very vocal Thistle support. Before the start, one Jags fan – in full Highland dress – is chanting over and over: 'One Des McKeown, there's only one Des McKeown. One Des McKeoooooooooooowwwwnnnn, there's only one Des McKeown.' After about the fourth chorus, Mowgli shakes his head and sighs about the dangers of strong drink.

I go into the game knowing 'One Des McKeown' needs to perform well. I'm feeling less secure than normal about my place in the team this year and realise the only way to secure the jersey is to make it hard for JL and GC to leave me out. Sounds simple, but that's football.

It finishes 0–0, with our performance better in the first half, possibly because we'd travelled for ten hours and perhaps also down to the heat and a lack of concentration. Personally, I'm happy and feel more like myself.

I'm my own worst critic and know when I have had a good or a bad game. Other notable performances come from Sandy Stewart (problem solved?) and Jamie Smith, who either shows why the club have paid money for him or whose room-mate's talent is rubbing off on him. Stephen Craigan also has a solid game. On a negative note, the mysterious Julian has had a nightmare and probably done his chances of a contract no favours. His communication, distribution and one particularly spectacular fumble let him down.

After the game – and some hospitality from our hosts – we head back to our hotel for a few refreshments. By the end of the night the boys are into drinking games and young Derek Lyle and Martin Hardie fall foul of one numerically challenging contest called Buzz. For anyone who's never played it, I won't bore you with the technicalities. All you have to know is that Del and Martin were soon the worse for wear due to their inability to calculate in multiples of six, seven and eight.

The evening ends with the infiltration of one of the wedding receptions – invited, obviously. How many weddings have you been at when guests turned up in shorts and flip-flops? Some of our guys have no shame, though. You couldn't paint a red neck on most of them.

Back home, my brother-in-law Martin – married to Carolyn's sister Mary – is having his fortieth birthday party. It's in full swing when I phone Carolyn after the game. It's the full marquee in the back garden, disco/karaoke and scores of friends and family members. It's not the first time I've had to miss a party, wedding, communion, parent's night, anniversary, doctor's appointment or any other type of family commitment due to football. And it sure as hell won't be the last.

Sunday, 23 July 2000

A free day, yet even when left to our own devices players prefer to work to timetables and structures. Ask them to think for themselves and they struggle. Footballers always want to know what time have they to do this, when to do that, who's doing this, who's in charge of that. Looking after themselves for a whole day is a daunting challenge.

Some of the boys have mentioned playing golf on the adjoining course, so I investigate organising a competition. After negotiations with the hotel and local pro, I acquire 8 sets of clubs for hire, 51 balls and tee-off times for the 10 who want to play. I also manage to charm my way to securing some donations to present as prizes and to add a little extra spice we sort out longest-drive and nearest-the-pin competitions.

Three groups go out – Martin Hardie, Dunnsy, Trigger and Jered; Danny, Jamie and Cammy; Derek Lyle, Willie Howie and Des McKeown. Handicaps are noted and it is agreed there will be Scratch and Handicap prizes. Eighteen holes, four-and-a-half hours and countless one-liners later we hijack a young Spanish lady to present this roll of honour:

> *Nearest the Pin – Martin Hardie.
> *Longest Drive – Derek Lyle.
> *Handicap Prize – Robert Dunn.
> *Scratch Prize – Des McKeown.
> *Worst Score – Trigger.

Allan Cowan takes some photographs and, several speeches later, the boys head off for a shower to freshen up for dinner.

Those who elected not to golf have either gone shopping in Belfast or lazed around the hotel. JL's been visiting a friend and upon his late evening return declares training for tomorrow morning and retires the players at 11 p.m.

Jamie and I watch BBC highlights of Tiger Woods completing the Grand Slam by winning The Open at St Andrews. He gets $600 zillion and a solid gold claret jug. I received a bottle of white wine for my day of triumph and a fat lot of good that is to a teetotaller. The only similarity is that we both wore Nike caps.

Back home, Carolyn has just completed 10.2 miles in preparation for her half marathon. She's dehydrated and unable to spend too long on the phone. Dani and Taylor are both fine.

Monday, 24 July 2000

Up bright and early and into my best Ruth Madoc impersonation.

Down for breakfast at 8.15 a.m., the restaurant staff ask whether the rest of the party are aware service stops at 9.30 as opposed to the previous day's 10.30. So, *Hi-de-Hi* style, I phone all of the rooms to advise of the change of plan.

Training is at eleven, and is designed to loosen off the legs for tonight's game against Portadown, but it also provides notable performances from Dunnsy and Mowgli. Both have torrid times and are neck-and-neck in the race for the yellow jersey awarded to the poorest performance of the trip.

A very, very lazy afternoon follows before JL names tonight's game. As suspected, I don't start, but will play the second half wide left, replacing Deeks. Full team: Kenny Arthur, Sandy Stewart, Stephen Craigan, Alan Archibald, Jered Stirling, Moorie, Martin Hardie, Ian Cameron, Deeks, Dunnsy and Mowgli. Second-half changes will be me for Deeks, Derek Lyle for Dunnsy, Trigger for Mowgli, David McCallum for Cammy, Willie Howie for Moorie, Jamie for Stephen and Danny for Martin.

Our bus to the ground offers a few reminders of the tensions still simmering in this part of the world. Portadown is an eye-opener, with its red, white and blue kerbstones, lamp-posts and bunting. Union Jacks and Red Hand of Ulster flags adorn every house. The boys aren't sure what to say and are glad to get their minds back on football as we arrive at Shamrock Park.

We're off and running in bright sunshine with a decent first-half performance, Martin Hardie scoring in its final minute to give us the lead. Best performances come from Martin, Mowgli and Jered, while Sandy is – again – solid and Stephen and Archie too.

Changes made, my first involvement includes a lovely crossfield pass after JL hints at me to release the ball earlier after I'm caught on it once or twice. He's not the world's greatest diplomat and usually conveys exactly what he wants in exactly the style he wishes. Tonight is no exception.

'Des, you c***!' 'Aw, for fuck's sake, McKeown.'

Funny how you always hear the shouts directed at yourself, yet don't always hear instructions to others. That's why it's fairly obvious when a player is ignoring the manager. However, my next meaningful involvement is to react quickest to a bouncing ball in midfield and time my header well to release Trigger for our second goal. This makes me feel better and hopefully JL too.

The game peters out and victory is confirmed with goals from young Willie Howie and David McCallum. I've had a sticky spell in the middle of the half but a good workout, with plenty of supporting runs in attack and defence. JL and GC are fairly happy and it's nice to have had two clean sheets.

No hospitality from Portadown, so it's back on the bus and a stop-off at Julie's Kitchen in Belfast for fish suppers. We mainly talk music on the way home with one or two surprising the group with their tastes.

Turns out Mowgli's a massive Elvis fan – a 50-CD box set is even mentioned – Danny declares admiration for Billy Joel and Deeks not only plays in the same area as me but has the same karaoke party pieces, 'Mack the Knife' and 'That's Life'. Looks sure can be deceiving.

I speak to Carolyn and Dani before they leave for Philadelphia tomorrow morning. Carolyn's been feeling rough all day after last night's run, but must be getting better now – she gives me my list of chores to do while she is away.

* Water the flowers in the garden.
* Take her car for a run to keep the engine ticking over.
* Put Dani and Taylor's old pram into the loft.
* Plant a new shrub.

I note each duty and wish both my girls a safe journey with lots of love. It seems a long time until I'll see them again.

Tuesday, 25 July 2000

After breakfast and checkout we hang around the hotel lounge for an hour for our bus to the ferry terminal. Some read, some sleep. Six or seven of us get back to Chasing the Ace – a stupid decision on my part, as I don't win a hand for the full hour. Stephen Craigan and David McCallum win plenty.

At the terminal, we find Scottish papers and catch up on the real world. Celtic are playing West Ham at Parkhead tonight in a game billed as The Return of Paolo Di Canio. Damian McKenna and I have been invited along by a client, but it'll be touch and go timewise. The two-and-a-half-hour Seacat crossing flies in, my money keeps flying out. I'm £30 down – hardly England Squad standard, but heavy enough for a part-timer. (Will I never learn that nobody can be good-looking *and* lucky?) Frantic phone calls back and forward to Damian keep him in touch with our progress and we agree he'll pick me up at Firhill at 6 p.m.

There are plenty of Celtic fans on board heading for the game and JL is getting pretty wound up – both by them and through worrying about the three pigeons he's got packed away down in the hold. He's a huge pigeon-fancier and regularly compares his birds to his players. During one demanding early session in blistering heat, one of the guys complained there was no water left. JL screamed: 'My fucking pigeons fly non-stop from France and don't need fucking water!' Need I say more?

The game is fairly entertaining, Celtic winning 2–1 with Di Canio scoring the West Ham goal, though it's a striker called Frederic Kanoute who catches my eye.

I rush home to reintroduce myself to Taylor (sometimes Carolyn shows the kids my photograph to remind them what I look like!) and after half an hour of kissing and cuddling I drop her off with Carolyn's mum Margaret – another saint – with whom she's staying until Friday night.

Back home to unpack, stick on washing and get ready for tomorrow's workload. In bed at 12.30 p.m. Asleep before the light's out.

Wednesday, 26 July 2000

Up at 6.15 for an 8 a.m. meeting in Glasgow with Car Wash. I'll be rushed off my feet the rest of the day. The phone's red-hot, as it was while I was in Ireland.

Met with Steve Wolstencroft, Sports Editor of the *Scottish Sun*, who's keen for me to write a fortnightly diary for the paper on my life juggling football, work and home life. It's an exciting opportunity and I intend to grasp it with both hands. The picture desk want to snap me in each of my 'lives' for the opening feature on 5 August – in a business suit, at Firhill in my strip and at home with the girls. I suggest they fly Taylor and I to Philadelphia to meet Carolyn and Dani, but they don't buy it. It'll need to be just the two of us on Friday night. We agree a fee and I agree not to do interviews with other papers. I'm sure the other papers will be well gutted.

At Firhill, the team is read out for our friendly with Peterborough United. I'm on the bench again. Could be a long season. Then again, while JL might be unhappy with me and giving me a warning that I need to improve, he might just be having another look at Jered Stirling.

I wish everyone luck – including Jered – and mean it sincerely. I'm a great believer that it's a squad game and although for the first time in my career I may be looking at a place in a squad rather than a permanent shirt, only one person can change things – me.

The first half goes OK, with Deeks brilliant despite being out of position at right wing-back. Jered's also doing well on the left, while David McCallum, Martin Hardie and Trigger also look the part. Then Martin signals that he's struggling with a hammy, so there is going to be a change at half-time. The other subs are three teenagers and a 20-year-old, but the way I'm feeling, I'm not convinced it'll be me who goes on. But yes, come half-time I get the nod from GC – and go in as a straight swap in centre midfield. It's not a position I've been accustomed to during my career, but I'll give it a go.

It feels like 20 minutes before I get a touch, but I manage a lovely switch of play and after this I'm involved fairly regularly and quite happy with my contribution. I might even have scored. Late on, ref Bobby Orr – who I'm negotiating with for his company's office supply contract – blows for a foul when the advantage rule would have left me one-on-one with the keeper. When I challenge Bobby over his decision he tells me that he was trying to save my embarrassment because he knows finishing's not my strong point. Cheers, pal.

JL and GC are fairly satisfied with a 0–0 draw. Top men have been Deeks, Jered and the three centre-backs. We've played well enough overall without carrying a real cutting edge.

On the injury front, Martin's hamstring is tight, Stephen Craigan has a slight groin strain, Trigger's taken a calf knock, Ian Cameron's ankle is swollen from a knock in Ireland, Moorie's blisters have been rested and Doc's ankle is no better. Walter the Vet is going to be busy!

Thursday, 27 July 2000

In Falkirk early on with Graham, then back to Glasgow for the rest of the day. At lunchtime I bump into a good friend, Adrian McKenna – brother of Damian and known as Ziggy.

Ziggy's the classic case of a full-time footballer (he started at Hibs) who wasn't going to finance the lifestyle he wanted through football, so who decided to go part-time and concentrate on a career which will now be earning him treble his wages at Easter Road. Our relationship's been a little strained since he defected from Oyez to one of our major competitors. I feel slightly let down by him as I've done everything to help his career, yet he turned his back on me despite an unbelievable offer to stay. I respect his decision to go because he's doing what he thinks is right for himself, his wife Alison and their three young kids – but in my eyes what he's done was a bit like Mo Johnston signing for Rangers after agreeing to go to Celtic. Ziggy's also turned Judas for 30 pieces of silver and betrayed Reg and me.

Of course, this is becoming more and more regular in football, with players signing long-term contracts which they immediately begin working their way out of. What was the point of signing it in the first place? In Scotland we've seen van Hooijdonk, di Canio, Cadete, Viduka – Celtic sure can pick 'em – and in England you can count Anelka, Emerson, Hamman, Barmby, Unsworth and Hasselbaink as players who've been anything but honest with their employees. Someone shakes a bag of money at them and before you can count to ten they're swearing allegiances to a club they don't even play for yet! Football is being well and truly shafted by these individuals, though managers can also prove to be less than reputable. For instance, a very good friend of mine was released by Club A this summer. Having agreed terms with Club B, the manager of Club C offered him a contract. My friend explained he'd given his word to Club B and would keep it. Club C's manager then openly tried to persuade my friend to break his word and to sign for them instead. Thankfully, my friend has principles and said no. If only there were more like him.

Late in the afternoon, while doing my paperwork in Leonardo's, up comes my old Albion Rovers boss, Lisbon Lion Tommy Gemmell. He tells me that he and the other members of Celtic's 1967 European Cup-winning squad are being entertained tonight by Martin O'Neill, who's just taken over at Celtic and wants to speak to them collectively. It would be most unlike the Lions to turn down hospitality.

After a swift red wine, Tommy wishes me all the best and asks me to pass his regards to JL and GC. As he leaves, I realise how blasé I am about meeting guys like him – in my life I talk to men others treat as gods, men with international caps and medals galore. But that's the beauty of football. A stationery salesman (and often stationary left-back) can mix with legends and not be reduced to a quivering wreck because, although my ability is nowhere near theirs, there's some sort of respect between professionals. I like that.

I also like the fact that training tonight is not too heavy, mostly leg-loosening after last night's game, though at the end GC takes those who didn't play the full game for some extra work. For the first time in my career, I'm one of those working on the training field instead of the playing field. Some of the guys ask if the manager has explained to me why I wasn't playing. Are they asking through surprise? Or rubbing it in? I tell them all the same thing – no! JL never mentioned his thinking to me and I don't expect him to. His next move is up to me.

I take Taylor out for a McDonald's and promise that tomorrow night she can sleep in my bed and we'll cuddle all night. Carolyn and Danielle phone around midnight, then it's lights out.

Friday, 28 July 2000

Glasgow all day, looking forward to having Taylor at home tonight. After I finish work at 6.00 p.m., I pick her up from Margaret's and we get ourselves beautiful for our photo-shoot with *Scottish Sun* photographer Michael Schofield. Half an hour's snapping and then it's curry, *Friends* and bed with Taylor. It's good to hold someone.

Saturday, 29 July 2000

A restless night ends when Taylor wakes me at 9.30 a.m. We started off in bed together, but when she fell out at 3 a.m. and then I put my foot in her face for the tenth time I decided it wasn't the ideal preparation for today's game. I took her through to her own bed and after that I slept like a baby.

After pre-match beans on toast, I drop Taylor at my mum's and head to Firhill for a noon photo-shoot in my Thistle strip. Rather than head home again, I hang around until our 1.45 p.m. reporting time for the final pre-season game against English Third Division side Chesterfield.

As the season approaches it seems our numbers are dropping and the boys mention how few bodies are in the changing-room. The Mysterious Julian is no longer with us and one or two injuries magnify the problem of carrying a small squad.

JL and GC name the team at two and I'm in from the start. I'm operating as a left wing-back – we call it the Graveyard Shift because of the thankless ploughing up and down the touchline. Jered is on the bench. The full team is: Arthur, McWilliams, McKeown, Craigan, Smith, Archibald, Moore, Lennon, Dunn, Hardie and McGrillen. Subs: Lyle, Stirling, McCallum and Howie.

I'm well aware that I need to perform well after Jered's good display on Wednesday. The pressure is mounting and I really do feel I'm playing for my future

After our warm-up, JL and GC give final orders and organise set-plays and we're off. My first involvement is to miscontrol a long crossfield pass that gives the ball away. Not a good start and unfortunately it gets worse.

The first half is a personal and collective disaster. We're outclassed, outpassed and out-manoeuvred by a very tidy side. I have a shocker – everything I do is wrong, everything. My distribution's painful and the bench don't miss me about it. Once, when I've had to knock the ball long into the inside-left channel and a towering defence mops it up, GC gives me dog's abuse for losing possession. For the first time I can remember in my career, I snapped and shouted back at him, saying I had no options because no one was moving. GC shouts back and so do I. It's only later I think of the significance of this episode and analyse my behaviour. I'd never have dreamed of shouting back at a manager before – in fact, if I was a manager and someone talked back to me, I'd sub him. This was how my old Queen of the South boss Billy McLaren worked. When he spoke, you listened. I can't believe I've been so disrespectful to GC and can only put it down to frustration at knowing how badly I was playing, at giving the ball away and because I know I'm doing myself no favours.

Half-time comes, we're 1–0 down, and JL goes to town. He slaughters everyone for lack of movement, lack of composure, lack of urgency, lack of ability. He doesn't single anyone out, but Moorie and I know we've probably been the two worst offenders.

Willie Howie replaces Moorie and the overall display's much better. Me? I suppose it couldn't have got any worse, so I'm much happier with my second half. One worry is that my legs feel heavy and as others feel the same perhaps our pre-season programme has not been as successful as planned. Hopefully games will tone up our match fitness.

I'm subbed by Jered after 75 minutes and JL says well done, but he must be complimenting my workrate. It finishes 1–0 and the biggest plus is Willie Howie, who performs exceptionally for an 18-year-old – if he holds down a place it won't be long before clubs are sniffing.

JL's main concern is that we've failed to score in three of our four serious pre-season games. The saving grace collectively is we're unlikely to face a team as good as Chesterfield again. Personally, it's that Moorie's performance makes me feel a little better.

Monday, 31 July 2000

After a lovely Sunday with Taylor, it's back to the grind in Glasgow. The last day of the month always means ensuring the guys have processed all orders to generate as many sales as possible. Reg is on and off the phone regularly with updates.

Today's papers call the Chesterfield game one of two halves. Willie Howie gets some good press, which is great for him. Players at our level revel in any media coverage as there's so little of it – though one not-so-happy news item appears in the *Daily Record*, where JL says: 'I am looking for a left-back.'

I am numb.

I know I haven't played well, but for him to say in the national press that he wants to replace me is a shock. Do I knock JL's door down and demand to know where I stand? Do I ask away? Ignore his comment? Or use this criticism as a spur to prove him wrong? I know my ability and, when called upon, it's up to me to prove he doesn't *need* another left-back. The article also says Jered is having talks with JL today.

Looks like my season might not kick off on 5 August after all, even if my newspaper career does. After discussing my first column with the *Scottish Sun*, I head for training. GC is off watching Livingston, who we've drawn in the Bell's Challenge Cup, so JL is assisted by masseur and general handyman 'Disco' Dave Wiseman.

JL sets up some fairly heavy running exercises with the final run-through timed. Out of all the players, yours truly is quickest. Is the criticism working already? We go on to do some finishing exercises and the mood is very good, with everyone winding everyone else up – chief victim is Tid, who's on the next field with the Under-18s. On Saturday morning, he'd taken his kids to play Celtic and lost 3–0. Or that's what he told everyone, right up to the manager and the chairman. Turns out they actually lost 8–0 and the boys give Tid pelters for lying. The guys reckon his job must be under pressure and the season hasn't even started yet!

Training brings a few knocks – Cammy aggravates his ankle injury and steps out, Deeks' groin tightens during shooting practice and he takes a precautionary back seat, and Alan Archibald slips and cuts his kneecap open. He needs ten stitches and must be a doubt for Saturday.

Into the bargain, Jered's not happy with the part-time terms on offer and he's not sure about signing. At this rate I might play at Arbroath by default.

FIVE

Tuesday, 1 August 2000

THAT'S THE THING about having two jobs – there's always the chance that *one* of your bosses will be happy with you. In my case, while I might not have blown JL away in pre-season with Thistle, it seems I've had a phenomenal July as a salesman. Our monthly sales meeting tells us figures are generally better than expected and I'm delighted at my own performance.

Steve Brown, director of Electronic Office Supplies for our parent company OyezStraker, has come up for the meeting and it's a long, busy day – we're right through from 8 a.m. until 6 p.m.

I rush home to visit my mum and dad then spend some time with Taylor before sitting down around nine to start my paperwork with AC Milan's centenary game against Real Madrid on telly in the background. Real win 5–1, but in truth they've put out their reserves and it only goes to prove these pre-season kickabouts really do mean bo-diddly. If you want an example nearer to home, look at Queen's Park. Last season they were well and truly gubbed in every friendly, but went on to win the Third Division title.

After another body circuit, it's lights out around 12.30 a.m.

Wednesday, 2 August 2000

Funny how a few positive words from above can work wonders – on the back of yesterday's figures and Steve Brown's talk on his side of the business I'm flying as I make my calls across flash-flooded, thunderstruck Glasgow today.

Later, I'm at the Nuffield Hospital in the city's West End for a check-up on the shoulder problem that saw me suffer *eight* dislocations last season. I've been on an intensive physio programme and the consultant, Ian Kelly, is happy and says that I don't need surgery.

At Firhill that night, the home dressing-room is more like the beauty counter at John Lewis – there's moisturiser, hair gel, aftershave and deodorant everywhere. Anyone who's anyone is packing a toilet bag – except JL, who always ponces other people's kit – and that can only mean one thing. The team photo.

Mowgli's admiring himself in one mirror, Kenny Arthur's checking his blond streaks in another. Trigger and Moorie are scraping off stubble and goatee respectively. Me? At 30 and with a receding hairline, I don't kid myself on. Nothing I could do will change these looks.

As the snappers snap happily away, JL cracks jokes and moans that his seat's wet, but we all know he's more worried about his hair. He's plainly had an appointment today for a fresh demi-wave and just before the cameras appeared he's done his usual and disappeared to lacquer his barnet to death. If only he was as worried about his dress sense.

Posing over, it's down to the floodlit Firhill Complex to work on set-plays for Saturday's game at Arbroath – but although I'm heavily involved, I'm not taking it as a guarantee of a shirt. GC seems to be getting a team in shape, but JL's been known to fly by the seat of his pants and change things at the last minute. By this time, actually, JL's made his excuses and left for a Business Club function back at the ground. I'll be along later to join in a steak-and-wine-tasting evening. Anything for a free dinner!

Alan Archibald trains and will probably make Saturday. Ian Cameron and Derek McWilliams also take part – but Deeks has to pull out again due to his thigh strain. Steven Craigan isn't around – he's spending the night in hospital after severe headaches.

Speaking of which, I get home at 11 p.m. to find the lightning's knackered the house's electrics – my burglar alarm wakes up the street by blaring for 15 minutes when I try to reset it. At midnight, I finally sit down for the first time today to watch the Sky Sports headlines – or would have if the satellite system wasn't also jiggered. I go to bed wondering when I'll find time to let an engineer in to fix it.

Carolyn phoned from Washington tonight. She and Dani were at the White House today. They're fine, but missing Taylor and me. The feeling's mutual.

Thursday, 3 August 2000

Steve Brown comes with me on a few appointments in Glasgow which could result in plenty of new business. After he heads for the airport, I use Firhill as an office until training at 5.30 p.m.

Again it's set-plays, this time with JL involved and again with me in the thick of it all. When JL says he intends to play a 3-5-2 on Saturday I wonder where – or if – I fit in. Maybe wide left of the five? Or left centre-back if Stephen isn't fit? Then again, Jered Stirling's signed a one-month contract, so maybe I'll be on the bench.

I'd say there are only seven certain starters – Arthur, Archibald, Smith, Lennon, Cameron, McGrillen and McLean. Just about everyone believes he has a chance of one of the other four places.

After training, club skipper Danny Lennon reads out the bonuses and appearance money on offer for the season. The main debate is over unused subs – those of us with appearance fees in our contracts are unhappy that the club now want to deny us that unless we come on. My argument is that a guy good enough for the bench is getting no more than a guy in the stand.

In many of our experiences, other clubs pay appearance fees irrespective, but Danny washes his hands of it and says it's a matter for players who have appearance fees in their contract. He hasn't. The players affected ask Moorie and myself to argue the case.

We corner JL, who takes the club stance. A heated debate – not to be confused with an argument – takes place over the wording of the contracts, which says an appearance fee will be paid to any player *participating* in a first-team match. I'd say a player on the bench is still participating and that the club is playing with words. JL and GC don't agree.

Allan and myself leave the office no further forward but I will phone Alan Dick tomorrow and Moorie will see him after training.

Friday, 4 August 2000

One day to the big kick-off.

A few appointments, lunch with a client, pick up boots from Greaves for Jered. Most of my clients want to know if I'm playing. I can't answer 'yes' with any confidence.

JL phoned Alan Dick at home last night to report his conversation with Moorie and me. The suggestion is we're causing a dressing-room revolt. I explain that we're representing all the players, not just ourselves. All we want is clarification of a very ambiguous contract. Alan agrees and says he'll speak to players individually. He guarantees that if I'm on the bench but don't play I'll pick up 50 per cent of my appearance fee. I'm happy at that because I don't intend spending too many games on the bench. But I tell him I'm unhappy that Danny didn't get involved on our behalf – maybe if he had, JL wouldn't have thought Moorie and I were only looking after our own interests. I'll be telling Danny that from now on he should be our voice, along with one or two senior pros.

It's been reported today that we've signed Swedish striker Peter Lindau, a hit with the fans while on loan from Ayr last season. His arrival will add even more optimism around the place and might also change JL's personnel and tactics for tomorrow.

Saturday, 5 August 2000

It's here at last. Christmas all over again. But will Santa Lambie give me what I want – a starting place away to Arbroath?

The excitement of opening day is terrific. I love it, always have. Doesn't matter who you play for or who you're playing, it's special. Before all that, though, there's stuff to do.

Taylor came in beside me about half-five, I got up at eight a.m. after a fabulous sleep and started getting organised – breakfast, get Taylor's clothes together for a stay with my sister Anne Marie and her husband Stuart, take her over there then pick up a copy of the *Scottish Sun* to see the launch of *Des's Diary*.

Usually we break our journey to away games and have a pre-match meal but today we're meeting at Firhill at 10.30 a.m. to eat in the Aitken Suite below the main stand. I pick up Moorie on the way and drop in to see Tid to get his thoughts on my debut column. He likes it.

When we arrive at the ground, most of the boys have already started their toast and beans or scrambled egg. I choose beans and eat to a chorus of comments about the diary – 'How much did you get for that?' 'Where'd you get the bulge in your shorts from?' 'What a load of pish!' etc. My mobile's already been ringing with various friends and fellow players commenting on it, but I knew the boys would deliver the most abuse.

Peter Lindau has signed but is struggling with a stomach problem. Stephen's also ruled out thanks to his headaches. Like every other player, I'm thinking only of how these injuries affect my chances. My best chance is if JL sticks with his 3-5-2. If he goes back to 4-4-2 I expect to be on the bench – at best.

JL and GC appear at eleven and declare that they're going to read out the team and give their talk just now, as the Gayfield dressing-room is too cramped for a comfortable discussion. So, here it comes. Am I in or out? Has all the sweat been for nothing? I'm hearing JL read, but only listening for the name 'McKeown'. I look at the magnetic tactics board and see it's laid out on a 3-5-2. Is that good for me?

Come on, gaffer, read my name. He's still going. He's at No. 10 now, it's Mowgli.

'. . . and 11, Des McKeown.'

Des McKeown? That's me! I'm in! Now I can grasp that the others he's shouted out are Arthur, McCallum, Stirling, Lennon, Smith, Archibald, McWilliams, Cameron and McLean. Now I can relax and prepare for the season.

I'm playing left centre-half and feel part of the bigger picture again, even if only because of Stephen's bad luck. I don't care. In football it's up to the player wearing the shirt to show he should be in the team. As my old Thistle team-mate Paul McDonald said to me when I was getting pelters from the fans during my first season: 'You're only 90 minutes away from being a hero.' And he was right – no matter how I got in, I know a good 90 minutes could help me stay in. The amazing thing is, I've never played this position for JL, so I take some confidence from the fact that he thinks I can do the job.

JL and GC give the same speech that rings round every dressing-room on opening day – the one about this being where the real stuff starts. They also tell us there are to be no cards played on the bus – my feeling is they don't want anyone's focus damaged by losing a packet on the way up.

Most clubs have an away-trip card school, sometimes with serious cash changing hands. You can see why gaffers would worry about a boy who'd just chucked away £500. The QoS card school was brilliant and made journeys fly in. It was me, Stephen Cody, Cool Hand Duncan Campbell – the lucky bastard who usually cleaned up – Colin Campbell, John McLaren, Andy McFarlane and occasionally Jim Butter or Colin Harris.

On this occasion, the boys are not too down about the ban because Deeks has brought *Carlito's Way* on video and we settle down to watch Pacino at his best. The film ends in perfect time for us to arrive at rainswept Gayfield, perched on the edge of the North Sea and buffeted by the obligatory tornado.

In the tearoom, Karen and Margaret say I seem a lot happier than last time, though they're not to know how close I was to being pissed off all over again. As I chat to Arbroath guys like George 'Ginger Geordie'

Rowe, Jimmy Thomson, Ian Cardle, John McAuley and Craig Hinchcliffe, it's interesting to see how others pass the time before it's time to get the working clothes on. Some fidget with the match programme in the tiny dressing-rooms, some inspect a good-looking playing surface, others huddle together in groups discussing team selection, some don't know any of the opposition, have never played here before and are trying to figure it all out! I have my cup of tea and head for the dressing-room.

JL names the subs – not sure why he delayed this – then goes for a smoke as we start getting stripped. GC puts the set-plays up on a board. Walter the Vet straps up ankles and sees to blisters. Disco Dave Wiseman does some rubs – though the old football adage says that good players don't need them and bad players don't deserve them. Personally I don't *need* one, but I like to have one as part of my preparation. Do I deserve one? Ask JL at ten to five.

There must be 1,000 Thistle fans in as we run out. They outnumber the home support two to one and to a man we applaud them. The rain has subsided and the sun has appeared but – right on cue at five to three – someone cranks up the wind machine. We shoot with it first-half.

The Arbroath boys are flying in at us. We want to build from the back and play through midfield, but they're stronger and taller and want the ball forward quicker. Their set-plays will cause any team problems with their height and from one of them three minutes from half-time Ginger Geordue Rowe equalises Trigger's strike from five minutes earlier.

Our goal is the result of some neat passing and a great cross from Jered Stirling and overall we've played some great stuff. I'm very happy with my contribution – I've used the ball fairly well, won most headers in my area and not been beaten on the ground in our final third.

JL's fairly happy at half-time but Trigger's blamed for not marking Ginger Geordie at their goal, although Kenny's also told to come off his line more.

It finishes 1–1 and, despite Mowgli missing one from two yards out, we'll take the point. I've done OK and feel as if the ghost of 6 May has been exorcised. This time I'm smiling at Karen and Margaret as I head for the bus.

Back in Glasgow, I treat myself to a night out with Car Wash and Thistle's very own Stephen 'Harry Handsome' Docherty.

Sunday, 6 August 2000

Took Taylor to the pictures to see *Stuart Little*, then did paperwork. Missed out the body circuit as my back's sore from yesterday.

Monday, 7 August 2000

Training tonight before tomorrow night's CIS Cup-tie at home to Airdrie, a tough game against a First Division side run by former Scotland striker Stevie Archibald and bolstered by around ten continental signings.

The session does little except loosen off our legs, though we also work on throw-ins. Stephen Craigan trains and, although JL says nothing, I've a feeling that means I'll be on the bench.

Paul Sturrock has resigned today as manager of Dundee United. Most assume the decision is health-related after his past coronary problems and they're half-right – Luggy tells the world he is simply heartsick of football. He says it has consumed him 24 hours a day for 20-odd years and he needs a break. To me, this further underlines the complexities a part-time player or manager faces trying to mix football and business – we too are consumed 24/7 by the game but still have to do our day jobs. Part-timers are no less committed than the likes of Paul Sturrock. We just don't have the vehicle of full-time football employment to prove it.

Tuesday, 8 August 2000

Another 6.15 a.m. rise, even though we have the cup-tie tonight. When midweek games come around, a part-timer can't allow his life to revolve around them. The wheels of industry keep on turning and by lunchtime so is my stomach – I'm starving but I only have time for a chicken roll and some fruit, hardly ideal nutrition for 90 minutes on the pitch. I take on plenty of water to keep myself well hydrated.

My final meeting is with John McDonagh of Scottish Legal Life. He also happens to be assistant manager of Ayrshire club Muirkirk Juniors and we talk hopes and plans for about half an hour.

I'm first to arrive at Firhill. As the hospitality suites prepare for their corporate guests, I blag a cup of tea and a pint of iced water. The others arrive and we speculate on the line-up – everyone thinks Lindau,

Craigan and Mowgli will be involved at some point. I reckon Trigger might be on the bench beside me.

Come 6.45 p.m. I'm listening for my own name again but this time it arrives at No. 14. So, I was right – but wrong on a few other selections. Michael Brown has replaced Kenny Arthur in goal, Stephen's in for me, Martin Hardie starts instead of the injured Deeks and finally Peter Lindau replaces Mowgli, with Trigger staying in. JL finishes his talk by saying he would like to speak to me and I follow him to his office.

'Des,' he says, 'I know you're disappointed and so you should be after Saturday . . .'

. . . so at least he thinks I did OK . . .

'. . . but Stephen has been excellent in pre-season.'

'I know,' I tell him. 'And I also know if he'd been fit on Saturday, I probably wouldn't have started.'

He makes no comment on this but goes on: 'Then there's the problem at right-back. If we had one I'd go back to 4-4-2 and you'd be left-back, but I don't, so I can't.'

I appreciate the chat.

Soon after, when I'm getting rubbed down by Disco Dave, Stephen himself comes over and as good as apologises for me being dropped. I tell him I'm big enough and ugly enough to accept JL's decision and not to worry about me – but, again, I'm grateful for the gesture.

So now comes a big decision – how to warm up. By warming up away from the first eleven, I might look like I'm in the buff – but by joining in with them I might get too prepared too soon. The last thing you want as a sub is to be ready to rock then sit on the bench and get stiff. I decide to do some of the squad's warm up but not the shorter, sharper movements. Then I do some stretching and mobility exercises on my own.

Back in the dressing-room, GC can't tell us who picks up who on set-pieces – simply because Airdrie are such an unknown quantity. Archibald has literally brought in a full team of foreigners, so it's down to the players to designate who marks who. I go round all the lads and wish them luck, spending most time with debutants Michael Brown and Peter Lindau.

Airdrie are soon in control, central midfielders Jesus Sanjuan and Toni Calderon catching the eye, and after 15 minutes our lack of knowledge on set-pieces is highlighted as defender Alfonso heads the opener.

Five minutes later I start warming up behind our goals, but as I jog back to the dugout Alan Archibald – who's been outstanding – shouts to me that he's twisted his knee. Another five minutes and I'm on. I spend the rest of the half trying to get the pace of the game.

Mowgli replaces Peter Lindau, still recovering from his food poisoning, and unsettles the Airdrie defence at last. When he goes down in the box after 55 minutes, Ian Cameron sees his spot-kick saved – but ten minutes later Trigger scores from the edge of the box and Firhill erupts. Martin Hardie has two good chances, Mowgli sees a tremendous strike saved and we head for extra time.

As the clock ticks towards penalties, I chase a ball deep into our own corner and keep it in play so we don't have to take a throw near our own bye-line. I turn and play a pass inside to Danny but two Airdrie men are on him, dispossess him, and in the struggle one of them goes down. Ref John Underhill gives a foul but his linesman signals – wrongly – that it was inside the box and the decision is changed to a penalty. Austin McCann makes no mistake from the spot and Moorie gives me dog's abuse for not kicking the ball long. I assume he'll not be alone, although I feel I was fairly justified in playing the pass.

The game ends with a mêlée after Jered's tackle leaves an Airdrie player writhing, but over the piece it's been anything but dirty. The only booking was for me after I slowed one of their strikers down a little unfairly.

As expected, JL and GC throw my pass to Danny at me, who boots a clothes basket in frustration. I know how he feels but I say the pass to Danny was on and Stevie Craigan backs me up. I tell GC and JL to get the video and see for themselves. I'm not trying to blame Danny, I'm just saying what I thought at the time. JL and GC are using hindsight to say it wasn't the best option, that if I'd kicked for Row Z Airdrie wouldn't have got a penalty.

Once we all cool off, I head into the Aitken Suite for a few pints of iced water. I always go in, win, lose or draw. Fans respect you more when you don't just mingle with them after good displays, though I don't stay too long tonight. Carolyn and Dani are home tomorrow.

Wednesday, 9 August 2000

A restless night. Awake at five, I lie for an hour re-running the penalty incident and thinking about seeing my wife and daughter again. The champagne is in the fridge, the flowers are ordered and I leave a card to them from Taylor and myself as I head for work.

The papers don't mention my pass, just that Danny gave away the penalty.

This afternoon I'm at Haggs Castle Golf Club for a corporate day with one of my clients, solicitors Biggart Baillie, and as soon as the round's finished I phone home to make sure the girls are there then hit the road. We have a lovely evening talking about their trip and about what Taylor and I have been up to. We gab until I am dead beat.

Thursday, 10 August 2000

Can't wait for work to end so I can get to Firhill and see the video evidence. JL's in a meeting with the chairman when I get there, but half an hour later he comes looking for me. We go to his office to watch the tape along with Stephen Craigan and Disco Dave.

It's not totally conclusive. Danny *was* available in space but the Airdrie players closed down very quickly. In hindsight, a launch up the park might have been more advisable. I hold my hands up.

Training is not too demanding after Tuesday and bearing in mind the coming game with Stranraer. Archie should be fit, so the best I can hope for is the bench. Martin Hardie's struggling with a neck injury, David McCallum's hamstring's tight, Peter Lindau's fine and Deeks is still out, though Doc is getting closer and closer to fitness.

GC chins me about the video.

'So what d'you think now?'

'OK, in hindsight I might have been better shelling it.'

'Yeah? Well, actually I've watched it and reckon your pass wasn't as bad as I thought. It was Danny who came short and looked for it.'

Odd. I'd never criticise a player who offered an option to a team-mate.

Friday, 11 August 2000

Most managers would frown at what I did today. But sometimes there are things a part-timer simply cannot get out of – in this case, a work's golf outing.

You're right, 18 holes round Cowal Golf Club in Dunoon followed by hospitality is not the ideal way to prepare for a game. But what can I or Graham 'Car Wash' Connell, my colleague and Queen's Park midfielder, do? Anyway, we're both naturally fit, so hopefully we'll be fine.

I'm away at seven in the morning and home at 9.30 p.m. after not only a fabulous day but also my lowest ever round – a scratch 76. During the day, John McDonagh talks about the Giffnock Soccer Centre he runs.

'Tell you what, we've got an eight-year-old there who'll *definitely* make the grade.'

My ears pricked up.

'Really? How can you tell that a kid as young as that will make it?'

'I just can.'

This starts a bit of a debate in which I argue that too many kids are discarded at 13, 14 and 15 and that clubs miss out by not tapping into 18-, 19- and 20-year-olds. Until then, the attitudes of these boys are not truly formed and attitude is a footballer's most vital asset. OK, so I wouldn't include the Figos, Zidanes and Bergkamps in this. But for the player of average ability it's all about how much they want to put in. GC always argues with this but I usually come back by asking: 'How many schoolboy players should have made it? They had loads of ability, but where are they now?'

Saturday, 12 August 2000

Billy McLaren is a tax inspector who eats, sleeps and breathes football. He managed me at Albion Rovers then paid £5,000 to take me to Queen of the South. Now he runs Stranraer and today he brings them to Firhill. He's a fascinating guy, someone who'd talk about the game all day and all night, and a highly intelligent man with a vocabulary unsurpassed in my football experience. However, he's better known for passion and emotion – let's just say his instructions are never misunderstood. Billy isn't shy to pat you on the back but neither will he shirk from kicking you up the arse! Queen's fans used to chant 'Psycho, Psycho give us a wave' at him, and he usually did.

Up at nine, I get the papers then organise breakfast for Dani and Taylor while Carolyn's at the gym to train for her half-marathon next week.

Over my pre-match spaghetti hoops on toast, I read that we've signed a right-back, Emilio Bottiglieri, on a month's loan from Hibs. Does this mean JL will go 4-4-2 and I'll be left-back? I know the answer before the team is named at five to two because the magnetic tactics board JL and GC carry into the dressing-room is set out 3-5-2. I'm on the bench with Moorie, Willie Howie, Derek Lyle and Michael Brown.

Robert Dunn is the only fit player not included and his frustration is simmering. He talks of needing to get away and it's obvious he did not expect to be involved – despite it being August, he's turned up with a jacket which could double as a duvet.

During the team talk, JL and GC ask me how I think Stranraer will play. They appear to feel I have the best knowledge of the Second Division and regularly ask for my input.

I see Billy just before the game and shake his hand as we make for our respective hutches.

We go in 1–0 up through Martin Hardie's goal and at half-time I optimistically change from moulded boots to studs thanks to a sudden downpour. Fifteen minutes in, with Ian Harty having hammered an equaliser, the subs are sent out to warm up. As on Tuesday, I get a message that one of our lads is struggling. This time it's Martin and on 63 minutes I'm thrown into central midfield. Three minutes later, Peter Lindau secures a 2–1 win.

JL and GC congratulate me on my performance but the real stars are Paul McGrillen, Stephen Craigan and Man of the Match Archie. The dressing-room is in great mood, if you ignore a couple of obvious exceptions. Moorie and Dunnsy are on suicide watch. Moorie did not get on and is talking of speaking to JL on Monday. Dunnsy's sitting there going: 'Well, at least you got stripped.'

Sunday, 13 August 2000

With Carolyn on a ten-mile run, I take the kids to see my folks then head up to watch juvenile club Campsie Black Watch play. They're managed by my uncle, Gerry Marley, who has possibly been the biggest influence in my career, a truly remarkable man who I would trust to advise me on any situation. Gerry devotes himself to the club in a way that will never be seen again – how many football bosses of the future will be awarded the MBE for services to the game as he was two years ago?

While I'm watching the game, people I haven't seen for years come up and comment on my new *Scottish Sun* diary. Later, while we're out for a meal at Guidi's in Coatbridge, Carolyn says she didn't realise the game meant as much as my first column illustrated. This astonishes me but I'm also happy I can hide my disappointment from the family. Maybe now she truly understands my feeling I won't hear any more negative comments about my football life. Doubtful, though.

Monday, 14 August 2000

My thigh hurts and I'm wary about training tonight, when we'll be doing short, sharp work before tomorrow night's Challenge Cup-tie against Livingston. I spend the day stretching at every possible opportunity – in offices, lifts, cupboards, even coffee shops. People must think I'm not the full shilling.

Livvy are cash-rich and favourites to win the First Division title this season, so the tie will be a hell of a test for us. Everyone's fit bar Deeks and Martin Hardie, who's nursing a sore neck but is away working on Stornaway in any case.

Moorie and I take the warm-up and plenty of abuse as well. My thigh feels fine. GC splits us into two teams, reds and blacks, for a game of possession. The blacks are truly awesome – or are the reds just shite? Whatever, the blacks begin to bounce on one leg and cover one eye to give the reds a chance. Still they keep the ball. Thank God I'm one of them.

Afterwards, JL tells us to report at 6.30 p.m. tomorrow night, a problem for me because of business commitments. He tells me to ring him during the day. Before I go home, Walter the Vet and club doc Alan Robertson give my thigh a going over and say it's fine.

Tuesday, 15 August 2000

Lesson Two in how not to prepare for a game of football – yes, sports fans, I'm golfing again. This time the clubs get lugged to Kinross, where we're sponsoring the SBA Golf Day. I've asked for an early tee-time so I can get back for the game and Car Wash Connell needs the same deal as Queen's Park are at home to Montrose.

First, I'm in Kinross for a 9.30 a.m. appointment with Ray Hardie, then head for the golf club to grab a cup of tea, a couple of bacon rolls and some chocolate – I told you it wasn't the ideal preparation – before hitting the course. On the tee, I tell my partners to forget their golf shoes and wear running spikes instead.

Three hours, 25 minutes and 85 blows later, my thigh feels fine and my mind's been on nothing but Livingston. I run off the 18th green, dump my clubs, change and drive off at warp speed, closely followed by Car Wash. By the time the rest have had high tea and picked up their prizes, I hope to be ploughing into a flying winger.

As it happens, I'm the first of the boys at Firhill and am met by

Thistle's answer to Abbot and Costello, kitmen Ricky and Chico. Their current catchphrase is to wait for a group of three players to go past and say: 'Good guy, good guy, wank!' Ricky, a definite good guy, makes me a cup of tea and I feel very awake and fresh.

As the rest arrive, they question my decision to play golf today. I tell them I had no choice, but they plough on, saying there's no way they'd be fit to play after 18 holes.

At 6.45 p.m. the magic board shows we're playing 4-4-2. JL names a team with eight changes from Saturday, including yours truly at left-back. Stevie Doc makes his first appearance of the season after his ankle problems. Dunnsy and Moorie have a smile on their wee faces again.

Livingston, meanwhile, have named a full-strength side. We're up against it but by half-time it's still 0–0 and we're doing OK. My legs feel good as we re-emerge into a monsoon, thunder and lightning. It's my shoulder that does me in.

Twenty minutes from time, Barry Wilson spins me and I fall. I know right away that the bloody thing's dislocated again. That's nine times since the start of last season and if nothing else it's made me an expert at manoeuvring the joint to let it pop back in. I've done it so often the guys have started calling me Riggs, after Mel Gibson's character in *Lethal Weapon*. He had the same problem – sadly, he also has loads more hair and money.

Back in the game, I'm feeling fine but things run away from us as a team. Livvy bring on my old boys club team-mate Gerry Britton and young striker Mark McCormick and the former turns the latter's cross in before Wilson makes it two right at the death.

Still, JL and GC seem happy. The feeling is we've let a good side off the hook by missing too many chances. I head straight for an ice-pack and the doc gives me anti-inflammatory tablets. As I head for my car, a punter shouts: 'We're gonnae need to get you a bionic arm, Des.' Maybe, but could Steve Austin play 18 holes *and* 90 minutes in nine hours?

Wednesday, 16 August 2000

After a restless night, a difficult morning. The shoulder makes it hard to wash, to dress, to get in the car, to change gear. Now that last night's adrenalin has ebbed, the pain flows.

That night it's still hard to sleep and I'm tired as I leave at 7 a.m. on Thursday for a meeting at our Clydebank office on how to computerise our purchasing records. By evening, though, the shoulder has eased enough for me to do my stomachs at training.

We've got a free weekend coming up because of international matches and the lads are planning what to do with it. Some fancy a couple of nights in Newcastle, though it clashes with a night out we'd planned for players and their partners. It's no big problem for me because Carolyn's at a wedding that day, so she'll probably do her thing and I'll do mine.

JL's cracking jokes and the mood's night and day compared to this time last season, when we'd lost four out of four. OK, so we've only won one and drawn two of our first four this time but the atmosphere is fabulous and everyone's up for it.

Peter Lindau has rushed back to Sweden after his pregnant girlfriend is taken ill. Having been in the same boat when Carolyn was expecting both our girls I know what he's going through. It's a miracle that Dani and Taylor are with us today after being born extremely premature. I hope Peter enjoys the same happy ending.

Friday, 18 August 2000

Bought a PC today. Like football players, they appear too expensive, too complicated, obsolete after two or three years and need careful handling to show their true potential.

See? Not just a handsome left-back but a philosopher too.

Saturday, 19 August 2000

Lunchtime, sunshine, optimism's in the air.

I've made the kids breakfast, been to Tesco, put on the lottery ticket. I've laughed like I always do when Dani and Taylor do the catwalk with Tim Lovejoy off *Soccer AM*. Then it's spaghetti on toast, kisses and goodbyes.

I'm hooking up with Moorie and Michael Brown to meet the team bus at the Crowwood Hotel just outside Glasgow for the short trip to Stenhousemuir, but on the way I nip into William Hill's and put on a fixed-odds coupon. The first team I take is Partick Thistle and I'm sure just about every other guy in the team will have done the same. We're feeling good about ourselves.

But not for long.

Teatime, hometime, and a chill wind catches our aching bones. We've been thumped 4–0. Football knows exactly when to show six studs to your feelgood factor.

Looking back, the boys had started to seem on edge the minute we got to Ochilview. It was only quarter past one, half an hour too early for most. It feels like hours before JL names a starting eleven of Arthur, Docherty, McKeown, Hardie, Craigan, Archibald, Lyle, Cameron, McLean, McGrillen and Stirling. However, he doesn't tell us what system we're playing, so I break the silence and ask. He says 4-4-2. Little else is said to us as a group.

Then at last we're ready to go but the game isn't. Kick-off's held up as groundsmen peg down a stray bit of net at the end we're attacking. The Thistle fans amuse themselves by chanting 'Reject, Reject' at our former striker Isaac English.

They mocked too soon.

After half an hour, our defence collapses and Zak gets the second of Stenny's three in ten minutes. He celebrates by doing a Klinsman right in front of our punters. They look as happy as JL when he gets us at half-time. We've been booed off the park and the abuse continues in the dressing-room. Everyone gets it but young Derek Lyle takes it badly and gives some back. JL says he's hooked and Del continues with the verbal. Changed days indeed – when I was his age, there wasn't a manager alive who'd have allowed a player to give him lip like this.

Jamie Smith comes on, we go 3-5-2 with me inside Jered in midfield, but once Archie is red-carded for alleged violent conduct – ref Garry Mitchell is up with play and books him, then changes his mind on the say-so of a linesman 30 yards away – our misery is completed when we concede a fourth goal. It's the worst defeat since I signed in June 1998.

It doesn't matter that we've been unlucky, that we've had so many chances the sponsors have made Stenny keeper Garry Gow Man of the Match. We've been gubbed. JL and GC blame our attitude, saying we didn't appear hungry enough and got what we deserve.

Back home, Carolyn has her half-marathon tomorrow and turns in early. My mind is racing from this afternoon and I stay up doing paperwork until three in the morning.

Sunday, 20 August 2000

In our house, today belongs to Carolyn – but the papers belong to Chris Sutton as he arrives as a £6 million Celtic player with two goals away to Hearts. How fickle football can be. Only weeks ago, Sutton was being branded a £10 million flop after his nightmare season at Chelsea. At Parkhead, the fans were mourning the loss of Aussie mercenary Mark Viduka. Few thought the new guy could lace the boots of the old. Now it's 'Mark who?'

The kids and I go to see Carolyn finish the Glasgow Half-Marathon in two hours five minutes, a fantastic achievement. There's a fabulous atmosphere and among the crowd of runners I see a fella in a Partick Thistle shirt but keep out of his eyeline. The last thing he needs after yesterday is to waste oxygen shouting abuse at a lousy left-back.

Monday, 21 August 2000

Spent today in and around Dumfries with my colleague Craig 'Elvis' Williams. By close of play I'm two hours' drive from Firhill and by the time I've clocked up 240 miles and sat in endless traffic jams I'm thinking about giving training a miss. Throwing a sicky is something I've never done, and even though I could see it as fair enough I plough on, getting there just in time to hear GC promise us 'a bleaching' as punishment for Saturday. We run, run and run some more. And then, for good measure, we do some running.

Back at Firhill, JL goes on some more about the goals we lost at Ochilview but the boys seem more interested in what's happening on *Big Brother*. Everyone but me seems enthralled by this hidden-camera TV drivel – hence the reason I'm pushed out of the conversation.

Dani and Taylor are in bed when I get home. Dani's had a busy day too – she started Primary Three today and by teatime she'd phoned me and counted to ten in Italian. She'll be doing a degree in Nuclear Physics by Primary Seven. Taylor, meanwhile, has started nursery full-time and is knackered. So too is her daddy.

Wednesday, 23 August 2000

Second bleaching of the week tonight – they give us the ball a lot but basically only to disguise miles of running. The muffled whinging behind JL's back proves nobody's fooled.

Thursday, 24 August 2000

Big developments at the day job. Oyez are in negotiations to buy our biggest competitor in the legal stationery market – who just happen to be the company our old mate Ziggy defected to not long back. I've always believed that what goes around comes around and Ziggy might also find it to be true soon.

Training's not much fun tonight. We spend most of it loitering while JL works with the strikers. There's more muttering as boys wonder why they're hanging around for nothing. Did I say the mood was night and day from last season's downer?

Back at Firhill, most of the lads are deep in discussion about the backless, low-cut, split-to-the-pants dress TV presenter Kelly Brook has almost worn at Brad Pitt's latest film premiere but I'm having a far more disturbing chat with Ian Cameron.

Cammy's been jinking up and down left wings for years. Started part-time with St Mirren while he was at uni, qualified as an accountant, went full-time and did well at Aberdeen before working his way around the game and settling back here. You'd think he'd have had a good life. Instead, he's basically telling me that he hates football. That's right. *Hates* it. See, he always had talent. Enough of it to make a good living, no problem. It's just that, in his mind, everyone around him wanted him to make it more than he did.

If Cammy could have had his own way, he'd have finished his studies, got a good job and played five-a-sides every spare night he had. It's not that he hasn't enjoyed being in the game for a living. He feels as lucky as the rest of us that he gets to kick a ball for money. It's the training and the tactics and the transfer upheaval and the coaches – most of all the coaches – that spoil it for him. He'd be just as happy with jumpers for goalposts, five half-time, eleven the winner. That way no one would be yelling from the touchline, telling him to do something he didn't feel like doing. Still, I suppose it happens in every walk of life. People go along, making a half-decent wage and getting pats on the back without ever really enjoying themselves.

And so we pulled into Lochinch and he got out the car and went through yet another session of the stuff that makes him unhappy.

And if he really means it that sometimes he hates football, he'd find a soulmate tonight in Carolyn. She's not happy that I've promised to be home by quarter to eight but that by eight I'm just leaving Firhill.

Arrive home to an atmosphere.

Saturday, 26 August 2000

Cammy turned up today to find he was injured. It must be true, it was in the papers. And what's more, the manager said so. The wee man took it to mean he wasn't going to be involved against Berwick Rangers.

Moorie hasn't been sure whether or not to declare himself fit. He missed Thursday's training with an Achilles injury but wants to get back in the plans. Then again though, there's a free Saturday coming up because Scotland are playing, so he could give himself time to recover properly. In the end, both he and Danny decide to sit this one out.

Archie is suspended, so I'm guessing that I might play left centre-back in a 3-5-2. For once, I guess right but others don't look so happy – not least Kenny Arthur, who's lost the gloves to Michael Brown after the hammering at Ochilview.

It's ten to three, though, when the biggest change is sprung on us. That's when we learn that we're switching from specific marking duties to covering zones. This throws us – we can't believe we didn't work on it on Thursday. We're thrown again when we run out to find Berwick have nabbed our usual end of Firhill for the warm-up. They've got one over on us right away – and ten minutes later they get another when Michael misses a cross and they score easily. Right on half-time, Trigger misses a sitter and we're booed off. JL and GC join in the abuse once again. Every one of us gets it in the neck, Mel Bottiglieri is given the hook and Deeks thrown on.

It takes until five minutes from time for us to equalise. Martin Hardie, on for Trigger, gets his head on Jered's cross and spares at least some of our blushes. But if we're feeling a little better about ourselves, the gaffers are not. If half-time was an explosion, full-time is Vesuvius. Both of them are purple with anger. They're calling us lazy, cheats, not good enough. The feeling is that if we're not willing to work on the pitch they'll run us at every other opportunity – full-timers morning and nights, part-timers on Sundays. Privately, I think this is nonsense and you can see the same thought on every face. We're all thinking: 'Sure, that'll make us better. That'll develop us as a team, bolster morale.' Or, ditching the sarcasm: 'That's not worth a fuck.'

As we go back out for our warm-down, you get the feeling optimism is at rock bottom. You'd be wrong – it plunges even deeper when we get back in and GC announces: 'Everyone in at ten o'clock tomorrow!'

I see red.

'Any chance of the manager bringing us in on Tuesday night and Friday night as well?' I hear myself shouting. 'Just so you can totally fuck everyone up?'

GC's not impressed and squares up to me aggressively, his bulky frame making me look even skinnier than usual.

'Is that what you think then?' he's saying. 'Because you could always find a new club or take a free. Is that what you want?'

I say no and I'm about to say more but Deeks steps in to defuse the situation. Not that I'd have raised my hands – Deeks would have been picking me off the floor.

At this point Trigger takes a brave pill and says he doesn't like being referred to as a cheat. Now GC turns on him but this time no handbags are raised. It's best we leave it and get changed before someone says something they regret.

News of my barney with Gerry soon filters through to the Aitken Suite but I try to play it down because my main worry now is Carolyn's reaction to the news that we're training in the morning – followed by me going to the Old Firm game at Parkhead with my pal and financial adviser David McDonald. I can hear her now!

Anyway, pretty soon GC comes in and pulls me aside. He says he's delighted that I feel angry enough at the result and his reaction to it. He says it's nothing personal and I agree. I tell him he's not the first person to square up to me and probably won't be the last. It's just a pity everyone who squares up to me is six foot tall and the same across. Well, except for Carolyn. She's quite rightly livid when I tell her what's what. How many times have I heard her moan that 'I always have to change *my* plans to accommodate *your* football'?

The first frost settles early on the McKeown household this year.

Sunday, 27 August 2000

After a night in the spare room, it's time for more punishment.

As I drive to training, I wonder what they'll do to us – run us? Talk to us? Show us the video nasty and point out our mistakes? Of the three, I'd take running – mainly because it'll take the least time but also because it'll reduce the chances of tempers fraying in any discussion.

At Firhill, half an hour before the bleaching, it's obvious some of the boys didn't bother cancelling last night's plans. The jovial mood suggests two or three are still half-drunk, but the laughter soon subsides as training kit is handed out.

Not many seem to share my desire to run it out instead of talking it out but, to be fair, an hour later and it's all been pretty tame – even if those nursing hangovers might not have seen it that way. JL sits us down, tells us how disappointed he is in us and what he now expects. The one bonus is that the part-timers don't need to report until Wednesday night.

Before leaving, I tell JL that I'll be in Budapest at our annual salesforce conference when we play again in a fortnight. He jokes that I could have arranged it to clash with the Scotland game next week and not missed a game. Fact is, had I known about the game when the conference was being arranged, I might have done just that. The irony is, we're playing top-of-the-table Queen's Park at Hampden, so Car Wash will also miss the game – though I'm sure they'll miss him more that we'll miss me!

Spend late afternoon and evening making it up to Carolyn and the kids. We go out to eat – but I still end the day watching football highlights on telly. I'll never learn.

Monday, 28 August 2000

Today's papers are chocca with coverage of the Old Firm – and no wonder after Celtic's incredible 6–2 win. By the time David and I got to our seats, Chris Sutton had already scored and by 11 minutes it was 3–0.

In an atmosphere that made the hairs on your neck stand up – I've still got some there – Martin O'Neill's side fought like hell for each other but also had individual genius. Their fourth goal and the first of Henrik Larsson's pair, a spinning chip on the run over Stefan Klos, is one of the greatest I have seen in the flesh. The man's truly world class.

Rangers, meanwhile, were at sixes and sevens. Summer £3.6 million signing Fernando Ricksen gets pelters for being subbed after 23 minutes of torture at right-back. Sometimes you wonder what the gap in class really is between some of the millionaires and the paupers. Would I have done any worse than Ricksen in the same situation? I'd like to think not.

But enough of the big time. I scan the dailies for our match report – and find JL slaughtering every one of us just as he had to our faces, calling us cheats and duds. Various clients phone me to comment and

Graham, who I'm on business with in Falkirk, wants to know what went wrong. I tell him the story but say I still think we'll win the league. As his side are already seven points ahead, he gives me a wry smile.

At night, I do a circuit at the Westerwood and feel stronger than ever. I've completed my pre-season routine with ease then go home for some paperwork and ironing.

You heard . . .

Wednesday, 30 August 2000

Two days to the end of the Oyez financial year and it's all hands to the pump. I've hit my target for the month but our Aberdeen man Ray Hardie is struggling. We have a heart-to-heart and he feels better. Graham, Stephen and Craig are also quite a bit away but I'm confident Stevie will pull through as usual.

On the transfer front, Rangers have signed Dutch international Ronald de Boer from Barcelona and are waiting on Welsh international John Hartson to pass a medical and complete a move from Wimbledon. I can't help thinking these are knee-jerk signings after the defeat by Celtic – a thought borne out when Hartson's dodgy knee scuppers his deal.

Nearer home, Jered Stirling is not being offered another contract at the end of his month. I'm surprised by this but also slightly relieved – it's one less left-sided rival to worry about.

Come evening at Firhill, a BBC crew are filming a Thistle season ticket-holder who's going off on tour as a Britney Spears lookalike. Archie, Doc, Mowgli, Trigger and I are filmed with her and I'm nominated to stage a mock interview with her. The producer asks if we think she looks like Britney, to which Mowgli says: 'Listen, mate, *I* look more like Britney!' Anyway, the good old Beeb agree to donate £100 to our night-out fund for our help.

After a session which is basically running, Trigger declares that he needs another job to help pay the bills and fill his time. He even considers asking to go part-time and work full-time but isn't sure how to approach JL. Once again, I'm left contemplating my own quality of life. Although I make a lot of sacrifices, I still have the best of both worlds – a real job that pays for my life *and* my football. Trigger is envious and asks me if I can get him a job as a tea-boy. I tell him I'm not sure he could handle the responsibility.

Thursday, 31 August 2000

Last day of our financial year and we're looking for something like £40,000 in sales by close of play to secure the office staff's annual bonus. It's not looking good – and that will be hard for the staff to take because we've only missed the target once in ten years and they've got used to the extra cash to pay for holidays and Christmas presents.

After a manic effort, I arrive at Firhill to find out that JL is organising a bounce match between all the players because he can't find opposition for a practice match to fill our free weekend. I'm marked down to play in what appears to be the reserve team along with fringe players and a handful of youth-team boys. I assume this is because I'll miss the next game because of Budapest – but the more I think about it, the more I worry.

Maybe I need my contacts in but I'm beginning to make out some writing on the wall.

Friday, 1 September 2000

I believe the word is 'Phew'. At today's sales meeting, it turns out we made last month's target thanks to a last-day turnover of £60,000. God knows where it all came from but who's complaining?

We're given new mobiles with new numbers in sequence throughout the salesforce. Bugger. So many people have my old one it'll be a nightmare letting them all know.

Monday, 4 September 2000

Now, cutting my hair is a 30-second job. But when your barber's a Thistle diehard, it can somehow stretch to half an hour.

Jimmy's shop in the centre of Glasgow is plastered with fantastic football memorabilia, including a huge picture of the team that beat Celtic 4–1 in the 1971 League Cup final. The legend of Thistle as the Great Unpredictables is such that even when they led 4–0 at half-time, cynical fans still expected to go home having lost 5–4!

The boys are flying tonight, gabbling tales of their free weekend. The full-timers had an all-day session after training on Friday and Moorie then had a party on Saturday night. Some of the lads are paying for it all now – but they're still on a high.

The night ends with some five-a-side and a scrap – best pals Robert Dunn and Derek Lyle fall out, threats are made and next thing punches are being thrown. GC and Moorie dive in to pull the two straw-weights apart, but they're straight back in about each other. Del eventually goes up the tunnel, leaving Dunnsy behind. Then Mowgli loses the plot when Stevie Craigan shoulder-charges him but this time they let it lie and have a laugh.

JL's quite happy to see the feuds, delighted that the boys care enough to come to blows with their friends. He's old-school and I agree with him to an extent – the boys are so close that obviously there will be times when there's a clash, but it's only healthy if things are smoothed over as quickly as they have been tonight.

Wednesday, 6 September 2000

Last training session for five whole days – I'm taking my kit to Budapest, but somehow I can see myself being dragged round bars and clubs instead of gyms.

I'm flying at 6.30 a.m., so JL's letting me work on my own before the rest turn up. As I jog out of the tunnel, I can hear him all the way from his office moaning that his bloody bastard mobile phone's knackered.

Most players reckon training alone is soul-destroying but I enjoy the tranquillity. I can let my mind wander through business, football and family without interruptions. Training never bores me, it's a release from everything else.

By the time I've done a solid hour – 20 minutes lapping the track, bounding up and down the terracing steps, sets of press-ups and stomachs – the rest are getting changed. I wish them well for Saturday and head home for some kip.

Thursday, 7 September 2000

Ray and I leave Cumbernauld at 5.00 a.m. to pick up Stevie McCall en route to Glasgow Airport where we're meeting the rest of the sales team, plus a guest – business consultant Paul di Giacomo, who'll be giving us his input on the psychology of closing sales. He's also a football agent and his son Paul is a striker with huge potential at Kilmarnock.

In Budapest, Elvis and I unpack and head for a street café where we sit and pose in the rain. What a ridiculous idea – would we do the same if it was drizzling in Glasgow?

Friday, 8 September 2000

After a day discussing our policy on client entertaining, thrillseekers that we are, we go on a city tour which teaches us that just about everyone has had a shot at owning Hungary at some point. It seems to be the geographical equivalent of Lee Chapman.

And then comes my once-a-year experience.

I hit the bevvy.

Usually when everyone else has a session, I stick to the water. But on the Friday night of each of our overseas sales jaunts I break my teetotal rules and try out the national drink, straight. Last year in Poland it was vodka, the year before in Munich it was schnapps. Tonight, I become best pals with palenka, which is Hungarian for turpentine.

After a dozen or so I can safely say that for the first time in my life I am genuinely pissed. My head's fine but my body has gone and as I try to co-ordinate feet which want to go in the opposite direction from each other, I remind myself why I'm teetotal. The upside is that for the first time in my life I can truthfully class myself alongside Gazza, Bestie and Greavsie!

I stagger back to the hotel and phone Carolyn, who talks me through the extensive media build-up to tomorrow's Queen's Park–Thistle game. Suddenly I get the same feeling I do every time I go away on business at weekends.

God, I'm going to miss my Saturday playing football.

In an instant, I'm sober again as my mind juggles with the potential consequences of being AWOL. It'd be easy to hope Thistle lose or maybe even play badly and scrape a win. Possibly the ideal scenario for the missing player is that the team plays well apart from his replacement, who has a Chernobyl. Me? Call it palenka poisoning but I hope we not only win but the man in my shirt has a blinder. I'd rather go home to find Thistle closer to the leaders and have to fight my way back into the team, rather than get the shout by default. However, I know the truth is this trip might well jeopardise my position. The best case scenario for the club might well turn out to be the worst case scenario for me.

Saturday, 9 September 2000

Today my team-mates will run out at Hampden Park while I attend a discussion on marketing strategy, potential for increased turnover and gross profit through new business and continued development within our own client base. Whoop-de-doo . . .

It's an odd feeling for Graham and me because we should be facing each other across a halfway line, not a table in a hotel meeting room in Central Europe. What's more, while I at least have a chance of playing next week, Graham hasn't – he's off to the Olympics in Sydney as soon as we're home. His mate David Somerville's representing Great Britain at judo.

After work's finished, we relax for an hour in the Gellert Spa, one of the oldest in the city, before heading off to find a pub with Sky so we can watch the results come in. A couple of red herrings later, hallelujah! We walk into Beckett's Bar, an Irish theme joint, and there on the big screen is lovely Rodney Marsh and his pals to make us feel right at home. Celtic fans Reg, Stevie and Paul go up in the air at news of Henrik Larsson scoring against Hibs after 12 minutes. Craig and Ray, our resident Bluenoses, are not so chuffed. Graham, Dunky and I, meanwhile, wait for news from Hampden.

Half-time comes and goes with no score, but on 61 minutes Danny Lennon's name comes up on the screen and the rest of the pub is left wondering why a baldy guy and a beardy guy are leaping up and down. Graham hangs his head. He knows if it stays this way we'll make the rest of the trip hell for him. Then it's my turn to have a long face when Elvis reminds me that if we hang on for the win it could knacker my season. I think hard about this for a few seconds and decide I'd rather be happy for the lads today and remain confident of being needed somewhere along the line.

Thistle do hang on, as do Celtic, while Rangers only draw at Dundee – a mixed afternoon for our squad. We decide to go someplace where we're all neutral, so nip ten minutes across the city to watch Ferencvaros play FC Lombard in the Hungarian League. We sit among the very partisan home fans for a game which is no higher a standard than our own First or Second Division and finishes 2–2.

Just to prove how neutral they are, Reg and Stevie show their appreciation for Lombard's two stunning goals and we feel the need to claim that we're not with them. There were only 6,000 there but I can honestly say I've never felt hostility like it – even from Carolyn. Every decision is disputed, every opposing player abused beyond belief. Fans – and not just young ones – are running the length of the stand hurling verbal abuse and actual missiles at the Lombard team, at the ref, at his linesmen. One player has to be subbed after being hit on the arm with a firecracker.

I couldn't help wondering what the atmosphere must be like at somewhere like Galatasaray – and also how weedy some Scottish players seem when they claim to get a hard time from supporters. They want to try being here. Sure, I've had experience of the boo-boys. My first season at Thistle was dogged by abuse from the terracing, although I have a decent relationship with them now. I fully understand their right to give out stick – they pay the wages, after all – but I still wouldn't wish it on my worst enemy. And in any case, what they subjected me to back then seem like compliments now compared to the mayhem around me in the Ferencvaros stadium!

Still, it's a cheap night out – by the time we've been for a post-match McDonald's and taken taxis back to town, we find we've spent less than a fiver each. The Celtic and Jags contingent want to go back to Beckett's to celebrate a good day, the Rangers and Queen's Park whingers to drown their sorrows. A live band is playing oldies and, as always on these trips, we play our game of Spot the Celebrity Lookalike – last night we met a girl who was a ringer for Worzel Gummidge and tonight we see Olive Oyl, David Niven and Mo Mowlem get down on the dance floor.

The night ends with Graham becoming the only Queen's Park player to score today. What a pity away goals don't count double.

Sunday, 10 September 2000

Back to business, but in pleasant surroundings – we discuss E-commerce while cruising down the Danube. Later we fit in some shopping but, although buying for Dani and Taylor is easy, I'm stuck on what to get the wife who has everything. I decide to get her something at the airport and head back for some kip before one last night on the town.

Reg treats us to a fabulous Hungarian meal before we hit a club. Sunday night in Budapest isn't exactly buzzing but the good news is we spot Worzel again . . .

Monday, 11 September 2000

Home to news of a fuel crisis that could not only have a huge effect on the day job but on football as well. The guys are trying to remember how much gas they have left.

As Ray drives me home it's as well he has three-quarters of a tank left because every garage forecourt is mobbed and long queues are forming. He reckons he'll have enough to get him back to Aberdeen. We pass Firhill and suddenly I can't wait for training tomorrow night.

Taylor's waiting on the doorstep for me – or maybe for her present – and Dani comes bounding out too, but Carolyn looks shattered and me being away is getting the blame. It's great to be back.

Tuesday, 12 September 2000

Despite leaving home at seven, I still have to queue for ten minutes to fill up at Cumbernauld. The crisis is escalating and weekend fixtures are in doubt.

After a long day when Budapest catches up, I iron for two hours then do some stomachs before catching up on reports of Saturday's game. Archie played left-back and did well. Looks like the big coat for me.

Wednesday, 13 September 2000

Think about tonight's training session all day. Can't wait to see the boys, be back among it all again, hear the feedback on the win at Hampden.

Arriving at Firhill at 5.30 p.m., I see only one other car. Immediately the light bulb goes on above my head. Is training off? Alan Dick confirms it – injured players are to report at half six but no one else. Alan says I could do a session then but I say I'll go to the Westerwood instead.

I'm gutted. Not only did I want the crack, I realise my last chance of even winning a place on the bench for Saturday might have gone – I'll miss tomorrow night's session because of work. Later, I phone JL and he says there was no point dragging everyone in because of the fuel crisis. He's also forgotten I wouldn't be there tomorrow night. Cheers. I tell him I'll try and re-organise my schedule so I can work with the full-timers on Friday morning.

Thursday, 14 September 2000

Entertaining clients all day at Ayr Racecourse – Reg, Elvis, 12 females and me. The last race isn't over until 5 p.m., so we're not back in Glasgow until seven, by which time training's already finished. Bugger.

Those of the girls who are still *compos mentis* don't want their day out to end, so with Reg off to Parkhead to watch Celtic v Helsinki in the UEFA Cup, Elvis and I are left to chaperone them. We end up in the Horseshoe Bar, where every night is karaoke night. Elvis lives up to his name and I belt out 'That's Life' and 'Mack the Knife'. I even get a standing ovation, which is more than I can expect in my football career for a while.

Friday, 15 September 2000

Phoned Firhill to confirm to JL I'll be in this morning. They tell me training's cancelled again.

Why do they call me Lucky?

I'm pretty sure now I won't feature against Stirling Albion tomorrow but I still go through my Friday night ritual of a curry and *Friends*.

Saturday, 16 September 2000

This morning's papers don't even mention that I'm available for selection. I think that tells me all I need to know. Still, I have to wait for the formalities. Just after 1.30 p.m., GC tells me JL wants to see me. There can only be two things on his mind – he's either going to play me but warn me that I better do the business, or he's not involving me at all.

Guess which?

You can't argue with his decision to stick by last week's sixteen, especially when I haven't trained all week. That's twice he explained these things to me when he didn't have to. However, just as I'm leaving his office he says: 'I just hope I'm not cutting my nose off to spite my face – I think you could do me a turn today in a couple of positions.'

I'm dumbstruck. He thinks he needs me but won't use me out of loyalty. Football is bizarre.

After an hour of knocking my pan in on the pitch and up and down the terraces, I feel a pang of jealousy as I see the lads go through their final preparations. I feel strange, as if I've no right to be there. It even felt odd when kids asked me for my autograph, even though they do it to me and everyone else every week. Maybe I should go inside for a shower and stay out of their way. Instead, I go back to the dressing-room with them and wish everyone the best of luck. I sincerely want every one of them to do well and for us to win. JL tells me that if I see anything from the stand that he misses to come to the dugout to let him know. I appreciate the thought but I can't see me taking him up – he's like a caged lion during games and if I break his concentration I may just end up as his prey.

We cruise to a 3–1 win that could have been eight but for Albion keeper Chris Reid. My big coat could get a lot of wear this winter.

The real disappointment is that while players, management and fans celebrate afterwards, I feel out of place. I haven't contributed and it seems I'm on the outside looking in – a feeling enhanced at night when I attend a school reunion and people want to talk to me about the result. What did it have to do with me?

Monday, 18 September 2000

Spent yesterday with the girls. It's good to get back to work for a rest. I'm with Jags-daft Dunky for calls in Glasgow. He believes Saturday was as well as he's seen a Thistle team play in years.

I pack it in early to get ready for a night entertaining clients at a St Andrews Sporting Club boxing do, but only after a solo session at Firhill under JL's beady eye. He seems fairly happy with the shift I put in and by the time the rest roll in they take great delight in slaughtering me as I change into a tux.

JL wants me back for another solo shift on Wednesday. The rest have the night off.

Tuesday, 19 September 2000

A late night but no lie-in. I'm up and running again at 6.30 a.m.

Wednesday, 20 September 2000

Five o'clock at Firhill and it's just me, Ricky the kitman and a handful of the youth team. David McCallum's coming in for a solo session about half-six and the only other senior pro around will be Cammy, who's taking the youths because Tid's on holiday in Barcelona.

What a lovely chance for a wind-up.

I give Andy Gibson, the star of this year's youth team and already on a pro form, a tug.

'Hey, wee man, were you boys told why Tid's over in Spain?'

'Holiday, innit?'

'Nah, that's only the cover.'

'Aye?'

'Aye – he's actually been invited by Barca themselves to check out their youth set-up.'

Gibby's a cocky wee guy and he's not sure whether to buy this. But another little prod and the need to be in the know outweighs his street sense.

'Ask yourself why Cammy's taking the session,' I've gone on. 'It's because Thistle are having to suss out who could take Tid's job.'

'What, so he's really . . .'

'Really in the frame. Barca are checking out the best young coaches in the game and they reckon yer man's one of them.'

Now I've got him hook, line and sinker. The top man's been topped and he can't wait to swagger back and tell his mates the news.

With that I start my fourth solo stint on the spin. I should have been a marathon runner. As I finish, David arrives. It's the first time he's trained on his own and he quizzes me on what he should be doing.

'Well,' I tell him, 'I've done a 20-minute run, six horseshoes, six sets of terracings, 600 sit-ups and 100 press-ups.'

'Oh,' he says. 'I think I'll sort myself out, then.'

Carolyn's working tonight, so I keep one eye on Dani and Taylor and the other on the telly as Rangers win 1–0 away to Monaco. It's a fabulous result – the only downer is having to suffer the abysmal commentary of Archie MacPherson and Tommy McLean.

Thursday, 21 September 2000

A special day indeed – not only am I to train with the squad for the first time in a fortnight, but it's also my ninth wedding anniversary.

I have some meetings with Dunky in Dunfermline, an area I covered for Oyez years ago. It's nice to catch up with some familiar faces. After that, I have a meeting about my next *Scottish Sun* column – until now it's been pretty much ghost-written but the feeling is it's going well enough to suggest that pretty soon I'll be able to write the whole thing myself.

What a terrifying thought.

Training tonight reminds me why I'm *not* a marathon runner – they don't get to enjoy the kind of dressing-room atmosphere we have right now. The mood's brilliant and confidence is high again. It's also good to kick a ball for the first time in ages.

JL tells us to be at Firhill at 12.50 p.m. on Saturday for the bus to Greenock to play Clydebank. I've an outside chance of being on the bench but I'm taking the big coat just in case.

And now, the small matter of celebrating my wedding day. A quick change and Carolyn and I are off for a meal at Guidi's in Coatbridge then a rare trip to the movies to see *Snatch* – the girls are staying at Margaret's, so we're in no rush to get home. And with my prospects of a game on Saturday, why should I be?

Friday, 22 September 2000

All week clients have been commenting on how well Thistle are doing. They mean well but it only rams home to me how small my part in the revival has been. When results go well and you're in the team, you feel great. If you're not, it's a nightmare.

Saturday, 24 September 2000

Nevertheless, whether I'm going to play or not I still prepare the same as usual. Same food, same time, same place as always. Over my spaghetti on toast, I read the papers and I'm unhappy at the headline on my column – it makes it sound as if I felt hard done-by at not being involved in the Stirling Albion game, which couldn't be further from the truth.

Watch the first half-hour of Man U v Chelsea on Sky before going to pick up Moorie and Del. The weather's good, so I leave the coat behind.

Bad shout.

The wind's whipping around Cappielow and, as ever, Greenock has forgotten to pay its bill to the suppliers of sunshine. I check who's wearing what. Moorie's got a coat, so I ask to borrow it on the assumption that I'll be seventeenth man.

Another bad shout.

Like they say, never assume – it makes an ass of u and me. I am, in fact, sixteenth man. Bonus. Just getting the boots on again, especially when it's so unexpected, is a thrill and as I get my rub from Disco Dave I'm reminded yet again to take nothing for granted, especially as I get older. To prove this is true, the sun even peeps through as we kick off against a Bankies team littered with ex-Premier League stars – Rab McKinnon, Brian Welsh, Brian Hamilton, Derek Ferguson and player-boss Tommy Coyne. These are guys who can still cut it but who've been forced down the leagues because of the flood of foreign imports at the higher levels. That really gets to me.

By half-time it's 0–0 and not pretty and I can imagine the mood in the dressing-room. I'm only imagining it because we subs have stayed out in the tropical heat to warm ourselves and take abuse from the Bankies fans, who hate anything to do with Thistle. One shouts at me, 'Go back to Dumfries, ya bastard!' As I've never lived down there, I can only assume they're referring to my time as a player there – and in particular to the goal I scored which stopped them winning the Second Division in 1997, a goal made even sweeter by the defender I outjumped being one Car 'Graham Connell' Wash.

Anyway, back to the present and we make them even angrier by going ahead with a controversial goal – Trigger's been offside but not interfering with play, then joins back in and rolls in the rebound after Mowgli's shot is parried.

Five minutes later, Rab McKinnon is red-carded, but if we think we're cruising against ten men we're wrong. Clydebank equalise and JL rings the changes. Cammy comes on for Mowgli and ten minutes later the whole formation switches as I replace Moorie. We've gone 3-5-2, with me at left wing-back and I'm out to make an impact. Sure enough, within minutes it's 2–1. To Clydebank. I've not even had a touch when Brian Welsh heads the winner and the tin hat goes on our day when Martin Hardie's sent off for retaliation.

This time, I wish I was still outside imagining the mood in the dressing-room. No such luck – there's no escaping JL and GC's rant at our collapse. It's back to the drawing board. And now you have the flip-side of feeling like an outsider when things go well and you're not playing. When it goes wrong and you're a bit-part player, your chances of a game increase dramatically. Still not a happy scenario, though.

Thistle programme editor Tom Hosie wants to interview me – he usually does after bad results, because he knows I'm not the kind to snub him to be alone with my thoughts. So there I am, back out on the pitch, half-naked. Why? It's impossible to dry yourself in the Cappielow dressing-rooms. They're too hot and too damn damp because of the steam from the old-fashioned communal bath.

My old team-mate Derek Ferguson goes by and asks if I'm still using the sunbeds. Am I that pale blue?

Monday, 25 September 2000

A pleasant Glasgow holiday weekend over, we turn up for training and find out we'll be working around the edge of the pitch. You don't need a PhD to work out why.

Yes, folks, it's the obligatory post-defeat bleaching.

It's not the running that gets to the guys in these situations – in fact, some of us think we don't do enough of it. Personally, I'd have one running session a week. It's not a hardship. No, it's the thought that it's designed as a punishment that grinds you down. It's typical old-school psychology – give them a night off if they do well and run their arses off if they don't. JL's too long in the tooth to change his ways now.

Deeks has been released after a terrible time with injuries. He's also been finding it hard to train three nights because of family commitments and may now quit the game altogether. Everyone wishes him well.

Dunnsy's back for the first time since his straw-weight bout with Del. It turns out that although, in GC's words, 'I've hit ma wean harder', Dunnsy actually suffered a hairline fracture of the jaw. Needless to say, he's now known as the man with the glass chin.

Finally, Moorie's on suicide watch again after his Achilles flares up. The wee man just can't get an even break and I'm reminded of the old saying that you're either born good-looking or lucky. God knows what Moorie did in a previous life, though, because he's neither.

Wednesday, 27 September 2000

My last call before training is, handily enough, at Firhill. After Antonia gives me the club's stationery order and makes me a cup of tea, Alan

Dick spots me and questions the content of my newspaper diary. Turns out he reckons I may be sharing too much of what goes on in the dressing-room with the public. I disagree and argue that I've given Thistle nothing but good publicity. He says that's probably right but adds that I've been hinting at disharmony between myself and the management. I totally refute this and tell him I have an excellent relationship with JL and GC – and, what's more, neither has said a word about being unhappy with what I'm writing. I tell Alan nothing's done behind anyone's back, that it's all discussed openly in the dressing-room.

Yes, I've been asked regularly by fans if it's true I've fallen out with JL and/or GC – some have even suggested I've told JL I won't play unless I'm left-back. If only I had that kind of clout – when your ability's as limited as mine you play where they put you.

Thursday, 28 September 2000

Before training, I ask JL what he thinks of the diary. He says he has no problems but that 'a couple of people' have mentioned that the content may be too revealing. I wonder who those people might be – Alan Dick and the chairman, perhaps?

The session's short and sharp, with the emphasis on a small-sided game. I'm lucky enough to be in the yellow team, which wins every time. Poor Moorie, his Achilles eased, gives another memorably awful performance as captain of the hapless reds.

'Ah, who cares?' he says when we tease him gently. 'Ah've never been a trainin' player, ah keep the good stuff for Saturdays.'

He has a point. Many guys look terrible in training but perform in games. Others would play for Brazil if it was down to their work during the week but can't hack it for real.

Last year we had a boy here called Eric Paton. He could do things in training you wouldn't believe, yet his career is yet to take off. Same went for my old Queen of the South mate John McLaren, the brother of revitalised Kilmarnock winger Andy. Yet one of the best central defenders I've played with, Jimmy 'The Silhouette' Thomson, was a disgrace in training. He looked like he'd never played before, yet nine Saturdays out of ten he was magnificent.

Moorie only has to master that last bit now and his theory will be watertight.

Saturday, 30 September 2000

Today we play Forfar, a team I could have been turning out *for* instead of *against*. Their manager Ian McPhee, an old Airdrie pal of mine, offered me terms at the same time as Thistle and, even though I turned him down, I admired the way he went about things.

I pick up Tid, who tells me JL's not planning many changes from last week. That means the best I can expect is the bench again. However, there's a strange face in the dressing-room. It's only when JL announces the team at 1.50 p.m. that we find out he's French, his name's Gregor and he'll partner Danny in central midfield. His job will be to supply the flying wingers, Moorie and McKeown. Yes, that's right – I'm in. My first start since August 26 and I can't wait.

Sandy Stewart makes his first start in any game, Martin's suspended, Lindau has flu and Jamie Smith's dropped. Dunnsy returns from Siberia to warm the bench.

JL barks final instructions, hard enough for us to understand sometimes, never mind Gregor, who gets told something along the lines of: 'Right, Georgie, get fucked in early doors. Let's see what yer madea and try and keep their heids doon by pressuring the ba'.' He looks dumbstruck but it doesn't show in his performance. He plays well, we have a lot of the ball – but, you guessed it, we can't make it count. Still, JL seems happy enough at half-time and his plea for patience plays off when Mowgli's fouled in the box by keeper Stuart Garden, who walks for his protests. Trigger waits until the new man takes the gloves then slots the kick away.

Kenny Arthur's having nothing to do in our goal, yet he ends up picking one out when Archie is dispossessed and they equalise. The natives get restless and abuse flies. JL gets the brunt but no one is spared and you can understand why. The nearest we come is a header from yours truly which bounces down, up and onto the bar with the sub keeper beaten. We trudge off to a hail of boos.

For the second week in a row we've failed to beat ten men and disappointment is etched on every face. JL and GC go over and over and over the importance of killing teams off as well as keeping our concentration at the back. It's nothing we don't know.

In the Aitken Suite, the punters are in shock – but the talk I hear of sacking the manager is way over the top. I keep well out of it and simply tell them the players are well behind him.

At the heart of the post-mortem is wee Dave Cubbage – well, I say wee, but he might not be. I've only ever seen him in his wheelchair. That might not sound too politically correct, but if you met him you'd know he doesn't believe in all that nonsense. He's a remarkable guy who's become a good friend and who I've promised to celebrate with the next time I score. It was almost today. I wonder when – if? – it'll actually happen.

Back home, something's missing. Turns out the kids are staying with Margaret, so Carolyn and I can do our own thing.

A bad day is looking up at last . . .

SIX

Monday, 2 October 2000

AFTER AN HOUR'S TRAINING yesterday morning, JL and GC debriefed us on Saturday's game. Their main concern was the goal we lost. No one disagreed.

Today, confusion reigns at the day job sales meeting. No one seems quite sure if we've met our targets individually or collectively and the mood is low. We've worked our butts off for this moment and yet we're left in the dark. What an anti-climax. Reg spends most of the day trying to get answers from Accounts, but by close of play at 4 p.m. we're no further forward – and what's more, Stevie, Elvis, Peter and I have a plane to catch. We're flying to Birmingham and then heading on to Milton Keynes for an e-commerce conference. It's 9.30 p.m. before we're eating in our hotel and the boys are knackered. The rest stay on for a beer in the bar but I head upstairs to work on my next *Scottish Sun* column. It's going to be on the need for consistency in football and I'm using the analogy of how my mum bakes cakes. Trust me, it'll work.

Tuesday, 3 October 2000

A day's coaching on the company's new on-line ordering system – not exactly Las Vegas, but it has to be done – before I head for a gym session at a nearby hotel. Elvis tries to keep up with my 24-minute treadmill routine and gives in after a gallant ten.

After a few sets of stomachs and some skipping, it's back to the hotel for a meal before the biggest challenge of the day – trying to get a taxi into the town centre. We give up after an hour and 45 minutes and hit the sack. But not before changing our colleague Peter's alarm call from 7 a.m. to 5 a.m.

Wednesday, 4 October 2000

Another action-packed, fun-filled day in front of our PCs ends with us dashing to the airport in a bid for me to get back in time for training. As our tickets are non-transferable, this will only be possible if Silver Tongue McKeown can sweet-talk the check-in lady into bumping us from the 7 p.m. flight to the 4 p.m.

Two minutes later – two? I must be losing my touch – we're sorted and belting for the gate. Back in rainy Glasgow, the traffic's murder and I half-think about going straight home before deciding to head for Firhill. When I get there, the car park's empty. Is this déjà vu or have I seen this before? It is and I have – once again, Alan Dick confirms that training is cancelled.

The bonus is a night with the girls and a recital from Dani, who's had her first organ lesson today.

Thursday, 5 October 2000

One of my appointments today is with Eddie McMurray, MD of Thistle's main sponsors DH Morris and a Jags fan man and boy. He's confident about our title chances – and has a go at fans who've been dishing out abuse during our recent blips.

'I'm all for opinions,' he says. 'But surely we should all be pulling the same way?'

Later, just before training, club photographer Tommy Taylor asks if I'll pose for a picture with Thistle historian Robert Reid and a bloke called Bernard Stocks, who's just finished writing a book, listing – wait for this, stat fans – all winners of past and present, major and minor competitions involving Scottish League, senior non-league and junior clubs.

Tonight we train on the pitch at Firhill as JL shapes a team for Saturday's game away to Queen of the South. Mark McNally has appeared out of the blue, which suggests he'll play at Palmerston. He's been playing in Iceland but the season's over and, although neither he nor JL are saying much, a delay to the start of the session gives the game away. We've finished our warm-up and I ask JL what he wants us to do next. He says to hang on, he's waiting to see the chairman about something. I assume that something is clearance to play Nally on Saturday.

JL asks where I'm working tomorrow. I assume from the question he wants me to work with the full-timers because there's a chance I'll be involved on Saturday – probably at wing-back in a 3-5-2 – but although I'll be in Glasgow I'm facing the busiest day in the world and there's no chance of me coming in. In the end, he doesn't get to work out a team plan because it's only as we're leaving that he sits down with the chairman.

Before we go, Ricky and Chico hand out new tracksuits to be worn to all games. Let's just say they will win no awards at Milan Fashion Week.

Back home, I feel a niggle in my left hamstring and take some anti-inflammatory tablets. I want to be up for the cup on Saturday – especially with Elvis and ten of our clients from the Dumfries area in the stand watching me.

Saturday, 7 October 2000

Elvis traps at the house for eleven. JL's given the OK for me to drive to Dumfries, as we're meeting clients at Palmerston at one o'clock, 45 minutes before the bus gets there.

My column's in the *Scottish Sun* again today. It's an analogy between my mum's home-baking and building a good football team and I'm happy with it, bar the fact that a sub-editor has chopped out what I thought were some funny lines. OK, maybe they lost something in translation.

Driving to Dumfries always brings back happy memories. I loved my time with Queens and have had the odd notion to retire down there – the people are nice, the air's clean and you're within striking distance of Glasgow and Manchester as well as the coast.

The local football club is a model for all communities, a fabulous environment to play in, well run and supported by people with great pride in the team. Walking through the doors there is like going home. From Margaret and Dick in the office to Kevin the groundsman, everyone makes me welcome. The fans are good to me – diehards like Brucie the programme editor, big Ian Black the club historian, supporters' bar regulars wee Wullie, Frankie, Gail, Eileen, Ross, Jim, Alec, big Davie, Pam, Vanessa, Natasha and barmaid Donna always want to know how I'm doing.

But the warmest welcome is always in the tearoom, where Princess Doreen and Lady Vi hold court. Both are about 5 ft tall but with giant characters. Each time I go back I swap them a box of chocs for a peck on the cheek. Doreen cycles to and from the ground, rain, hail or shine, with her home baking and bread for the sandwiches hanging from the handlebars in plastic bags. Everyone's 'my darling' to her, except the players, who are all 'my weans'. Vi's just as special, a lady with no bike but also no airs or graces. She and I share the same love of Frank Sinatra and have been known to duet on 'Fly Me to the Moon'. And both, before you start getting ideas, are way past retirement age.

Yes, it's a great club, full of great memories and great people.

Here's hoping they're all miserable as sin tonight.

Mind you, Thistle have their fair share of devoted ladies. Take mother and daughter Assunta and Antonia Kerr, who eat, sleep and breathe the club. I can count on one hand the *training sessions* they've missed. They turn up religiously with bottles of water for the lads and are always at away grounds when the bus pulls in. Just for good luck, Antonia now works in the office at Firhill. Now *that's* a labour of love.

Elvis and I check into the Cairndale Hotel and are at Palmerston for 12.45 p.m. As our guests arrive in the ground's hospitality suite, each wishes me the worst for today's game. I tell them I'll have to get picked first. They laugh but I'm deadly serious.

On my way to the dressing-room I meet Queens chairman Ronnie Bradford, a good friend and yet the main reason I left the club. Although Thistle had approached me and I was very interested, I didn't want to walk away from a club who had given me the best four years of my career. I was torn and arranged a meeting with the then manager, Rowan Alexander, and the board. Rowan did everything in his power to keep me but Ronnie said I was holding a gun to the club's head. For me, this was nonsense – Queen's were offering me more money than Thistle and the stumbling block was the length of the contract. I was so angry I made up my mind on the spot that it was time to go. Still, Ronnie and I met on the first day of the next season, shook hands and agreed it had been nothing personal. He reckoned he'd been acting in the club's best interests and would like me to return one day – words he backed up with a substantial bid turned down by JL last season.

Ronnie introduces me to new Queens boss John Connolly, an old St Johnstone mate of JL's, and then I join up with our boys. Every one of them gives me dog's abuse about the diary.

'Yer maw's cakes? What a pile of shite!'

'Where the fuck did that idea come from?'

Even Ricky the kitman shakes his head and says: 'Dessie boy, we need to have a chat . . .'

Above
HAIR TODAY...
me (and lovely curly locks) on my wedding day, 21 September 1991, with Carolyn and (from left) her dad Dan Durick, St Isabel, St Margaret, my dad Billy

Left
GONE TOMORROW...
me on Carolyn's brother Gary's wedding day, 31 March 2001, with Taylor (front left) and Danielle

Right
ON THE LINE ...
and I mean my career
as well as the ball.
A pre-season friendly
against Chesterfield
and my face is already
a mix of concentration
and fear

DON'T
GIVE UP
THE
DAY JOB

Left
THE ODD COUPLE ...
JL tries to protect his
bouffant from the wind,
while GC does his best
impression of Blakey from
On The Buses

Above
I'LL BE THERE FOR YOU . . .
with Angela McPhie, who I
visited in hospital after a
major operation and who
remained a friend and a fan
right to the end of the season

Left
**BUT WILL I BE THERE FOR
HIM? . . .**
John Connolly gave my career
the kiss of life in November,
but by May I was left unsure
of my future yet again

DON'T
GIVE UP
THE
DAY JOB

Above
SO WHAT NEXT?
Lee Evans-lookalike
Allan Moore keeps his ears
open for his next career move.
Mind you, those lugs can also
pick up Radio Azerbaijan

Right
MY HAIR'S THIS GINGEY . . .
George Rowe, making Bonnie
Langford look like a brunette.
And you know what rhymes
with gingey? Stingey!
Enough said . . .

DON'T
GIVE UP
THE
DAY JOB

Left
MUD, SWEAT AND TEARS . . . slithering at Palmerston in one of my final games for Thistle – and it's only September

Right
TAXI FOR McKEOWN . . . back playing at Firhill again in April, but it needed a transfer to get me there

DON'T GIVE UP THE DAY JOB

DON'T GIVE UP THE DAY JOB

Left
INTO THE VALET ...
Graeme 'Car Wash' Connell
doesn't know what to do
with his hands without a
chamois and a bucket in
them

Below
**ELVIS HAS LEFT THE
IGLOO ...**
workmate Craig Williams
loves me tender after a kick-
about had us all shook up
during our Arctic safari in
March

Right
**MA CAR
CHAMELEON . . .**
the legend that is
Ronnie McQuilter
kindly throws on
some dark leisure
wear so we can
pick his bright
yellow tan out from
his bright yellow
car. And he has
another pair of
shoes the same in
the boot

RON 9

DON'T
GIVE UP
THE
DAY JOB

MERRICK

MERRICK

Left
**THE UNACCEPTABLE
FACE OF SCOTTISH
FOOTBALL . . .**
Pretty Boy Peter
Weatherson does his
tribute to the Elephant
Man. And he also has
Merrick on his boots

DON'T GIVE UP THE DAY JOB

ON HIS BIKE AGAIN . . . the one and only PK works out in between free transfers. Does his bum look big in this gym?

I take it from that he's not impressed.

Neither, can I say, are many of us impressed with the pitch onto which will squelch a Thistle team reading Arthur, Doc, McKeown, Crags, Nally, Archie, Lindau, Lennon, McLean, Stewart and McCallum. On the bench are Mark Brown, Moorie, Howie, Cammy and Mowgli. As suspected, we'll play 3-5-2 with me ploughing – and in this rain, I *mean* ploughing – a furrow up and down the left flank. Playing wing-back is tough enough without having to run through porridge. Still, at least I'm playing – and if I'm struggling, the chances are my opponent will be as well.

By half-time we're 1–0 up – Trigger again – and so far in control the concern is we're not out of sight, a concern justified on the hour when Queens equalise. Now, for the first time, we're on the back foot and JL shows his hand.

On come Cammy for the tiring David McCallum, Mowgli for Peter Lindau and William Howie for Sandy Stewart – except that when the No. 11 board goes up, I think that's my number and start to trot off. I'm nearly at the touchline when Archie shouts that I'm actually wearing No. 3. Luckily, no one else seems to have noticed my stupidity.

No one, that is, except that bastard Elvis, who gives me pelters all night.

Mind you, I might as well have been off the park. While we were on top I'd been well involved but now I seemed to be running the length of the park and back without ever getting a touch. I've had more throw-ins than kicks. How out of it was I? Far enough for one Thistle punter to shout: 'McKeown – you're shite! Put that in yer column!'

But just as the mood was turning against us as a team, supersub Mowgli got a touch to Cammy's corner and we won it with two minutes to spare. The wee man's first goal for the club had got us out of jail.

Our problem is we're not killing teams off and JL and GC let us know all about it in the dressing-room – but we're still 11 points better off now than after a quarter of last season and only one off the top of the table. Now the bad news. We're in for training tomorrow and I have to tell JL I'm staying down here on business and won't make it. He only accepts my apology when Walter the Vet says he'll give me a solo workout on Monday night.

At night, Elvis and I watch Scotland struggle to beat San Marino and Ireland get an excellent draw in Portugal as the World Cup qualifiers kick in, before the two of us meet up with Ian Black for a night out. Most Queens fans we meet reckon Thistle are the best team they've faced this season.

Hit the sack at 3.30 a.m.

Sunday, 8 October 2000

Up early, read how we made heavy weather of yesterday's win then drag my even heavier legs up the road. I'm taking the kids swimming today while Carolyn goes running and I'll spend most of my time in the jacuzzi.

That night I'm out for the count early doors, with legs like Gyproc.

Monday, 9 October 2000

It's raining cats and dogs. I'm soaked between the car and the office and as I sit gently steaming I can't wait to train on my Jack Jones tonight – if only I knew then it was going to get even better. I arrive at Firhill to threats from Ricky and Chico that if anyone lays a single stud on the pitch they'll be hung. And so I do 35 minutes of non-stop pounding up and down the terraces in a merry downpour. It's a routine that would drive me daft if I didn't vary my stride; every step up and down, then every second step and – you guessed it – every third step. By the end, my thighs and calves are screaming but I push myself through a short body circuit indoors and feel like I've put in a good shift in difficult circumstances.

Home for pasta, paperwork and many zeds.

Wednesday, 11 October 2000

Life today is dominated by the death of Scotland's First Minister Donald Dewar.

I met him two years ago at The Scottish Football Writers Association dinner. He seemed a keen football fan who was very patriotic towards the national team, so perhaps it was fitting that they were playing tonight. The players wore black armbands and stood for a minute's silence before the World Cup qualifier against Croatia in Zagreb. He would have been proud of what happened next, Kevin Gallacher's goal levelling an early Croatian strike and leaving us top of the group.

I didn't see the goals due to training. JL had forgotten the game was on and it took a bit of player power and some gentle nudging from GC to bring the session forward to 6.15 p.m. We accepted our 45-minute gutting and were away by 7.30 p.m. to catch the second half.

Before I head off, I ask JL if he's planning to bring us in every

Sunday from now on. This would be a popular move, as it'd give the boys Mondays off. He says he fancies the idea because it gets aches and pains out of our legs but doesn't commit himself. Then he says to me, 'You're still a hell of a popular bloke at Queen of the South, eh?'

'I think so.'

'I get the feeling that one day they might offer you a coaching job down there.'

'Yeah, I've heard that as well, but I've never really given it much thought. Why?'

'They've made a bid for you.'

This takes me aback, so I joke, 'I take it you said you weren't interested.'

'No,' he says with a straight face. 'I told them to come back with more money.'

I don't know if he's kidding or not but for the first time I'm seriously wondering if he doesn't want me anymore. If he's serious, it means he'd let me go to QoS if the money's right. On the other hand, the fact that he's told me of their interest suggests he's in no hurry to offload me. All I can do is concentrate on trying to make him keep me.

I watch the second half from Zagreb with Moorie over a bowl of home-made soup at Tid's. He should have chucked football years ago and become a chef.

Later I head home to watch highlights of England's 0–0 draw in Finland. I am heartbroken for them. There's huge media attention on this game following Kevin Keegan's resignation minutes after Saturday's 1–0 defeat by Germany at Wembley. Howard Wilkinson's taken them to Helsinki but just about everyone bar JL's been linked with the job permanently. Keegan was the people's choice last time round but this time it appears the FA will take their time to get the right man. Keegan, not for the first time, seems to have got out of the kitchen just as the heat's been turned up. How similar his managerial career has been to the man who took over his No. 7 shirt at Liverpool, Kenny Dalglish.

Sir Bobby Charlton – a former five-a-side team-mate of mine, though that's another story – blasts the FA for even suggesting they will consider a non-English coach. He says foreigners may be OK for smaller, developing nations but that it would be an insult to national pride to consider one to run England.

Pardon my French, Sir Bobster, but what a load of old pish.

Is he saying English fans would not support a team who trounced Brazil because the man coaching it was Italian, French, Spanish or Scottish? What if a foreigner won them the World Cup again? Would they not parade it through Piccadilly Circus because of the shame? Is Sir Bobster seriously trying to tell us nobody can teach the English anything about football? After tonight's miserable performance, he has to be joking.

Thursday, 12 October 2000

At a meeting with Elvis at one of his top clients, Salon Services, their accountant Mark Northway doesn't have too many compliments for JL or GC. This is because Mark's a Falkirk fan and Falkirk fans still shiver at the thought of the time my gaffers spent in charge at Brockville. Versions of events back then differ depending who you talk to – the anti feeling amongst the fans was fed by unhappy players leaking stories to the press. JL and GC were made out the bad guys from day one of an unhappy spell, though they'd tell you it from the opposite angle.

Before we leave, I blag a freebie five-litre bottle of shampoo. We may not win on Saturday, but at least our hair will be soft and manageable. Later, we go to Hamilton for a call at electrical retailer Stepek. Sadly, they turn down my request for a 28 inch Dolby-surround widescreen telly for the Firhill players' lounge.

Friday, 13 October 2000

School holidays mean lovely quiet roads but disquiet in the McKeown household. This is because while normal daddies can take the same week off as their kids, a footballer cannot. The best I can offer Carolyn and the girls are a couple of days in Nairn from Sunday.

Today's also my mum Isabel's sixty-sixth birthday and on the way home from work I pop in with cards and gifts. Carolyn is going for a night out with all the female members of the family tonight to celebrate, so it's just Dani, Taylor and me for the usual pre-match *Friends* -and-curry ritual.

Saturday, 14 October 2000

Bad omens from the off today. I arrive at Moorie's in my club tracksuit to find him in a proper suit. Ditto Del when we pick him up. In the dressing-room at quarter to two, only Cammy, Jamie and me are in leisurewear. The guys explain they felt it was better to look smart for home games, which is fine, but no one told the part-timers – and it means I'll be wearing a suit six days a bloody week.

JL names the same starting eleven as last week as we prepare to take on Arbroath, complete with my old QoS mates Ginger Geordie, Jimmy the Silhouette and Marvellous Stevie Mallan.

The crack pre-match is superb, the pattern post-kick-off predictable – we hog the ball and control the game but can't score. I waste the best chance of the half by blazing Stephen Craigan' fabulous cross over the bar and Trigger's raging because I didn't square it. Maybe he's right, because come the second half he shows me how it's done with an opportunist strike to keep his goal-a-game run going.

It's at this point that we flash back to last week. Once ahead, we fall away and Arbroath take over. Once again, I spend my time running up and down the line without the ball. Once again, we throw it away at the death.

We're eight minutes from a scrappy win when Arbroath equalise and this time we can't conjure a winner despite throwing on all three subs. To make things worse, Mowgli goes down in the last minute under The Silhouette's tackle and may have damaged a cartilage. Me? I suffer a jarred back, take a kick in the calf and pop my shoulder again. Am I getting too old for all this?

JL and GC put on the same old record afterwards about killing teams off but this time Danny leads the counter-argument that we should be able to protect a 1–0 lead. I disagree – at 1–0 a single mistake can do you in. If we get that extra goal, we'll grow in confidence at the back. The one we lost today was a mixture of errors – Archie's in the frame but three or four others were involved. I played a part when I hit the turf under an – *ahem*! – accidental trip by Marvellous Mallan and left a gap.

Still, a couple of beers and the boys loosen up. Allan 'Travolta' Moore is leading an assault on the discotheques of Glasgow by Danny, Del, Trigger, Archie and Doc. Despite loving the odd night out or twenty, I head home. There's training in the morning and then we're off to the Highlands, so I need my kip. Yep, I'm definitely getting old . . .

Sunday, 15 October 2000

I awake to find my back and calf still sore but the real worry's this shoulder. The time's coming when I'll have to take a decision on whether to write the season off and get it sorted.

As the lads drift in, events of the previous night are pieced together. Danny confesses that after leaving to catch the 1.30 a.m. bus to Harthill he fell asleep, woke up in Edinburgh and had to get another bus back at three, finally getting home at four. The rest have had no such disasters but are still the worse for wear. Danny blows the cobwebs off by taking us on a seven-minute run that leaves some struggling. GC then sets up more running before we play a small-sided game for the best part of an hour. Everyone feels heavy-legged by the end and is gasping for bottles of water. Enter JL and his unique homespun philosophy.

'Nah, ye shouldnae be drinkin' water,' he yells, 'it's tea and coffee ye need. Get plenty of it down ye before games and ye'll be fine.'

Later, we watch a video of yesterday's Arbroath goal and the main culprits fingered are Archie, Nally, Stewart, Kenny and me. It would've been easier to excuse those *not* to blame.

The drive to Nairn takes four hours, including a lunch break at Aviemore, and once at the hotel we head straight for the leisure club. Dani and Taylor both love the pool.

Tonight is a milestone in Taylor's young life. For the first time, she goes to bed with no bottle and no pull-ups on and wakes without having had an accident. One day she will read this and hate me for telling you.

Monday, 16 October 2000

My shoulder's giving me grief.

After breakfast we take the girls to the Black Isle Wildlife Park to see deer, zebras, snakes and birds of prey, before getting caught in a downpour and heading for the shelter of a cinema in Inverness. It's still raining when we leave.

Back at the ranch, Carolyn takes the girls swimming while I work on Saturday's column.

Tuesday, 17 October 2000

Home again and ready to get back to the grind – and believe me, life *is* a grind right now from a football point of view. My shoulder stops me doing a body circuit tonight, and with recent results and the thankless role I'm playing, everything's a bit of a downer.

For the first time in my career, I'm already feeling like I need a break from the game to recharge my batteries. I'm back to the low of the last six games of last season.

I'd kill to take the family away on a real holiday.

Wednesday, 18 October 2000

When was that break in Nairn? Last year? It feels like it as I chase my tail around Glasgow, trying to dodge the jams caused by Donald Dewar's funeral procession.

Come evening, I manage my stomachs but the shoulder stops me doing upper body work. No one here likes missing out on training – the work ethic is the best I've ever known in the game. Before each session there are maybe eight or nine guys doing weights and the numbers are growing all the time. Previously you were lucky to get two or three doing extra work.

JL takes us onto the pitch tonight and tries out exercises he picked up watching Celtic's Under-21s train yesterday. At first he's dischuffed with the quality but soon he's enthusing – even Moorie's having a blinder.

Dressing-room chat tonight is about our Christmas night out. Most teams go out in fancy dress – last year I was Captain Hook – but there's a different idea this time. Pyjamas. It's a brilliant plan which most of the guys are right up for. It strikes me I'll have to buy a pair, but it'll be worth it for the laugh.

Suddenly, football seems a happier occupation again.

Thursday, 19 October 2000

Reg the gaffer agrees to help me with a couple of deals I'm trying to close – but on one condition. I have to find him a shop that sells bacon sandwiches just how he likes them. Which isn't so much well done as cremated. I've never met such a fussy eater. He could make a living as a complainer. Even when I find the required provider of scorched pig, he says the place is too warm and we have to leave. Still, he helps things go smoothly with my clients, so I'll forgive him.

Business done, I make the mistake of logging on to the Internet to visit some Thistle websites. It's a mistake because I'm getting a doing left, right and centre from the fans. Comments range from 'he's pish and doesn't deserve a place' to 'Lambie MUST drop this guy' to 'he's got no pace and doesn't tackle. Obviously it's not his job any more!'

I wish they'd say what they really feel.

On digging deeper, I do find one or two positive comments. One fan says he 'enjoys watching Des play and he does not merit the level of abuse that he receives. However he is not best suited to midfield and Lambie should use him as a left-back in a flat back four system.' Another states that 'Des is nothing more than an honest pro and deserves everything that the game can give him. He does not deserve to be singled out for stick.'

I've obviously been oblivious to this level of abuse and, while I respect their right to dish it, I'd rather everyone was behind all of us than just some of us.

I will endeavour to prove to them that I am, in fact, *not* pish.

Friday, 20 October 2000

Rumours abound of a new signing as we prepare to visit Stranraer, who are grinding out results and doing well.

Tid phones to tell me Michelle is pregnant again. That's all very well but does he think I'll play tomorrow?

Saturday, 21 October 2000

Sick on the bus down to Stranraer.

Sick when the name McKeown was not mentioned in the sixteen.

Sick again on the bus home.

What a beautiful day.

JL didn't crack a light that I'd be out when we met at Firhill for our pre-match meal and the mood on the way down was great – plans for the pyjama party grew arms and legs, with someone suggesting we get dressing gowns to check into the nightclub cloakroom and Moorie saying we need our names and numbers on the back. Then, about 20 minutes from Stair Park, I feel ill and spend the rest of the journey in the loo. No one told JL and after a cup of tea and some air I felt great again. No point worrying him.

As if it would have.

As the team was read out, I wasn't in the eleven. When he named the subs and I wasn't among them, it took a couple of seconds to sink in. Then Cammy says, 'I made it. Did you?' All I could manage was a weak, 'No.' I got up, wished everyone all the best and walked out with fellow Siberian citizens Dunnsy and Willie Howie. I told them I now realised how bad a player I was when I was preparing to sit beside them in the stand. Truth is, though, they're both young guys with good futures. I'm not. At my age I can't be happy wearing the big coat. For only the second time in my career, I've been bombed because of my ability and not injury or work commitments. It hurts as badly as it did back when QoS left me out at Berwick.

Thankfully, Dunnsy is an old hand at killing time before games and helps me through the void. I pop out to watch the lads warm up, go and see the doc about a pain I have in my jacksie and to get my annual flu jab, then discuss how Stranraer will play with GC.

Before kick-off, I go to the dressing-room to shake everyone's hand – yes, even the manager's – and I'm soon out of my seat as Moorie hits a screaming volley to make it 1–0. Then I sit down again as I realise I'll never hear the end of it from him.

Half-time comes with us ahead and them down to ten men. On the hour it's game over when Peter Lindau's weak shot squirms through their keeper. I'd told Dunnsy earlier that it'd take something special to beat this keeper but that was because I did it last season. It's now a stroll and Trigger scores for the sixth consecutive match to tie it up. We come in joint top with Clydebank and the dressing-room is buzzing. It's been a good day. For the team. Me? I vomit again on the bus and spend the rest of the journey sleeping.

We go out for a meal at night and the more I think about what's happened the more I feel that JL has changed the team for the sake of change, to be seen to be doing something. Sandy had been dropped to the bench, much to his disgust, while Martin Hardie came straight back in from a three-game ban and Jamie Smith's return came just in time to stop him putting a down-payment on an igloo. The reshuffle had meant guys playing out of position and for me the performance was no better than those that had earned us so much stick in the previous two games. The bottom line, though, is that JL ended up with a 3–0 win and thus the defence rests.

Sunday, 22 October 2000

I'm a crazy, mixed-up kid at training this morning. One minute I'm angry, the next envious, the next again apathetic.

I'm angry because the boys can see no reason for me being dumped yesterday and everyone chins me to find out if JL has explained things. Each gets the same answer – no, and I won't be asking him to. Better players than me have been dropped and if JL expects a chap at his door it won't be this chap.

Then I'm envious, which is understandable. The other guys enjoyed their Saturday night knowing they'd earned their corn for 90 minutes. I didn't because I hadn't.

Apathy? I can't help that one because it's eating at me that perhaps I have nothing more to offer the club and maybe I should accept it's time to move on.

That night, while driving to Aberdeen for a meeting in the morning, my mind's doing cartwheels working out what to do next. I could say nothing and hope to get back into the side sooner rather than later. I could play well, forget my bad spell and everyone would be happy. I could fail to get back in and JL could tell me I'm surplus to requirements. What then? Stay and fight to prove him wrong or try to find another club? Or perhaps JL's already decided I'm extra baggage and is actively trying to sell or swap me.

For a fleeting second I even consider hanging up my boots and becoming a coach.

On balance, it's most likely that JL's trying to shift me. I'd even bet he'll contact QoS to fix up a swap for a boy called Sandy Hodge. He's out of favour down there but JL likes him and he plays in my position.

Watch this space.

Monday, 23 October 2000

Every customer I meet today wants to know how the football's going. All I can do is grit my teeth and tell them the truth. The mobile's also red-hot with calls about my non-appearance at Stranraer. Most assume me shoulder's knackered – I tell them no, it's just cold.

I get home at about seven to find preparations underway for a big event tomorrow. It'll be Taylor's fourth birthday and we've booked her a party. She's too excited to sleep.

Tuesday, 24 October 2000

Taylor's sleeping when I leave for Dunfermline at seven but I phone her from the car to sing 'Happy Birthday'. She's hyper. And soon, so is her daddy. His day goes like this:

> 9.00 a.m.-11.30: First appointment.
> 11.30-12.15: Drive to Glasgow for second appointment. On phone the whole way.
> 1.15 p.m.: Second appointment.
> 2.30: Third appointment, also in Glasgow.
> 3.30: Drive to Cumbernauld to visit client with Car Wash.
> 4.45: Head home.
> 5-5.45: Tidy up day's paperwork.
> 5.45: Go to Taylor's party.
> 6.45: Head for Milton of Campsie to pick up mum, sister Veronica and nephew Sean and take them to our house for Taylor's family party.
> 7.30-9.30: Party, body circuit, dinner.
> 9.45: Drive mum et al. back home.
> 10.30: Home, feet up.
> 11.30 p.m.: Zzzzzzzzzzzz . . .

Wednesday, 25 October 2000

Glasgow, Edinburgh, Dunfermline then Glasgow again. It never stops. By teatime at Firhill, I can feel my hamstrings tighten up so badly – after 1,000 miles in 72 hours – that I'm not sure whether to train. My mind's made up when I hear we're working on the astroturf. Instead, Walter the Vet tells me to stretch off and avoid heavy running. I stick to skipping and body work.

JL's in a good mood. When I tell him about my hammies he says, 'How the fuck can your legs be tight?' I reply, 'Well, it wasn't because of Saturday – you never fucking picked me!'

It's all a laugh but the serious side is that the last thing I need right now is an injury. Doc's crocked and with several others complaining of flu symptoms, I need to be available. Walter reckons I'll be fine to train tomorrow night.

Thursday, 26 October 2000

Won back a client today, three years after I lost them. Result.

At training, my hammies loosen off as the session goes on but I doubt JL would lose any sleep if they went twang right now. The best I can hope for at Berwick on Saturday is the bench – and even then only thanks to Doc's injury. It's between me, Dunnsy and Willie for the vacant seat and if I miss out to two lads who've been miles away from a game, JL's message will be loud and clear.

Saturday, 28 October 2000

Got in the car to head for Firhill, then got out again to check the big coat was in the boot.

It's impossible to second-guess what JL will do today. As I found to my cost last week, he always has a surprise up his sleeve – my hunch is that his latest will be to bring Dunnsy in from the salt mines. He's been training with Bury all week and if I was his gaffer I'd be thinking that his spirits would be high.

By the time we're in Shielfield's away dressing-room, though, I've so convinced myself I'll be out that I'm almost disappointed to be named at No. 16. Now I need to motivate myself from scratch in case I'm needed. Dunnsy and Willie are in the stand again and obviously Dunnsy hasn't been listening to the team properly because he asks me what I fancy doing until kick-off. I tell I'm him on the bench and his face is a mix of embarrassment and disappointment.

It's cold and wet as we warm up and Berwick get at us with a strengthening wind at their backs. Kenny gifts them the lead and we're up against it, but great work by Danny sets Trigger up to score for an unbelievable seventh week on the trot.

We're level at half-time and finally I get my chance to perform. Every shot I hit rifles towards Michael Brown and somehow I feel like I'm contributing something.

The wind drops second half but we lift the pace and take the lead when David McCallum is fouled in the box and Trigger does the needful. If we hold on we'll be clear at the top.

As legs tire in the heavy conditions, JL begins to think about changes. First, Del replaces Peter Lindau. Then Sandy goes on for Danny, though this one takes five minutes to make while he waits for Danny to get as far away from the dugouts as possible so he wastes as much time as possible wandering back over. Then he tells me to get ready to take over from Martin Hardie but I predict to Cammy that the clock will run down before I get on. Five or six times Walter the Vet asks if it's time to get the boards up. Five or six times JL says to wait.

The final whistle goes while I am standing on the touchline.

Just call me Mystic Des.

Monday, 30 October 2000

Meeting in Aberdeen today with Les Dalgarno, senior partner of the city's largest legal firm and a big pal of Sir Alex Ferguson. We talk football for ages and his stories are brilliant.

Tuesday, 31 October 2000

Driving, driving, driving – first to Huntly, then Inverness, then three hours back down the road to Cumbernauld and my girls. No exercise tonight, just an hour in the bath.

Wednesday, 1 November 2000

At our sales meeting today, the wind-ups about Saturday's derby against Queen's Park have started. Car Wash isn't saying much but I'm giving him dog's.

'Admit it, you're only a bunch of amateurs.'

'We'll see.'

'What d'you mean "we'll see"? You're amateurs, no match for pros like us.'

I keep waiting for him to come back with a crack about how he's at least he's got a chance of playing whilst I'll probably be wearing the big coat again, but he keeps his powder dry. My only comfort would be that at least I'd still be paid more to sit in the stand than the entire Queen's team are getting for running about daft.

Good news on the day job front is that the team has hit its targets again and personally I've had a huge month. It's a nice consolation when my weekend job's faltering so badly.

Thistle call to say training's off tonight, and although JL feels we deserve a free night I don't think I deserve one. Hit the Westerwood gym instead.

The day ends with me working until 1 a.m. on Saturday's column. I resist the temptation to moan about being left out and have a pop at Car Wash – 'a guy who's had more free transfers than Airtours' – instead.

Thursday, 2 November 2000

JL's a superstitious guy whose motto should be: 'If it ain't broke, don't fix it.' He probably wouldn't be able to anyway. Still, master tactician or not, he's been named Bell's Manager of the Month – and to make it a double, Trigger adds Player of the Month to his membership of Mensa.

Friday, 3 November 2000

My usual Friday ritual bites the dust – but it's a small price to pay to see Taylor's face as she watches the fireworks display at Broadwood Loch. We're home in time for *Friends*, the time every week that I really start to get excited about the next day's game. Not tonight. Not when I know there's little chance of me taking part. The important thing now is to make sure I'm still up for it in case the shout comes. Stranger things have happened. But not many.

Saturday, 4 November 2000

Matchdays are starting to feel like Christmases when you know you're either going to get socks or Y-fronts. The sense of anticipation soon seeps out of you. Knowing you've little or no chance of starting is soul-destroying. It's a sad state of affairs when you'd be relieved to park your backside on the bench.

I'm at Firhill early to meet Reg the gaffer and some clients who're enjoying pre-match hospitality. Sadly, Elvis has gubbed his knee playing football last night, so old Dunky steps in as the table's Des McKeown – a late sub.

There's a match programme at every place setting and I'm shocked to see my handsome face staring back from ten covers. Autographs? Sure, no problem.

They've all stuck a few bob on Car Wash scoring the first goal. I can safely say I'd be a better bet – in fact, if they win I'll bare my arse in George Square at lunchtime. Car Wash himself, meanwhile, knows his limits. When I meet him outside the dressing-rooms, he offers to make me a cup of tea. I let him off for today.

Our treatment room is always the equivalent of a kitchen at a party – everyone meets there and it drives Walter the Vet mental. Trigger's on the table for treatment on the calf he injured on Thursday night. JL comes in and sees his star striker stretched out before him.

'Christ, what a big girl's blouse.'

'Don't panic, gaffer,' I tell him. 'I'm fit.'

'You? I wouldnae trust you to play up front.'

'You wouldn't trust me to play anywhere.'

And so it proves at 1.50 p.m. when he names the same side as last week, with me at No. 16. Dunnsy and Willie are in Siberia again, so it could be worse.

By kick-off 4,035 people plus bit-part players have taken their seats, but not me. I prefer to stand. JL's a bag of jaggies and turns every couple of minutes to ask what I've thought of this decision or that chance. I'm too busy saying silent thanks to above because Car Wash has met a teasing cross with his humph instead of his head and kept my arse covered for the time being.

JL settles when Martin puts us ahead but ten minutes later he's edgy again as Queen's equalise. It's happening to us again – though at least it wasn't Car Wash who scored. Just before half-time, Moorie duffs a shot across goal straight to Trigger who taps in for the eighth game on the bounce. Incredible.

As the second half fizzles out, there seems little chance of me getting a run and my chances move to remote when Del replaces the limping Trigger and Sandy takes over from the tiring David McCallum. Ten minutes from time, I loosen my boots and take off my tie-ups when Cammy gets the shout to go on for Peter Lindau. The only remaining drama comes when Car Wash has a great effort saved by Kenny. The city of Glasgow owes our keeper big time.

Back in a happy dressing-room, we find out Clydebank have lost. We're now four points clear at the top. It must feel great to have contributed. As the rest go out for a warm-down, I collar JL.

'I can't believe you put Cammy on before me.'

'Ach, Des, it was heads or tails. You lost.'

And you know what? I believe him.

Moorie's nursing a few sore ones from today but he's still on a high – he's going with Tid to a fancy dress party for Gerry Britton's thirtieth.

What else could they be going as but the Ugly Sisters? With those taxi-door ears and a swollen hooter from a Queen's elbow, Moorie will be the ugliest bird in history.

Sunday, 5 November 2000

Somebody please poke my eyes out with a stick.

I've turned up at Moorie's house to chauffeur him to training and the first thing I see is Tid sprawled on the sofa in a coma – still in dress, high heels and lacy hold-up stockings. The other Ugly Sis? She's still upstairs, identically dressed, lipstick smudged and mascara a mess. And she's not too keen to get changed.

So there I am, rolling up at Firhill with a half-cut thirtysomething winger in a dress and make-up. The boys went mental. Some still bear the psychological scars of seeing him in stockings. Especially seeing him do an entire session in them.

Thank God JL hasn't trapped. GC's keeping one eye on us but basically it's a loosener and a bit of fun – except for those who didn't play. We get the bonus of a 12-minute run followed by some shooting practice.

By the time I've dropped Moorie off he'd begun to sober up and Tid had emerged from his coma. The worrying thing is that this cross-dressing thing is catching. That night, at the annual Dukla Pumpherston charity dinner in Glasgow, GC parades the room selling raffle tickets. And wearing a French maid's outfit. I'm beginning to feel like the weird one for wearing trousers.

Monday, 6 November 2000

The rain's tipping down as I wake from five hours' sleep. We're due to play Raith Rovers in a bounce game tonight but it must be in doubt already. A lunchtime call to JL confirms the worst. My excitement about the chance of an actual game of football has been wasted.

Tuesday, 7 November 2000

Rangers fell at the first Champions League hurdle tonight. Again. Monaco have snatched a draw late on at Ibrox and the point's enough to let Galatasaray and Sturm Graz play out a virtual friendly knowing they're both through.

Gers fans will curse the mistake Lorenzo Amoruso made to give away the equaliser. They'll moan about injuries to key players at key times. They'll sigh that they've come so close a year on from being pipped by Bayern Munich. But whatever way they or anyone else looks at it, they've failed. Again. They've spent a shedload of money. Again. And got precious little return. Again.

Three years ago, chairman David Murray promised Rangers were ready to make the great leap forward in Europe under Dick Advocaat. He came with a huge reputation and was given a huge salary to achieve what Walter Smith could not – lasting continental credibility. Three campaigns later, what has the Little General achieved that the big electrician didn't? Jack shit. Sure, he won five of the first six domestic trophies he played for. But Walter helped them to nine titles in a row plus a pile of cups. That wasn't what he was hired for.

Advocaat has spent something like £75 million – not counting wages and bonuses and houses and cars and the rest – and has still not got beyond the first stage of the major Euro tourney. Of all his buys, I can only see genuine value for money in Stefan Klos, Gio van Bronckhorst, Claudio Reyna and Billy Dodds – though Kenny Miller will hopefully develop into a great buy at £2 million. But what about Fernando Ricksen, Bert Konterman and Andrei Kanchelskis? Ronald de Boer, Tugay, Neil McCann and Allan Johnston? Peter Lovenkrands, Dariusz Adamczuk, Stephane Guivarc'h, Gabriel Amato, Lionel Charbonnier and more? Throw in the likes of Michael Mols and Arthur Numan, on whom the jury must still be out because of injury, and it looks to me like the Little General has not exactly traded like a stock market whizzkid.

And then there are the players he's let go – Jonatan Johannson, banging goals in for Charlton in the Premiership after being let go for £2 million less than they paid for Kanchelskis; keeper Antti Niemi, a £400,000 snip for Hearts; Colin Hendry, signed in a blaze of publicity for £4 million then ousted almost immediately; Paul Ritchie, lured away from Hearts for free then sold for £500,000 before kicking a competitive ball. Ritchie's the one that really angers me. Rangers made it clear they wanted him and he made it clear he wanted to go, so much so that Hearts boss Jim Jefferies decided not to play him for the remaining six months of his contract. But did Rangers really want him at all? Or did they just not want Hearts to have him?

The Little General is often given credit in the media for nurturing Craig Moore's career, yet it's forgotten that he in fact punted him to

Crystal Palace and only took him back by default when the London club couldn't stump up the fee. Advocaat's damn lucky he never flogged the boy to someone with money!

Last but not least, there's Advocaat's handling of Amoruso. The only word for it is deplorable. He has quite openly tried to punt the Italian more than once, yet when he can't get a deal done he asks the guy to play and it's to Amo's credit that he continues to give his all. Last summer, when it looked like Sunderland would pay up, Advocaat went out and bought Ritchie and Konterman. Then the move broke down – and, hey presto, Amo was not only welcomed back, but also handed the skipper's armband. Yet just a few weeks ago he publicly humiliated a proud man by stripping him of the captaincy when his performances dipped. Not only were the fans and the press making Amo the scapegoat for another European disaster, so was his gaffer. How's that for man management?

My final indictment of Advocaat's reign is that he seems to have lost the spirit that held Walter Smith's dressing-room together through good times and bad. Smith forged the ultimate in camaraderie. They used to say that he had teams who won together because they drank together, and even if they sometimes took the latter to extremes, they were brilliant at the former. It seems from the outside that today's Rangers squad is split by cliques and there is a growing feeling that the Little General's own Dutch colony are immune from blame when things go pear-shaped. The blame for this can only lie with one man – the manager.

Perhaps Advocaat will pull things round and win another domestic treble but that's still not why he came to Scotland. Anyway, I have a sneaky suspicion that the arrival of Martin O'Neill at Celtic may soon underline the deficiencies I've laid out here. The Little General may be left giving thanks that the Irishman didn't arrive sooner.

Wednesday, 8 November 2000

Can't wait to get a good sweat on tonight.

During a crossing and finishing exercise, JL compliments me on my superb delivery. OK, so he actually yells 'Why don't you fucking cross the ball like that on a Saturday?' But in my current position, it sounded like glowing praise.

'Simple,' I've shouted back. 'I don't do it on a Saturday because you don't fucking pick me!'

After training we find out that Jim Jefferies has quit as manager of Hearts. I wind JL up that he's the only man with the credentials to replace him – after all, he did it at Falkirk.

'Aye,' he mumbles back. 'That'll be fucking right.'

Thank you, Oscar.

Thursday, 9 November 2000

I do a lot of stuff in my day job – selling, entertaining, debt collecting, even delivering now and again. This morning, though, I almost have to go 15 rounds with a van driver. He works for a courier company used by Oyez and he's delivering our stock to one of my clients. Except that the delivery point is on the second floor and he's not for humping the goods up there. He's for leaving them in reception for someone else to carry. But the receptionist isn't having it. She won't sign for the goods unless he delivers them to the right place, so he starts putting the stuff back in his van.

Enter gladiator McKeown, who happens to be in the building and gets a shout to help.

'OK, pal, how about you just put the stuff where it's meant to go.'

'No way.'

'Why not?'

'Cos.'

'Cos how?'

'Cos Ah'm no', OK?'

'No.'

'No whit?'

'No, it isn't OK. These are clients and you're delivering supplies they've ordered from me. Please just do it.'

Now, the boy's about 50 – but he clearly thinks he's still got the fighting ability of a 30-year-old. He squares up to me.

'You're messing with the wrong guy, son!'

Well, I'm no Lennox Lewis. But I was still well able to have a roll around the floor laughing before picking myself up and throwing the git out. Then shifting the damn stuff myself.

My good friend Craig Levein, manager at Cowdenbeath, is being linked with the Hearts job. I give him a call for the low-down – and a wee wind-up.

'Mr Levein? It's Hearts chief executive Chris Robinson here.'

'Very good, baldy.'

'How did you see through my disguise?'

'It was shite.'

'Ah.'

Anyway, he's pretty much in the dark about the speculation and isn't going to show an interest unless Hearts show one first. Wise move.

At training, JL sounds out the part-timers about the possibility of a week abroad in December. We've been given a bye in the first round of the Scottish Cup and he wants to use the break to build team spirit. Unfortunately, he'll have to build it without me. December's one of my busiest months and there's no chance of time off. Turns out all the part-timers are in the same boat.

Saturday, 11 November 2000

Another Saturday and the prospect of more socks and Y-fronts. But wait, it's worse – today, I get the equivalent of bath salts. I'm not even on the bench. Dunnsy and Willie will replace Del and me among the subs at home to Clydebank and, believe it or not, I'm more disappointed for Del. I was sure he'd get a start in place of Peter, who's been toiling.

Before I can get up to leave them to their preparations, JL starts laying into them. He says today's the last chance for some to prove their worth. It seems an odd way to motivate a team unbeaten in six and top of the league. Still, it's not really my problem. I'm not even high enough in his estimation to be among the ones getting a last chance. I now need to consider my future very carefully. I make a couple of calls to put feelers out.

It's only when I go to ask JL for a complimentary ticket for a pal – you don't get any unless you're stripped – that he explains things to me and leaves me more confused than ever.

'See, Des, Dunnsy and Willie were a bit down and I wanted to gee them up a bit.'

So that means Del and I get a boot in the goolies? Is that meant to make us sing 'Happy Days Are Here Again'?

'Anyway,' I ask him, seeing we're being open and honest, 'why was I left out of the team in the first place?'

'I don't think 3-5-2 suits you.'

'Right – so as that's the formation you've stuck by, is there any point me being here?'

'Course there is – we're bound to make changes and I'll need every man in the squad at some point.'

'That's fine for you to say, gaffer, but I need to play football. I'll be honest, this is the biggest dilemma I've ever had in football.'

'How come?'

'Well, do I stay and take the chance of getting back in a team that wins the league – because I've no doubt we will. Or do I give up the chance of winning something for the first time in my career and go somewhere for a game. You must see that, surely?'

'Of course – and you *will* play a part. And by the way, don't jinx us with that stuff about winning the league.'

Peter and Martin's goals give us a comfortable win in the end, although Kenny wins MoM for three outstanding saves and Nally and Archie are superb at the back. Results go our way and we're now six points clear. So much for me jinxing the run.

It could be a long, long season.

At night, Carolyn and I go to an engagement party for her brother, Gary, and his sweetheart, Gillian. It's a good night but I'd be lying if I said my mind was on anything but my own future.

I'm re-running my conversation with JL over and over in my head, trying to work out what it means to me. He's the guy who picks the team, he's picking it in a 3-5-2 formation and he doesn't think I fit in. Fact is, though, I don't think he knows where I *do* fit in. And, come to think of it, after 14 years in the game I'm no longer that sure either.

This is where football is a truly odd business. In what other job would someone employ you not knowing what they wanted you to do? Every other industry has Human Resources departments – they were called Personnel in pre-yuppie days – which try to get optimum output from staff by giving them optimum support. In football, this is left to one man. The manager – after all, the only other stuff he's got on his plate is tactics, negotiating transfers, picking the team and blowing up the balls for training. He wears more hats than a cricket umpire. And the fact is most managers I've known have been totally one-dimensional in their dealings with players. Their yardstick for output is simple – is he playing well? If so, pick him. If not, dump him. Very few know how to kick your arse one minute and cuddle you the next. It's all short-term.

In 14 years, I've never been interviewed by a manager to discuss my performances. Never once has a manager asked me what I think is wrong with my game – even though there's plenty wrong with it. Oh sure, I've been *told* plenty of times that I'm a diddy, but it's never turned into a discussion on how I can improve. You're *ordered* to pull your socks up or else you're out.

In general, managers lump all their players into one pigeonhole. They don't allow for one guy being shy or another over-confident or another having personal problems. You're either in or you're out – and when you're out, you're *really* out. Ask Dunnsy. And so I've got to 30 without truly knowing what it is I am good at on a football pitch. I've played left-back in a 4-4-2, left wing-back in a 3-5-2, centre-half in a four, sweeper in a three, centre midfield, left midfield and a left-sided marker. Which is my best position? Give in! I'd *guess* left-back but any one of a dozen managers might disagree.

Look at Paul Lambert. Successive gaffers at St Mirren and Motherwell knew he was a good player, but in what position? He played right-wing, left-wing, centre-mid, up front – you name it, he dabbled in it. But he never made a shirt his own and in consequence no bigger club was prepared to take him on. Next thing he's at Borussia Dortmund, who spot that he's ideally suited to hold in front of the defence and within a year he's winning the European Cup. Then Celtic are paying fortunes for him and Scotland can't do without him. Now you can't imagine him not directing the traffic for club and country. Why couldn't someone at home have sat down and worked out how to get the optimum output from such a talented guy?

In business, I know my strength is as a salesman and not an accountant. In business I have review meetings with Reg the gaffer to focus me on my performance, work on my weaknesses and confirm my strengths. To my knowledge this doesn't happen anywhere in football and I'm sure because of that both managers and players would initially be uneasy with it. But surely through time players would better understand what was expected of them and how their performances were evaluated.

At present in football, no news is good news – as in, the gaffer usually only wants to talk to you if you're having a Ricksen. But if players are not made aware of their strengths and weaknesses, how can they develop fully? Fact is, too many footballers are discarded because of a manager's failings, not their own. Who knows, I might have missed my chance to be Paul Lambert before Borussia even invented him.

Sunday, 12 November 2000

Training this morning proves one thing to me – my fitness is dropping. As much as I'm putting a shift in with the boys and in my personal sessions, the lack of games is taking its toll. I last kicked a ball on 14 October and with no reserve team to tick over in, my sharpness is receding faster than my hairline.

It's been Catch-22 for me – I've resisted doing too much on my own in case it affects me in training with Thistle. Now I have no choice. I need to build myself back up over the next two or three weeks and I start today with some extra running. I'll do the same tomorrow and Tuesday and, although I'll be working on Wednesday night, I'll be back with the boys on Thursday for another battering even though there's no chance of me playing against Stirling Albion on Saturday.

Craig Levein calls me later and asks if I'd fancy a month's loan at Cowdenbeath, who are going great guns in the Third Division. It would get me some games and fill in his problem left-back position, and I'd go in a minute, but I tell him JL might veto a temporary move because of how small his own squad is.

Monday, 13 November 2000

My mobile rings. It's Thistle's number. Straight away I reckon it could be JL telling me he's accepted Craig's offer. Not so, but half-decent news anyway – he's arranged a friendly tomorrow night at Albion Rovers. At last. Football.

Tuesday, 14 November 2000

Batter through business today with my thoughts on a pitch in Coatbridge, where in my mind I'm bouncing around like a teenager and hammering a Mitre again.

Me and the San Siro di Cliftonhill go back a long way. I had a happy spell with the Rovers, but long before then it was the first ground I ever had a trial at. I'll never forget the state of the place back then as long as I live. I was turning out for Dumbarton and didn't know what to expect – but I certainly hadn't bargained for an away dressing-room half filled by a huge ceramic bath which hadn't seen Domestos since the First World War. An old-fashioned water boiler hung on the wall above it but it seemed the stuff it heated came from the nearby canal. Another small worry was that it was lit by a naked flame about a foot away. Welcome to the glamorous world of professional football. Today, happily, the manky bath has been replaced by showers, which gives you a bit more room to swing a Moorie, plus they've filled in the window-sized hole in the toilet wall which left your business visible to everyone coming through the adjoining turnstiles.

Tonight is icy cold but at least it's dry. The playing surface is hardly Wembley but at least I'm on it. I'd have run about a cow pasture for a game. I'm playing centre-half and also turning out are Sandy Stewart, Cammy, Del, Dunnsy and keeper Michael Brown along with two trialists and some of Tid's kids.

Rovers send out a bunch of young pros with something to prove against a bigger club. Whenever I've played in the stiffs you want to be up against older guys who really don't want to be there. Your worst nightmare is facing weans with a cause. We play well enough, though, and win 3–1 with goals from Dunnsy, Del and Cammy. I'm happy with my performance and my fitness seems fine. JL seems satisfied with it all.

But if I enjoyed the game, I loved the hour I spent afterwards with Rovers manager John McVeigh. What a character – you couldn't dampen his spirits with a sledgehammer over the napper and his enthusiasm is infectious.

John's fighting an unfair dismissal case against his last club, Raith Rovers. Last December they sacked him amid newspaper reports that he bullied young players and recently there have been more stories about him acting the same way at Cliftonhill. The rumours are he's ordered kids who have a nightmare in training to strip and sing a song, so as soon as I'm in his office I ask if I need to do the same. He tugs at his shirt collar, something he does a million times in every conversation, and says, 'Hey sure, that's a loada pish!' And thus the ice is broken. I suggest he should double the age of his squad in one fell swoop by signing Sandy and myself. He says that he would take us in a minute if he had the money.

The rest of the crack is all about his film-making exploits with Robert Duvall and Ally McCoist. He's been involved from day one in a movie about a small Scottish club who win the cup against all the odds. His stories grow arms and legs by the second until my sides are splitting. I remind him of the day he tried to sign me when he was in charge at Thistle.

'I couldn't believe it,' I say. 'Not only did you get the sack the same day it was meant to go through, but Frank Sinatra died as well and he was my hero.'

'Aye,' he bellows, 'an' Ah *still* got the front page!'

Thursday, 16 November 2000

The sales team has stayed in a Glasgow hotel after a conference and a night out and the morning starts with a blind panic. As I approach Car Wash's room to make sure he's up, I hear disturbing noises which I can only describe as the sound of a head being smacked violently against a headboard. Now, Graham likes the ladies, but when I left him last night he couldn't have bitten his fingernails. Surely he hadn't pulled in that state? I go back to my room and phone him. No answer. I try again. Still no answer.

Urgent action is needed, so I go back along the corridor and rattle his door. The noise is even louder now – and I can distinctly hear Car Wash shouting verbal abuse that Channel 5 would put a sexual content warning on. My first thought is that he's picked up a m'dear after all and is – *ahem*! – entertaining her. My second is that a colleague we met yesterday, who is gay, has picked Car Wash up and is entertaining *him*. Maybe it'd be better to leave the boy to his own fate. However, back in my room the mobile rings with Car Wash's number on it. I'm not sure what to say to him.

'So, Graham, how are you?'

'Fine, now – but you'll never believe what happened to me!'

'I think I might have a clue . . .'

'No, honestly, you'll never believe it!'

'Honestly, love, I think I might. But try me anyway.'

'I've spent the last 20 minutes locked in the fucking shower. The door just wouldn't open – I even tried to climb out over the gap at the top. I could hear the phone ringing but couldn't get to it. I can't believe nobody tried to help me. I was shouting my fucking head off!'

'And the things you were shouting – would they have been the kind of things you wouldn't say if you were at tea with your auntie?'

'Sort of.'

'Ah . . .'

It's five minutes before I wipe the tears from my eyes and am able to admit what I thought had been happening to him.

I'm tired by the time we do a small-sided game. I'm on the yellow team, humped twice by the reds. But GC decides the third game's the one that counts and that each member of the winning team gets to 'work' an opposition player for a minute as a forfeit. We've soon got the game in the bag and pick our victims – but Moorie, who's wearing red, erupts and refuses to do the punishment. GC bites back and we're into a shouting match.

'I've worked hard,' the wee man shouts. 'Pick on someone else!'

It's pretty obvious he's referring to Peter Lindau, who seldom looks interested in training and rarely bursts a gut for his team-mates. Worryingly, he's also getting that way on Saturdays. He's a different player from the one we brought on loan from Ayr last season, and while you can accept poor performances, poor workrate gets on everyone else's goat.

Moorie loses the argument and does his minute's punishment.

The boys put his outburst down to PMT.

Saturday, 18 November 2000

Trouble before I even head for the game – the *Scottish Sun* sub-editors have put a headline on my diary that suggests I'll be walking out unless JL picks me. What I'd actually written was that I'd have to consider my future if I wasn't involved soon. It's a subtle difference but one which could land me in bother. I decide to play the headline down if the management challenge me. My conscience is clear.

When I come back from Tesco with the shopping, Carolyn says a lady has phoned to ask if I'd call her to talk about her daughter, who's in hospital. Carolyn thinks the girl's called Angela and goes to Firhill in her wheelchair. Straight away I know who she means. Angela's in her early twenties and Thistle daft. She goes to every home game with her dad Billy. She's also been through four serious operations recently to drain fluid from her head. How humbled am I to find out that, when asked what she'd like to cheer her up, she'd said she'd like to see me?

I feel small. Here's me thinking my world's crumbling because I can't get a game of football – and there's a young girl fighting for her very life who believes meeting me would somehow help her recovery.

Truth is, two other tragedies this week have underlined just how lucky I am and prove that things we take for granted are suddenly made special due to the misfortune of others. Take Alan Stubbs. The Celtic defender battled back from testicular cancer last year but now the disease is back and appears to have spread. You can only hope he battles through it again. Nearer to home, my cousin Catherine died last night. She was only in her thirties, with a husband and a young son. Her life was only beginning. And I think *I* have problems . . .

Maybe JL's read my mind and realised I need a lift because when we get to Forthbank he tells me I'm on the bench. Del and I are back, Dunnsy and Willie are out again.

The first half is like Little Bighorn, with Stirling having eleven

General Custers while our injuns camp in their half non-stop. Martin Hardie's fourth goal in four games finally puts an arrow in their hat. Guess what, though? We die with our boots on. Custer and his troops break and we struggle. Out of nowhere, Trigger sidles over to the bench during a stoppage.

'Gaffer?'

'What?'

'Any chance of asking Peter to run about a bit?'

'*What*? '

'Ah said, any chance of asking Peter to run about a bit?'

'What? WHHAAAATTTT??!? *You* fucking tell him to run about!!!'

Needless to say, Peter doesn't run about any more than before and is involved in the breakdown in play that lets Stirling equalise. Cue the entrance of Del.

Sandy replaces Moorie next before – *ta-raaaa*! – I come on for the tiring Martin. Seven minutes to change the game and I very nearly manage it with my first touch. Trigger squeezes the ball front post but my shot's blocked and we end up holding on for a draw.

JL and GC lose their rag afterwards and name names they felt stopped playing at half-time. Call me selfish but it crosses my mind that I've an outside chance of playing in the QoS game next week.

Oh, and nobody even mentioned my diary headline.

Sunday, 19 November 2000

Angela's smile when I walked into her hospital ward brought a lump to my throat and will stay with me forever. Her face beamed as I gave her flowers and a CD. Moments like these make you realise how much football clubs mean to their supporters. The fact that I could bring some joy to a sick girl just by being connected with Thistle underlines how lucky I am to be in the game.

The lads are going to a Race Night at Firhill later and it's bound to turn into a session. I won't be with them. I'm going to Celtic stalwart Tom Boyd's testimonial dinner in Glasgow.

Monday, 20 November 2000

My avenues of escape are being blocked off one by one.

I had three clubs in mind should I need to leave Firhill – Stranraer,

Forfar and QoS. But Stranraer manager Billy McLaren gave former Thistle trialist Jered Stirling a go at the weekend and he scored twice. Strike that one off. Queens, meanwhile, have been linked with former Scotland left-back Tosh McKinlay. Strike that one off too. And finally, Esther, my old mate Ian McPhee has resigned as manager of Forfar. Another door slams in my handsome face.

On the day that grumpy old Victor Meldrew dies on screen, it may be fitting to admit that 'I don't belieeeeeeeve it!'

Wednesday, 22 November 2000

So it looks like I *will* play in the Queen of the South game on Saturday. But not for Thistle. Was it only two days ago that I ruled out my chances of returning to Palmerston? It doesn't seem like it because tonight I open talks with their manager John Connolly. I'm going down there tomorrow night, hopefully to finalise things, after it became clearer than ever that my Thistle days were over.

Yet I have to admit JL was brilliant with me. It is strange how things came about but in the end it would appear my meeting tomorrow night at Palmerston will secure my transfer out of Firhill. I'd only gone into his office to tell him about a couple of signings Queens were hoping to make when he caught me off guard.

'I'm told you're one of them.'

'Me? Haven't heard a thing.'

'I have. The board accepted a bid today and gave Connolly permission to talk to you.'

'So what does that mean for me?'

'That's up to you.'

'Nah, come on – would you prefer a fee for me and my wages to play with?'

'If you put it like that, yes. You know the formation I want to play and you know where you stand at present. So, yes, I'd prefer to bring in another player.'

In that instant, my decision was more or less made. JL's honesty made it clear I'd be stupid not to speak to John Connolly. I phoned him from Firhill, said I was interested and that I'd phone him back after training.

It was a bizarre feeling to work out with the boys knowing I could be playing against them on Saturday, but with them not knowing I knew. By then I was sure that if Queens offered a good enough package, I'd be off.

Half an hour on the blower with JC took away any doubts about signing. I asked where his interest had come from, as he'd only seen me play once. He said everyone at the club spoke very highly of me and anyone else he'd asked said he'd be signing a player who'd give the same level of performance every week. He'd also heard I was good about the dressing-room and my attitude was not to be questioned.

'Next question. Where do you want to play me?'

'Left back in a 4-4-2.'

'What about the length of contract?'

'To the end of next season.'

All we needed now was to talk a deal and, as his initial offer was better than what I was on at Thistle, I knew there must be some more to play with. I put forward my own terms and he said he'd go to the board with it.

The only problem now was explaining to Carolyn that I'd be driving down the M74 the next night instead of taking her out for her birthday. As one trauma fades, another looms.

Thursday, 23 November 2000

Des McKeown, Queen of the South. It has a ring to it. Going to Palmerston saved my career once before and now I'm hoping it can do so again. When I went there six years back, I'd been going nowhere at Albion Rovers. Queens revitalised me. The situation now is frighteningly similar.

My meeting with JC and directors Tommy Harkness and Craig Paterson went smoothly. I didn't get everything I asked for but we met somewhere in the middle. We shook hands, they gave me my club tracksuit and I went to await my new team-mates.

First in was a familiar face, club captain Andy Aitken. He's done well since coming in as a kid when I was there. He introduced me to the rest but it was a strange experience to know your surroundings so well yet be a stranger. I sat and watched them, trying to remember names and form first impressions. They're the ones that last.

By the end of training, my impression was of a bunch with a good attitude and harmony. There was nobody I could say I didn't take to. Hopefully they'll feel the same about me. As for training itself? A different voice, a different emphasis and a different venue were the very lifts I'd needed for a long time.

Afterwards I went down to the bar beneath the main stand and met a

126 DON'T GIVE UP THE DAY JOB

few fans. They assured me I'd be welcomed back with open arms. I wish I could have said the same about home.

Carolyn was already in bed when I came in at gone eleven and wasn't too interested in my news. She was against me moving to QoS, saying the travelling would mean even less time at home. This had been one of my major concerns too, but on second thoughts I decided it might give me *more* time with the family. I'd only be training Tuesdays and Thursdays instead of Sundays, Wednesdays and Thursdays – and there was always the risk of JL dropping extra sessions on us at the last minute. The Queens squad was spread too far and wide – from Newcastle to Glasgow – for JC to do that.

I'll have to convince Carolyn that this was not only the right move for me, but for her as well.

Friday, 24 November 2000

Curry and *Friends* go past in a blur tonight as I contemplate my debut tomorrow. JC's all but told me I'll start and for it to be against Thistle is a hell of a coincidence.

My phone's been red-hot all day as news of the transfer spreads. Fans of both clubs as well as friends and colleagues have been very supportive – yet the whole business hasn't really sunk in with me yet. Maybe it'll hit me when I arrive at Firhill tomorrow and go into a different dressing-room.

Anyway, JL's kept his word that he'd use the money he got for me. He's brought back striker George Shaw, who played for him at Thistle before. Two guys making second debuts for new clubs in one game might be some sort of record.

Geordie's arrival, though, might ruin my plan to boot Moorie up and down the touchline all day. I've told the wee man of my intentions but he says he's been threatened by better players than me.

Saturday, 25 November 2000

I can't remember anticipation like this.

As I arrive at Firhill, I walk slap-bang into Thistle chairman Brown McMaster and a group from the hospitality suite on a tour of the ground. If one of them told me to remember to go into the right dressing-room, twenty did.

First off, I go to JL's office and wish him and the club all the best starting from tomorrow. He's with GC and Disco Dave and they say the same back. Next, the bootroom to collect my footwear. Ricky and Chico give me the usual abuse before wishing me good luck. Finally, before I get on with my life, a procession of handshakes and warm comments from all the lads in the Thistle camp. They don't think that I should have been sold and think it strange that JL has let Queens play me today. Others think there's something personal between JL and myself but I tell them no – in fact, I've nothing but praise for him.

My brother Gerry also makes an appearance. He's a cop based in Maryhill and the only member of the force who orders a hat two sizes too big so his hair gel doesn't get messed up.

The Queens lads are buoyant as they arrive. I sit alone, trying to focus on an unusual situation. I need to play well – to gain the respect of my new team-mates, to repay JC's faith in me, to prove JL wrong for not playing me, to silence the Thistle fans who'll give me dog's abuse. Plus, I need to get one up on Moorie.

I am my new team's only change from last week. It feels good to hear my name at No. 3. By the end of the warm-up I'm more or less sure of everyone else's name.

I hear one or two comments from the home fans before kick-off but the real stuff will come later. When ref Dougie Smith knocks the door for us to go out for real, the butterflies start. As I walk up the stairs to the tunnel, I'm really nervous. It's the first time I've felt this way in years and brings home how much the game means to me. I can't wait for my first touch. That's what sets the tone for your game and I need a good one. When it comes, to a few boos but nothing life-threatening, I hit a decent pass forward. We're off. Then, two minutes in, I slide-tackle Peter Lindau. Unfortunately, my knee sinks into the pitch, stretching my groin muscle further than it wanted to go. The pain is excruciating and I immediately fear it's game over. I get up and try to run it off but after a couple of minutes I tell Dougie that next time the ball goes out I'll need the physio.

Our physio Kenny Chichton wants me to come off. Not me, not today. I beg five more minutes, he says OK, and it eases. I know it's doing me no favours but I have to play on.

As the game develops I'm pleasantly surprised with our style and quality. One of our strikers, Peter Weatherson, catches the eye – though predictably it's Trigger who strikes first. We dig in and Warren Hawke equalises shortly afterwards, but in injury time – guess who that was added on for? – David McCallum scores to separate the teams.

It's been a painful 43 or so minutes but luckily Moorie is having a shocker and deflecting the abuse away from me. He's run balls out of play, tripped over himself, been cemented by yours truly and been the victim of the worst bobble I have ever witnessed in football. This is what friends are for.

Kenny works on me during half-time – though it's getting worse by the minute – and I soldier on until the end. We've lost but I'm hugely encouraged by what I've seen. Thistle will win the league but we've a chance to finish second. It's a good sign that the boys are so down.

JC's doing his after-match analysis when I notice a sign stuck to the mirror behind him. It reads, 'Nae luck, Des, nae win bonus tonight!'

This can only be the work of Ricky and Chico. I find the fat bastards and give them pelters but we end up having a laugh. I should have expected it.

In the Aitken Suite, the bargirls have signed a Thistle shirt for me, the boys still want me on their Xmas night out and Walter the Vet has agreed to work on my injury in midweek.

Groin but not forgotten.

Sunday November 26

2.20 a.m.: Ouch!
2.45 a.m.: Aaaaarrrgggghhhhh!!
3.10 a.m.: Oooooyyyyaaaahhhhhh!!!.
3.15 a.m.–10.00 p.m.: More of the same.

Sleep? Forget it. I've spent the full night twisting and turning like Frank McGarvey. As JL will confirm, there's not a position I'm comfy in. The pain was so bad I thought about going to casualty in the early hours and can't see myself playing for weeks. What a start.

Come morning, I call Walter the Vet and his straightforward advice has me lying on a chair in front of the TV all day. Carolyn and the girls are my legs today, carrying a bag of frozen peas from the freezer to my right thigh and back again for refrosting.

Looks like my home debut will have to be put on hold.

Wednesday, 29 November 2000

Now, if I was a full-timer, I'd have spent the last two days on a treatment table or in a swimming pool or a jacuzzi, generally being nursed back to fitness. As a part-timer, though, I've spent the last two days in Dundee and Aberdeen. All that driving's just the job for a damaged groin. However, the pain does appear to be subsiding. On Sunday it felt like bungee jumping with no rope. Now it's only like bungee jumping with the rope tied to your genitals.

Back in Glasgow, the Vet spends about 20 minutes on my bits. It's good to be in among the boys. They too were impressed by Queens and concede that a draw might have been fair. Or maybe they were just humouring a sick man.

Walter knows when he's hit the spot because I nearly go through the roof. This is the bit physios love, the bit where they cause untold pain. The more you writhe in agony, the harder they prod. It's their way of compensating for the fact that you play the game and they don't.

I'm packed off with a course of anti-inflammatories and an open invitation for more torture.

Thursday, 30 November 2000

Down to Dumfries for more treatment from Kenny but there's a queue. I get there at half-five but don't hit the table until 9.15 p.m. In between times I do 45 minutes' skipping and pop to the gym at the nearby Cairndale Hotel with fellow new boy PK.

Who's PK? Where have you been these last 15 years, living in a cave?

PK is Paul Kinnaird, a legend, notorious, a man who seems to be everywhere at once. He's 33 and it's remarkable to think this is the first time I've played with him, considering he's been with 21 – count them – 21 clubs in 18 seasons.

His patter is magic and time flies by.

When Kenny eventually gets round to me, he wastes no time in finding the sorest spot possible and jamming his fingers in up to the elbow. He diagnoses that I have fibre damages and says the best case scenario is two weeks. The worst is four. Physios always err on the side of caution. Players always look on the bright side. This is why I think I'll be back in a week.

SEVEN

Friday, 1 December 2000

LIVED TODAY like there was no tomorrow. Which there won't be. Like every Friday recently, I know I don't have a game to look forward to. Sure, I'm wanted again now that I've left Thistle but no way will I be fit to play for Queens at home to Arbroath. Hopefully this will be the last wasted weekend for a long time.

Still, the good news is we've hit our sales target again at work. Reg dismisses class at 3.30 p.m.

Saturday, 2 December 2000

Last night the rain never stopped and part of me didn't want it to. If I'm being selfish, I'd rather the game was off so I could play when it's re-arranged. But it's not to be. A pudding of a pitch passes a morning inspection.

KC has me in before kick-off for a blast of ultrasound on the groin. This time when his fingers go in they don't feel quite as much like knitting needles. I must be getting better.

Today, though, the real pain is in my heart. My mum phoned while I was on the M74 to say she'd called the doctor in to see my dad. He's been suffering from various chest infections for five or six weeks and things are getting serious. I asked Saint Isabel if she wanted me to turn the car round but she said no. The rest of the family was there and she'd phone me later.

Billy McKeown and I share a strange relationship. From an early age I realised he was very proud of me and that's been true of everything I've achieved in business and football. It's just that he's always had a strange way of showing it. He'd tell everyone except me how well I was doing, bowl on for hours about how I'd signed for Celtic or passed my degree. To my face, he's been my biggest critic. He's never told me what my achievements, as little as they are, mean to him. In fact, not only has he never conveyed his pride to me, he's always torn strips off me personally and professionally at every available opportunity.

When I signed for Celtic, I was 18 and studying at Jordanhill College. The daily physical sessions that were part of the course meant I was very fit, but they also meant that some Saturdays I wasn't running on a full tank. This was never truer than the day before manager Billy McNeill decided to play me out of position at centre-half in a reserve league game against Rangers at Parkhead. That Friday I went orienteering through Mugdock Country Park to the north of Glasgow and next morning I was meant to leave for a four-day skiing course at Aviemore.

Then I found out I'd been picked for the biggest game of my life.

The orienteering took it out of me. So too did the anticipation of playing in an Old Firm clash, even if it was between the second teams. I barely slept that night.

Next morning I piled my ski gear in the back of the car along with my football kit. Dad was to drop me at the bus station back in the city centre after he and my sisters, Veronica and Anne Marie, had watched me play. I looked for them up in the main stand during the warm-up. Usually at reserve games it was easy to pick people out but that day there were 15,000 in, a miniature replica of a real Old Firm crowd. The noise, all the party songs, the whole thing made my guts churn and my head burst. As I ran out of the tunnel for real, I knew Dad and the girls would be swollen with pride.

The game flew by. We went behind early but fought back to be 3–1 up early in the second half. Then Rangers came again and at 3–3 my legs started to cramp up with the effort of keeping them at bay. Add that to the exertions of the day before and the sheer nervous exhaustion of the occasion and I was entitled to be knackered.

Billy McNeill knew I'd given my lot, his assistant Tommy Craig knew it, the coach Bobby Lennox knew it, I knew it, everybody knew it. Everyone, it turns out, except my dad.

When the boards clattered and 5 went up, I came off to a standing ovation and the outstretched hand of the first Briton to lift the European Cup. He gave me a beaming smile and a big 'Well done', a sentiment echoed by Tommy and Bobby.

I was just sinking into a hot bath when I heard a muffled roar that could only have come from the away end. A young striker called Gary McSwegan had completed his hat-trick and finished us off. Still, as I left the ground I was happy with my performance, if not the result. I'd been blameless in their goals, had passed and headed the ball well and I even signed a couple of autographs for kids on my way to the car.

My dad's first words when I sat down will never leave me.

'You,' he said, 'are an embarrassment.'

It was a very quiet drive to the bus station. By the time I got to Aviemore on my own three hours later I wasn't in the mood to go out with the others and was consoled by a fellow student, Scott Morgan, who has since become one of my best friends.

I mention this episode because it says a lot about my relationship with Dad. Now, older and wiser, I understand his thinking a lot better. He's never meant me any harm. He just hasn't wanted to show how proud he was of me.

The same has gone for Veronica and my brothers Vincent and Gerry. Only Anne Marie, the baby of the family who studied to be a doctor, ever got any outward praise. He was obviously banking on her looking after him in his old age!

Over the past five or six years we've all watched Dad change from an active sixty-something who played golf every morning, to a sick man confined to bed with Progressive Supranuclear Palsy and whose only true comforts are watching Sky Sports and being with his family. I'm sure everything will be OK at the hospital but sometimes I think that he'd actually prefer to be taken, as he has no real quality of life. Isabel will let me know how things are ASAP.

Treatment over, I listen to JC's team talk. Again, there's a lot of sense. He names a side with changes all the way down the left thanks to PK also being injured. Our little section of stand will not be dull this afternoon.

Unfortunately, there's a lack of atmosphere about Palmerston compared to Firhill and only a couple of fans seem to be making any sort of noise. One guy just in front of us gives the boys some stick until PK says: 'Hey, you, ya arsehole – shut the fuck up and support the team.'

And he did.

The heavy pitch doesn't help a poor game, though it's right up Arbroath stopper Jimmy Thomson's street. The Silhouette, as he's known, is proud to tell you he's cleared the ball out of every ground he ever played on. When we played at Queens we used to take bets on whether he'd manage it. Example? On our first trip to Caledonian Stadium in Inverness, a ground with one extremely tall stand, we challenged him to do his party piece. Midway through the second half he swung his pipecleaner right leg and biffed one right over the roof and onto an oilrig. Few fans that day could understand why this big berk was standing in the centre circle with one arm raised like Denis Law, celebrating as if he'd scored the winner.

Despite Arbroath going down to ten men today's game finishes 1–1, no bad thing as I'm going to a party at Ginger Geordie Rowe's house and we wouldn't want the police involved.

It turns into a brilliant night, particularly after the news that dad has settled down nicely in Stobhill Hospital.

Sunday, 3 December 2000

After a visit to Walter the Vet at Firhill, I pick up Mum to go to the hospital. Billy's had a fairly satisfactory night, though he complains that another patient is out to get him. He mumbles the word 'drugs' and seems visibly worried. We assure him there's nothing wrong and assume he's imagined it all.

Later, JC phones to asks my opinion on out-of-favour Thistle trio Dunnsy, Del and Mowgli, though the man he really wants is Gerry Britton of Livingston. I phone Gerry, an old pal, and report back that, although he'd be interested, he wouldn't be available on a free. JC's now thinking about a loan deal but even that would depend on how much of Gerry's wages QoS would be asked to contribute.

Monday, 4 December 2000

Billy's doing fine.

Tuesday, 5 December 2000

Still not fit to train with the squad but get to Dumfries early and finish some paperwork in the bar of the Cairndale Hotel. Then I do an hour's body circuit on my own before getting some good news from KC – he reckons I might have a chance of facing Clydebank in the first round of the Scottish Cup on Saturday. JC, though, says not to push it. The league's his priority and he would rather I was fully fit.

Ronnie McQuilter's next on the treatment table with a sore back. Ronnie, like PK, is a lower-league legend. He's a funny guy with a bright yellow Golf, bright yellow hair and a bright yellow tan. Tonight, though, his car's off the road and I offer him a lift to save him hanging around for one.

To say the next hour or so listening to the thoughts of the Ronster is interesting is like saying PK's had the odd free.

'So,' I've asked him, 'how you enjoying it down here?'

And that's basically my part in the conversation over.

'No' bad. It was hard when St Mirren let me go after I'd come back from doing my cruciate. I was gutted, it felt like they shat on me a bit.'

I could see that. He'd been out for the whole year when they won the First Division and felt he was due another chance to prove himself. It never came.

'Anyway, after that I just wanted a game, so when King of the North came in I was up for the cup. I've lost respect for Tom Hendrie at Love Street now – it wasn't just me that got shafted, ma mucker Norrie McWhirter got done as well. He'd been there years and had injury problems and they let him go as well. That was a choker.'

It was odd listening to the serious side of a guy I'd only ever known before as a party animal, a big Casanova in the brightest kit Versace made. He always loved putting himself up as the guy with the hair – 'strawberry blond, by the way, no' ginger' – the teeth and the jawline. He's like Jim Carrey as *The Mask*, but without the mask. He's got the ability to be whoever he wants to be when he's out on the town. Yet here he was, pouring his heart out about how football had done him wrong. Then he started talking birds and normal service was resumed.

If Macca's had hunners, the Ronster makes him look like a virgin.

'Ah musta had fifteen hunner – so far,' he laughed, and for a second I almost took him seriously. 'Ah've been there, done that, given them the smile and we're off. Respect.'

Respect. That's his buzzword.

'And think about it,' he said while I slapped the steering wheel. 'Just imagine the damage Ah'd have done if Ah could play!'

And on he went. Brilliant stories, frightening patter. I nearly had the car through the central reservation about eight times. It doesn't matter if he really has done fifteen hunner sorts or spends every night in pipe and slippers reading the *Financial Times*. He's a legend.

Eighty-odd miles home flew by like a trip to the corner shop.

Wednesday, 6 December 2000

Saint Isabel phoned at 10.15 this morning to say Billy has not had a good night in hospital and that, ominously, the doctors want to see the family. I join the dots to reveal a serious situation.

I arrive to find Anne Marie watching over my dad, who is now wearing an oxygen mask. As the rest arrive he wants Gerry, a policeman, more than anyone else. Again, he seems very scared and talks of drugs and the man who wants to 'get' him. As he demands PC Gerry arrests the man, we fear he is hallucinating.

The doctor arrives, takes us to a side room and explains that we have a decision to make. Dad's condition has deteriorated dramatically and his voice box and throat are paralysed. They could operate to bypass his windpipe with a tube but that would also mean inserting a feeding line into his stomach. Even then, he might not be strong enough to come off the ventilator after surgery. On the other hand, we could let nature take its course, meaning he would pass away in his sleep within 24 to 48 hours.

It's Mum's shout but we all wanted the same thing. A peaceful end.

Billy would have thanked us for it.

There were a few tears as we went back to see him before putting together a plan to look after him in his final hours. I would go back into Glasgow to finish off today's calls, pay a flying visit to The Vet then spend the night with Anne Marie and Mum. Vince, Gerry and Veronica would relieve us in the morning.

I phoned Reg with the news, arranged for Dunky to cover for me, then told JC I wouldn't be at training tomorrow or available for Saturday. I found myself praying for more rain so the game would be off.

Back at Stobhill that night, Dad had been moved to a private room. With morphine settling his apparent paranoia, he was almost comatose. As night fell, his breathing became shallower and quicker. By midnight he was surrounded by Mum, me, Anne Marie and his younger brothers Thomas and James. Everyone took turns telling stories, mainly about his days as a player in the seniors with Dumbarton and the juniors with the likes of Bo'ness, Renfrew and Carluke. He always used to tell me that in those days junior football was the equivalent of today's First or Second Divisions, with crowds of six and seven thousand the norm. We used to argue about what level he'd play at today. Everybody tells me how good a player he was. Every time Carolyn's late father, Dan, cut my hair he'd tell me Billy McKeown was a 'beaker' of a player – I didn't know what a beaker was but he always said it like a compliment. I expect his death to inspire many more tributes, not only to Billy the man, but also to Billy the footballer.

The last time he woke was between 4 a.m. and 4.15 a.m. He had become slightly agitated and we asked for more morphine. It was then that all hell broke loose.

A man in his thirties was in the bed across from my dad's room and each time I'd gone in and out he'd acknowledged me. Eventually I said hello. He said he was sorry about my dad's condition and I thanked him. Then, at 4 a.m., he tried to burst into Dad's room, screaming that everybody was being conned and how the nurses were speaking in 'Zagreb' so nobody understood them. He was lucky I stopped him before Uncle James did or he'd have been enjoying hospital food a lot longer. Instead, I ushered him back to his bed and calmed him down. However, when the nurses and doctor tried to give him his medication, it became clear he was a drug addict with withdrawal symptoms and he hurled his water and tablets at my dad's window. Again I got to him before James but this time using a bit more force. Billy spent the next 15 minutes awake, roused by the man we had thought was a figment of his imagination. But in a daft way, I was grateful to the guy – because his outburst let me do something I'd wanted to do for a long time.

I told my dad I loved him.

It was a moment that brought me great peace but it was soon shattered. Uncle Tommy and Uncle James came back from having a smoke to find our friend across the corridor hurling missiles at three nurses and a young lady doctor. As I got there, the guy was looming over four cowering females with a heavy, high-backed chair held above his head. I pounced and got him in a half-Nelson until James got there. Between us, in the middle of a ward full of anxious patients wakened by the commotion, we held him for five minutes until the response team arrived. At the time, it was frightening. Now, it seems almost comical.

'Move one inch, pal,' snarled Uncle James, 'an' Ah'll break yer arm!'

'Don't you bother,' I whimpered. 'His arm's twisted round my arm. Break his and mine goes as well.'

'OK,' said James, 'd'ye want him on his back?'

'No way!' I've yelled. 'I'm right behind him!'

After what seemed like hours, maybe ten orderlies rushed in and pumped the guy full of whatever you need to pump guys like him full of to get them off the rampage. All we wanted was to get him off the ward. It seems scandalous that it took visitors who happened to be staying overnight with a dying relative to save defenceless staff. Still, those final 15 minutes when Billy McKeown was conscious were magical. He laughed, he cried and he knew we loved him. Whoever that guy across the corridor was, whatever he's doing now, we owe him.

Thursday, 7 December 2000

My dad passed away at three minutes to two this afternoon, cause of death Aspiration Pneumonia. I arrived 15 minutes later and cried.

Friday, 8 December 2000

Spent today organising the funeral, fitted in a three-mile run in torrential rain, then settled down for curry and *Friends* with Carolyn and the girls.

Billy wouldn't have wanted it any other way.

The good news is the rain dance had worked and tomorrow's game is off.

Saturday, 9 December 2000

Good old David Murray. Just when I need something to take my mind off my dad, he comes up with the goods big time.

You can always tell when Rangers have gone out of Europe again because their chairman starts blaming everything on the media. And so it goes in the wake of their AGM, where Murray has deflected all the blame away from himself, his manager and his collection of under-achieving millionaire players and firmly onto those who report on their failings.

Murray's an expert at pre-emptive strikes on the press just before they get to lock their sights on him. When things are going pear-shaped, he rallies the fans and convinces them there's a newspaper, TV and radio conspiracy against their club. And you know what? They always swallow it hook, line and sinker. And so when the shareholders gathered in the wake of Thursday's second European exit of the season, rather than question what direction Murray and Dick Advocaat are taking Rangers in, the hall rang to defiant applause about the media's role in their problems.

Rather than ask Murray why he has sanctioned so much transfer activity to put the club no further forward in Europe again, they pick on reporters perceived as enemies.

Rather than ask when Rangers will take that great leap forward, they curse their detractors.

Rather than ask why season-ticket prices are rising despite a poorer product, they question why the press are allowed into Ibrox at all.

Yet these shareholders are the same people who generated stories of unrest by venting their fury weekly at the performances of the team and certain individuals. This season it has been Amoruso, Konterman, Ricksen and Ronald de Boer who have been subjected to abuse. The manager has also started to take it in the neck. That's when Murray always knows it's time to get his retaliation in first. He knows he's next in line for a doing, so he gathers his loyal sheep around him and repels all boarders.

You have to admire his cheek in using what should have been a difficult situation to throw up a smokescreen around his own deficiencies. He told the AGM the press were singling out people for too much personal abuse and that this was out of order. He may well be right – but where was he when other individuals at other clubs were taking the same personal stick in the media? When Kenny Dalglish or John Barnes or Ebbe Skovdahl were being singled out for humiliation? When Chris Robinson or Eyal Berkovic were being thrown to the wolves daily? Mr Morals was nowhere to be seen or heard then because he was quite happy for anyone outwith his own club to be taking the flak. In fact, never mind outside his own club – outside his own *office*.

Monday, 11 December 2000

Dad was buried today in Lennoxtown Cemetery after a sell-out mass at St Paul's Church in Milton of Campsie. The whole family contributed to the service in one way or another and the numbers there to pay their respects was overwhelming. Tid, Moorie and Ginger Geordie all came, which meant a lot to me.

We held it together pretty well throughout, though favourite hymns brought a few tears. Mum did brilliantly. Her grieving will come later, I'm sure.

Father James Boyle, visibly upset at the loss of a friend, summed up Billy with great accuracy.

We're lucky to have a good family at a time like this because, although we all know Dad's death is a blessing, it's easier saying it than accepting it.

Now I need to get back to football. I need the boys, I need the catharsis of the wind-ups. The dressing-room will help me cope with the loss. What also helps is a bouquet of red, yellow and black carnations by the grave with a note reading: 'From the players and staff at Partick Thistle FC. Thinking of you at this sad time.'

This truly is a beautiful game.

Tuesday, 12 December 2000

The rain dance is still working, so it's back to training rather than sitting out a Cup-tie. Palmerston's waterlogged, as is the training ground, and as a result the quality of the session's not great. Or at least that's my excuse.

Still, I have no reaction to the injury and the patter's great. PK's going on about the fact that he's been promoted five seasons on the trot and won four titles with four different clubs. It's a remarkable achievement when you think how many pros end up with no medals to show for their careers. PK has more medals than a pilgrimage to Lourdes.

Big Ronnie, on the other hand, reminds us that he's collected more female friends than Hugh Hefner. As ever, his conversation revolves around these off-field victories. Between him and Medallion Man there's a wisecrack every two seconds.

After the week I've had, guys like Ronnie, PK and Moorie are invaluable.

It's no insult to Moorie when I suggest that his managers – and he's had plenty – would admit to remembering him more for his infectious personality than his abilities. But if success in football was down to one-liners, Moorie could have played for Brazil. Imagine Pele standing in front of a taxi with the doors open and you get the picture.

Football's full of guys who crack you up, masters of the one-liner, the put-down. Sure, it's often cruel, but the dressing-room's no place for shyness. You give it and you take it. One night years ago I was coming off training with Queens when wee Johnny McLaren, brother of Killie's Andy, shouts to me: 'Hey, Dessie, you did the work of two men tonight.'

'Cheers,' I said.

'Aye – Laurel and Hardy!'

There's no answer to that.

At Albion Rovers I played with a boy called Martin McBride whose brother Michael was our physio. One day at the 'San Siro', Martin's having a shocker when one of our other boys goes down injured. Michael leaps out of the dugout with his sponge in time to hear a punter in the rickety old kennel of a stand yell: 'Haw, while ye're there gie yer brother the kissa life!' And the great thing about grounds like that is that *everyone* heard him.

Stuart Miller was a boy who played for Dumbarton and Clyde and had buck teeth. Silky Hetherston used to say when he was a wean there were shutters on his pram. Anyway, he ended up as manager of Kilsyth Rangers and they're struggling for players. So one of his guys, who's having a nightmare, goes down with a head knock. The physio goes on and comes back with the news that it looks like the boy's lost his teeth. 'Never mind that,' says Stuart, 'tell him if he doesnae get his fucking finger out he'll be losing his jersey.'

Speaking of teeth, Silky also tells about when he was at Falkirk and they signed Yogi Hughes from Swansea. The big fella would later become a cult figure as a centre-half with Celtic and Hibs but back then he was a struggling centre-forward. Manager Jim Jefferies, though, had worked with him at Berwick and swore by him, so much that he spent £70,000 to bring him home. The dressing-room was not convinced. After training one day following a poor result on the Saturday when Yogi's had a stinker – funny how these tales all surround guys playing badly – Jeff's number two Billy Brown comes and batters on about how they could all take a lesson from the new boy's character.

'We need more guys like the big man,' says Billy. 'He's through in the bootroom taking his studs out with his teeth.'

'Very good,' says Silky, 'Seventy grand for a pair of pliers.'

Thursday, 14 December 2000

Life must be getting back to normal. I did more than 200 miles today and hit the sack at midnight.

Friday, 15 December 2000

For most at Oyez, the office Xmas party is the social event of the year.

For most. But not for me. Not when it's on a Friday and these nights mean something again.

Even though I'm teetotal, I've never liked being out the night before games. I've even called off from Thistle's pyjama party on Sunday because the Clydebank tie's back on for Monday. Carolyn and I show face but by the time we leave the cabaret is just starting. I'm not really in the mood anyway after the funeral.

Saturday, 16 December 2000

All last night's sacrifices are for nothing. JC phones to say Stenny's pitch is frozen, so yet another game is off. We can't even train because the weather in Dumfries is the same, so I do a road run and a body circuit before taking Mum and the girls to put fresh flowers on the grave.

After that I catch a bit of the Campsie Black Watch–Possil YM game, then go home to bed and get angry at Radio Clyde.

Their lower-division coverage is shocking. It's all SPL, SPL, SPL, with lip-service paid to the First Division and only brief mentions of the Second and Third at half-time and full-time. And if that's not bad enough, I then have to suffer the drivel of sportswriter Jim Traynor on the phone-in *Open Line*, talking about Scottish football having too many clubs and how we have to shut down those who aren't self-sufficient. He claims some clubs are draining the game of cash and that they 'need to find their level'. He actually mentions Forfar by name. My blood pressure rises by the second until I'm tempted to phone and slaughter him and the rest of a panel of know-alls who know nothing.

These panels are basically made up of ex-players and journalistic big-hitters who between them know enough about the lower leagues to cover half of a postage stamp. They fawn over the Old Firm and blame everybody for the state of our game, yet they could be doing so much for the lower divisions through media exposure. They should be generating interest in the game, not knocking it – especially when, contrary to what Traynor spouts, many smaller clubs *are* self-sufficient and suffering more from negative media tripe than from financial worries. It's interesting to note, too, that Dundee's two-goal hero in today's game with Kilmarnock is Steven Milne – a young striker who developed his skills last season on loan to . . . Forfar. Rangers' scoring sensation Kenny Miller also benefited from a spell at Stenhousemuir while he was learning his trade with Hibs. What would these kids have done without smaller clubs to give them a chance? Would Miller be a £2 million player today?

And, while I'm on a rant, exactly what money are the Forfars of this world draining from the game? They get washers through being on the pools coupon, from their share of SFA profits and from sponsorship deals. Occasionally one of them will rake in a couple of hundred grand from a Cup-tie at Ibrox or Parkhead, but big deal. The rest of the year the Old Firm are allowed to keep every penny of their gate money, so isn't it only right that once in a blue moon they give something back?

Jim Traynor claims to be a fan of Airdrie, a club which at the time of writing are most definitely *not* self-sufficient. Does he want them closed down too? Or will he make an exception for his pals?

Meanwhile, after the last of our so-called élite clubs crashed out of Europe this week, the Radio Clyde panel suggest this lack of success should be remedied by a massive investment in youth development – yet they want to close the clubs which breed future stars. Brilliant.

Rangers lost in Kaiserslautern on Thursday to go out of the UEFA Cup a few weeks after failing – yet again – in the Champions League. The panel suggests this is because Dick Advocaat can only attract second-rate players because of the standard of our game. Nonsense. It's down to poor investment on the coaching and playing side. Any manager who spends £74 million, as Advocaat has, should not be spending it on second-rate talent. In fact, no manager should spend £1 on second-rate players. Plus, if our game can only attract second-rate players, surely it can only attract second-rate coaches? Rangers must see Advocaat as one of Europe's best or else why did they pick him to do what Walter Smith could not? The fact is, though, he hasn't done any better in Europe than the man he replaced – a man who was big enough to walk away when he saw he was not producing what the club wanted. If Walter Smith failed, Dick Advocaat has failed. Will it take another £74 million before chairman David Murray realises this?

Deep breaths, Desmond, deep breaths.

Sunday, 17 December 2000

I can't resist it. I have to pop into Firhill for a while to see the boys on their night out.

As I park, I can already hear Mowgli doing Elvis on the karaoke. Inside, every player is in pyjamas, slippers and dressing gowns. Some have even taken up Moorie's suggestion of getting numbers on the jammy jackets.

Seeing them so happy and together almost makes me regret leaving – yet what's the use of being part of a great team spirit if you're not part of the team?

Monday, 18 December 2000

Woke up and remembered I'd booked today off work because I'd planned to be out last night, so it's a long lie until ten then a trip to see Danielle's school nativity play. She's one of the narrators and performs brilliantly. I'm really proud of her but where does she get her confidence from?

Home, change into my new club blazer and off.

By the time the team is named, Palmerston's starting to frost over, though the ground's soft underneath the crust.

Clydebank, another struggling club Jim Traynor would like to see shut down, have turned up with eleven fit outfield players and have only rustled up two subs – a keeper and last year's manager, Steve Morrison, who's officially retired. All this must make us favourites, but JC demands the utmost respect for them. I'm in at No. 3 for my first game in three weeks and my first at home for Queens in more than two years.

During a slithering warm-up, PK asks me what I think of his shorts. I glance down and realise he's not wearing official club issue. He says they make his bum look enormous. I take his point, as in his personal Reeboks it only looks huge. However, he still creates both goals to see us through to a second-round tie away to Elgin City. The ever-impressive Peter Weatherson scores each time and celebrates to his own tannoy signature tune. Just as Henrik Larsson wheels away to 'The Magnificent Seven', Peter gets 'Nellie the Elephant'. The boy's so ugly that he's talking about getting 'Merrick' embossed on his boots where Beckham has 'Brooklyn'.

Thursday, 21 December 2000

Maybe it's the hairline, but most people think I'm nearer 35 than 30. Tonight, though, I genuinely feel like a veteran for the first time in my career.

About an hour into training, assistant manager Ian Scott tells me I've done enough for the night and should head back to Palmerston with the others thirty-somethings for a massage from KC. I don't know whether to be angry or thankful. On one hand, I pride myself on my fitness and don't feel in need of a break. On the other, maybe it means they know they don't need to run me any more. Whatever the reason, though, it seems time is catching up.

Friday, 22 December 2000

Lunch with Elvis, Car Wash, Dunky and Ginger Geordie to mark the last working day before Xmas, after which I meet my old pal Claire Ronald for coffee before going to see my mum.

As I sit down with Claire, an elderly gentleman comes over to talk to me. Turns out he's a Firhill season ticket-holder heartbroken that I've been transferred. His words confirm to me that fans do appreciate players whose effort is constant even if their brilliance is rare.

Saturday, 23 December 2000

Queen's Park at Palmerston today in a game brought forward from Boxing Day to give us all a better break. A win today takes us over Car Wash's side, who have the best defence in the league but are finding it hard to score goals.

Before the game I give Doreen and Vi their Xmas box of chocolates – one simple way to make sure they keep the tea coming and put the best cakes and sandwiches aside for me.

Seven minutes into a game played on an awful surface – so bad it made me slice my first clearance into the stand, would you believe – 'Nellie the Elephant' plays again as Pretty Boy Peter scores, but within a minute Kevin Finlayson's unstoppable shot pegs us back. Twenty minutes from time, I swerve a shot against the bar – yes, *their* bar – but Car Wash runs the midfield and the day ends in more disappointment for us when Pretty Boy is red-carded for dissent and goes off with his trunk firmly between his legs. By the time we join him in the dressing-room, he's distraught. I hope his tears teach him a lesson and help him develop into the top-class striker we all feel he can be.

Sunday, 24 December 2000

While floods of motorists are driving back grumpily from last-minute shopping trips, I'm out running by the side of the road. I can almost hear them scream 'get a life' as they slog past me through the traffic. If only they knew that's exactly what I'm doing.

Monday, 25 December 2000

For once, there are some things more important than football and fitness.

Dani and Taylor have a whale of a time opening present after present before heading to Mum's for even more. Two binbags later we head home for dinner with Carolyn's entire family. It's fabulous.

Tuesday, 26 December 2000

Who's that clown out running in a blizzard at nine in the morning? Get a life!

Back home, I defrost myself with a body circuit, before luxuriating in a shower and then picking Mum up to take her to the football. Thistle vice-chairman Tom Hughes, who's also my accountant, has invited us as his guests for lunch before the game with Stenny.

My letter of thanks to the club for their kind wishes following Dad's death has been reproduced in the match programme and fans pass on their own condolences. I'm happier than ever now to have left the club on such good terms.

Mind you, they're also pretty chuffed with how it went – the guy they signed on the back of me going, Geordie Shaw, is the best man on the park as they win 3–0.

In the Aitken Suite, I meet young Angela, the girl I visited recently in hospital. We've kept in touch since and she phones about once a week. Mum's soon locked in conversation with her, telling her all my secrets. Highlight of the day, though, comes after I sign a couple of autographs for Thistle fans who then ask my mum for hers too. Underneath her name, they scribble 'Des McKeown's mum'.

That night, JC calls to ask if I know the boy Connell and is amazed when I tell him that he works for me. He asks if I'll call him to ask about a move. Car Wash not only confirms he fancies it but that, because he's an amateur at Queen's Park, he's free to move any time. JC can't believe his luck when I tell him.

Finally, tomorrow's Morton–Ross County game has been cancelled after the Greenock club went into administration. It's yet another case of a club spending more than it earns, then the chairman fleeing the coup when it all comes on top. How many more clubs need to suffer like this before football wises up?

Wednesday, 27 December 2000

Dumfries is snowbound. I'll be astonished if Saturday's game with Clydebank goes ahead.

Friday, 29 December 2000

The game's off already, so instead of treading Cappielow's slush we'll be bronzing ourselves on the beach at Southerness, down the coast from Dumfries. Car Wash will be there too. He's had permission from his boss Cowboy McCormack to talk to JC and I'm hoping the deal goes through – it would be nice to have him as chauffeur on Saturdays as well as a tea-boy through the week! But will the club run to white gloves and a peaked cap as well as a blazer?

Saturday, 30 December 2000

Ever tried to jog along a beach with ice and snow piled up along the shoreline?

Ever tried to jog along a beach with the sea turning into ice in front of your eyes?

Ever tried to jog along a beach?

Today we did all of the above – yet we managed a great session which was only ended by the tide creeping up on us.

The only reason I mention this is that when Dani and Taylor hear I've been at the beach tonight they'll think I've been paddling and making sandcastles. Not even the penguins were brave enough to paddle out there today.

Car Wash joins in and looks pretty close to signing. Turns out he'll be paid more than me but that doesn't bother me. Why should it? I'm amazed by how many players sign a contract only to declare a year or so later that they're unhappy with it. I doubt if there's a dressing-room in the country where someone isn't upset at what someone else earns. Contracts these days seem to have clauses covering just about every eventuality – goal bonuses, appearance money, signing-on fees, win bonuses, loyalty bonuses, sell-on percentages and more – so it's incredible to think any player who signs up willingly should need to get uppity at what the next guy's being paid. If I'm making what I think is fair, why should I care what anyone else gets?

But tell that to Pierre van Hooijdonk.

Sunday, 31 December 2000

Hogmanay, more snow and as much chance of us playing on Tuesday as of JL trying to re-sign me for the title run-in. With this in mind, I'm tempted to have a later night than planned tomorrow when Carolyn's family is visiting. If the game was on, I'd want everyone out by about ten. With the game likely to be off, I'll play it by ear.

Carolyn and I see in the bells before she and Dani go to a neighbour's party and I stay and watch *The Guns of Navarone* with a snoozing Taylor. Just call me the Wild Man of Scottish Football.

EIGHT

Monday, 1 January 2001

MY LIFE HAS CHANGED so much in the last year and so much is going on right now that it's sometimes hard to keep track. You feel like you want to press Pause and step away from it all, get a handle on everything. But life's not like that. Particularly not home life. As a new year dawns and resolutions are made, mine must be to try and make more time for Carolyn and the girls. I simply don't see enough of them. I'll try my best to change that.

Still, if things are sometimes frosty around the house, at least a thaw's set in down at Dumfries. Sadly, the extra water will surely make the surface just as unplayable as before. I guess tomorrow will end up as a training day rather than the derby against Stranraer.

Tuesday, 2 January 2001

Shockaroony! The game's on! Maybe I *should* sit by the phone to wait JL's call. Or maybe not, eh?

Car Wash won't be registered in time to play, which means he's been able to enjoy a normal Ne'erday – well, as normal as his life ever gets – and as we arrive at Palmerston it appears a few others have gambled on a postponement and done the same. The guilty men put their hands up to JC and he takes it well. I don't think he can believe the game's on either. In fact, I start to think he's been on the beer as well when he hands me the No. 8 shirt and tells me I'll be playing centre-midfield. It doesn't last, though. Young Danny Patterson has a nightmare at left-back and I end up in familiar territory – but whatever angle you looked at the result from, a 3–2 defeat was bad.

We only had ourselves to blame. We'd taken the lead. PK smashed one off a post from 25 yards and everything was looking tasty – until Davie 'The Virgin' Mathieson let one slip past him and the tide turned.

Then Danny got caught in possession and we were 2–1 down. I had a couple of fair cracks at an equaliser but then Steven Skinner lost the ball when we were going forward and Stranraer broke to make it three.

In a game that somehow seemed to last an eternity, we got one back when their keeper walked for a foul in the box, but it wasn't to be. We got what we deserved – nothing.

Wednesday, 3 January 2001

Talk at today's sales meeting was all about Car Wash's move to the only team called Queens he ever wanted to play for.

And then I went back to Firhill.

Nah, relax – it was only to see Walter the Vet. My hammies are as tight as two coats of paint and with the Cup-tie at Elgin on Saturday I need them loosened quick. There's no training tomorrow night, so I'll come back for some more ultrasound and heat treatment.

Friday, 5 January 2001

Last night's session with The Vet was a waste of time. The Elgin game's off already. We'd planned to stay up there overnight, so it's as well the call came before the squad set off – especially with some of the boys starting their journey in Newcastle. The game's now on next Saturday, so that day's league game with Berwick will move to midweek.

This is when the real complexities of part-time football kick in. Your full-timer doesn't really care where he's going. He just turns up and gets taken. Us guys have to rearrange day job schedules to let us get away on time for buses. None of us can ever afford to underestimate the goodwill around us that makes it all work.

Saturday, 6 January 2001

Before training, JC pulls me in to talk about signing targets. He wants me to find out why a certain player isn't getting a game and if he'd fancy it here. He also wants to know if one of Thistle's boys would be better than someone here at the moment. I say no, I don't think so. Then he digs me up on a couple of occasions against Stranraer when I could have done better. He thinks I've been pulled out of position too often and not recovered quickly enough when the ball's been past me. I take it on board and I'll try to sort it out next time.

Back up the road, I catch most of Thistle's 3–0 Cup win over Deveronvale. Martin Hardie gets another two – that's 11 for the season, superb for a midfielder.

Moorie, meanwhile, is well and truly bombed and I doubt if he'll start another game for JL. He feels the same way and I tell him now's the time to think about going part-time and looking for a real job. He says he's already thinking about it – he could end up better off financially that way as well as guaranteeing himself a game.

On a day when Radio Clyde again show their loyalty to the lower divisions by not having a football show – well, there's no SPL, why should they bother? – the big story is St Johnstone's sacking of strikers George O'Boyle and Kevin Thomas for allegedly taking cocaine at a Christmas night out.

Whether people choose to admit it or not, drugs *are* a problem in Scottish football. I personally know players and managers who use them and they're far from the first. However, it's no more of a problem than in the music industry, the legal profession, the media, politics and even the police force. The more people who take drugs, the more chance there is that footballers will be among them.

I'd never condone drugs but as this story grows arms and legs too many people are jumping on a bandwagon that needs to slow down. For example, St Johnstone are being praised for their stance but few are asking questions about the real motives behind it. O'Boyle and Thomas are both bit-part players – and, for good measure, bit-part players who have been on the long-term injury list. Might sacking them have been just that bit easier because they've taken more out of the club recently than they've put in? I wonder what the boardroom attitude might have been had the culprit been young Keigan Parker, their number one asset and probably worth well over £1 million. Answers on the back of a rolled-up £20 note.

Monday, 8 January 2001

After a day spent glued to FA Cup games on telly, it's time to prepare for our own shot at glory. The draw for the next round was made last night and we've got Airdrie at home if we get past Elgin.

The directors, of course, would rather we had the chance of Celtic or Rangers away. Every small club board does – and this year's lucky winners are – *ta-raaaa*! – Stranraer and Brechin. Billy McLaren's boys get Martin O'Neill's millionaires down at homely Stair Park, but Dick Campbell's Third Division promotion-chasers have the real dream-ticket of a trip to Ibrox. For the players, it's a fantastic chance to play at a huge stadium against top international players. For the enthusiasts who run Glebe Park, it's a lifesaving windfall that will wipe out their overdraft and, depending on the gate, finance them for up to three seasons. Not bad for 90 minutes.

Every year I cross my fingers for one of the Old Firm away in the Cup. Every year of my career so far I have been disappointed. Surely one crack at them's not too much to ask before I get the six-inch nails through the soles of my shoes? Last year was so nearly our year at Thistle. We made the last eight and landed a decent tie away to Ayr. We lost and they got Rangers at Hampden in the semis.

Thursday, 11 January 2001

Having spent the last day or so in Aberdeen, I have to report that the chances of Saturday's game going ahead are as remote as mine are of growing a ponytail.

After work, I go on the scrounge – I'm helping Uncle Gerry organise Campsie Black Watch's annual dinner and am rounding up auction items. That's where the real money's made at their kind of do.

First call is to Derek Ferguson, who's promised to get me a shirt from younger brother and Rangers captain Barry. Next up, football agent Willie McKay, a Milton of Campsie boy who went to school with my brothers Gerry and Vincent, but who now swans it in a Monte Carlo apartment and does big-time deals across Europe. Right now he's working on a deal to take Lorenzo Amoruso from Rangers to West Ham but he says he'll find time to get signed shirts from Marcel Desailly and West Ham strikers Frederic Kanoute and Paolo di Canio.

Last but not least, Craig Levein, now with his feet under the table as Hearts manager. He's been in the papers all week after ordering his players to cancel a week's holiday with their families and come in for extra training instead. The natives are restless but he tells me it's not been a spur of the moment decision. He genuinely believes they're not up to it physically – in fact, he reckons his £15-a-week boys at Cowdenbeath worked harder in training than guys making £200,000 a year.

He's taken on a difficult job at Tynecastle but he's facing up to it well and I'm sure he'll be a huge success. Before I hang up he asks me who

I think would be good enough to step up from the lower divisions and make it. I recommend Trigger and Archie and he says he might watch them on Saturday. The other striker I suggest he check out is our own Pretty Boy, who I say would be willing to work and learn at full-time level. Again, he says he'll have him watched at the weekend.

Sadly, he says he has no interest in the balding but perfectly-formed left-back I recommend.

Saturday, 13 January 2001

Watched Thistle draw with Stirling Albion today after a night in Elgin I will never forget.

The pitch up there passed a 1.15 p.m. inspection yesterday, so off we went. It's four hours up there but the trip flew by in the company of our ex-chairman Norman Blount. We talk football, football, football and he's great crack. But he's only the warm up act.

After dinner and a massage at the hotel, I retired with my esteemed team-mate PK to hear the full blow-by-blow account of his incredible career. Two solid hours of dreams, regrets, fall-outs, disputes and more frees than a church in Stornaway. Queen of the South are his – wait for it – *twenty-first* club in 18 seasons which have taken him from Norwich to Dundee to Exeter to Iceland and Ireland and back. He machine-guns me with stories, all told from a viewpoint so jaundiced it would have made Mao Tse Tung look like a milk bottle.

Are we sitting comfortably? Then he'll begin.

'Norwich, right? Ah'm just out of school.'

'So you're 12?'

'Aye, funny. Everybody wanted me. Ah had four years there, loved it. Played for the Scotland youth teams wi' Durranty and guys like that. But in the end Ah was homesick and wanted back up the road, so Ah went to Dundee United.'

'Like it there?'

'Loved it – but wee Jim McLean hated me. Ah got a runners-up medal in the UEFA Cup final against Gothenburg in 1987. Played in the Nou Camp the same season. But he never liked me. So one day Ah'm in the bookies when Ah get a tap on the shoulder.'

'McLean?'

'Naw, one of the youth kids. Tells me the gaffer wants to see me. But Ah've got a favourite comin' in and Ah'm not for budging. So 20 minutes later Ah get another tap.'

'The boy again?'

'Naw, McLean. He says: "Ma office, now." When we get there he hands me a piece of paper with a phone number on it. I ring it and it's Motherwell – he hated me that much he sold me to his brother Tam.'

'Did you ever get on with anybody?'

'Ask Moorie or Tid. They'll tell you. Ah'm a good lad. Never been in a dressing-room where the boys didn't like me. But outside, people get the wrong impression. OK, Ah've done some daft things – but the trouble is, it takes you two minutes to get a bad name and 20 years to try and clear it.'

I got his point. I'd heard a million stories about him before he came here, not all of them complimentary, but I couldn't argue that he was great to have around.

'Anyway, Ah did the swivel at Fir Park for a season, then Ah won the lottery – St Mirren came in and paid about £200,000 for me. Superb. Four and a half good years Ah had, even though the club was in a dip. Then Davie Hay and Gordon Smith came in and . . .'

'You fell out with them?'

'Got it in one. It ended up that we had an argument at training and Ah walked back a couple of miles to Love Street. The fans didn't like me much either – Ah got back in the team, but one day when Ah was on the bench at Parkhead Ah went to warm up at the away end – and they unroll a banner sayin': KINNAIRD'S LESS POPULAR THAN THE POLL TAX.'

'What did you do?'

'Ah went and did ma stuff in front of the Celtic fans.'

'So what next?'

'They put me on loan to Orient and Burnley and then Ah got the chance to go to Exeter – but their manager was Alan Ball and even I knew he hated Scottish boys. I lasted about 48 hours and was back up the road again.'

'Then where? You must have had some Air Miles!'

'Air Miles? Ah couldn't even drive. Ah was the only Premier League player with a Travelcard for the buses.'

'You should have been asking for a sponsored bike. Although I hear you've had a few of . . .'

'Enough! Anyway, next was Thistle. Brilliant. Lambie's the best manager Ah ever had, he got more out of me than anyone ever did. Mind you, he still freed me!'

'Didn't everybody?'

'Nearly – I've had about a dozen. I've lost count. After Firhill I signed for John Bond at Shrewsbury, then went to play for John McClelland at St Johnstone. That was OK.'

'But?'

'They let me go and Ah went back to Thistle for a spell, then won three medals with Derry City in Northern Ireland, went to Coleraine and then south to Bohemians.'

'Slow down, I'm getting travel-sick! How d'you get all the contacts over there?'

'It was the same manager every time, a guy called Felix Healy. When he got a new club, so did Ah.'

'What, you mean you kept getting him the sack? Shame he never went to Juventus.'

'Funny guy.'

'So what next?'

'Firhill again. Played in Europe for them.'

'Europe?'

'Inter-Toto Cup. Fantastic. Then Bert Paton took me to Dunfermline and we won the First Division – listen, Dessie boy, no' many guys can say they played 400 Premier games with six clubs. Some record, eh?'

'Not many guys can say they played with six clubs, pal.'

'Correct. So where was Ah?'

'Don't ask me, I'm dizzy.'

'Aye, Scarborough. Then Ayr, where Ah won the Second Division title. Then Stranraer, where Ah won it again. Then Ross County, where Ah won the Third Division and then got promotion from the second last season – that's five promotions in a row, pal, count them!'

'And then here? So are we going up?'

'As long as the old PK shuffle keeps workin'. It's never let me down.'

'So how come it never made you a superstar?'

'It nearly did. Ah just never got the credit for how hard Ah worked. All Ah did as a kid was practise controlling a ball and crossing it. But everybody thought it just came natural and that Ah wasn't a grafter.'

'So does it not get on your tits that so many guys you played with at youth level cracked it? Do you think they remember playing with you?'

'Aye, they remember – and here's how. We were playing England at Carrow Road when Ah was with Norwich, right? And we're getting a pumping. So at half-time Andy Roxburgh has us all sitting round the dressing-room from one to eleven – he always had us in order.'

'Par for the course with him.'

'Ah know. So he starts with the keeper and works his way round. Everybody's getting it, everybody's hopeless. So Ah'm at 11 and he's just finished on No. 10 when Ah stand up and shout: "The gaffer's right – youse lot *are* hopeless! This is ma home ground and Ah'm embarrassed. Get the finger out or youse are finished!"'

'So what did Roxburgh say?'

'What could he say? He agreed with me!'

In the end I could take no more and demanded he stop so we could get some kip.

We'd just put the light out when the party started through the wall. A bunch of girls were carrying a night out on into the wee hours and with the music and laughter and shouting there was no chance of us getting our heads down. We dozed on and off, but by about half-five we were done in. So PK phones reception: 'Any Stewart Grainger of me gettin' a sleep here?'

After the night manager sent for a translator, he pledged to try and sort things out. He phoned the party but got a rubber ear. Eventually, the bold PK took matters in hand. On goes the light and he leaps out of bed in his white boxers – one half jammed up the crack of his arse – and vest a size too wee, off to sort the girlies out.

'Right, Ah'll shut them up for good!'

'You do that, PK.'

Our door slams. Then: Knock, knock!

'What?'

'Listen, any riska you lot giein' it a rest, doll?'

'What?'

'Look, we've got a gamea football the morra. Gonnae turn the music aff and shut it?'

'Naw. Piss off.'

Their door slams.

'OK, then . . .'

If his bum looked big when he returned it was because his tail was between his legs.

'Good job, PK,' I've mumbled from under the covers. 'You really showed them, eh . . .?'

Sleep came some time in the night and seemed to last seconds before the phone was ringing. The clock said ten. It was KC.

'Game's off, chaps.'

'Bollocks.'

Totally cheesed off, we grabbed our stuff, had breakfast and got back down the road. And you know the sickening thing? There wasn't one of us who wouldn't have bet his house on a postponement by the time we'd got halfway up the road last night. Who the hell passed the pitch as playable anyway? Didn't they reckon on it getting colder overnight? I'm told it tends to do that in winter. Now we're looking at coming back up on Monday, which will be disastrous. Everyone will have to beg more time off work but the Newcastle lads like Pretty Boy will need *two days'* off so they can leave at breakfast and catch some zeds after getting home at six next morning. And if it's not Monday, it'll be Wednesday and the problems will be the same. Having said that, just for once I've not got a problem. As it turns out, I'm working with Ray in Aberdeen and Elgin on Monday, Tuesday and Wednesday. Sometimes this juggling business is easy-peasy.

And so I ended up at Firhill for the second half against Albion and a seat beside Craig as he checks out Trigger and Archie.

Hit the couch at night to watch a movie with Carolyn.

Sunday, 14 January 2001

On the way to Aberdeen today, JC phoned to say the game's off again tomorrow night.

Tuesday, 16 January 2001

Guess what? The game, rearranged for Wednesday, is off yet again. This is becoming an epic, or to put it another way, a pain in the arse. We're back on for next Monday when I won't be working up here. The SFA really are inconsiderate sometimes.

Thursday, 18 January 2001

Inverness last night, Glasgow today, Dumfries tonight. If they did Road Miles I could fly to Sydney twice a month.

Today, seven First Division clubs have announced they want to break away from the Scottish League and set up the so-called SPL2 because, as one chairman put it: 'We're fed up of being held back by the lack of ambition shown by clubs in the Second and Third Divisions.'

So let's look at the Magnificent Seven who've had enough, shall we?

Only Livingston and Ross County among them can claim to be cash rich. The others are living hand-to-mouth and in this we see the real reason for the proposed split. They want a bigger slice of the SPL cake, pure and simple. There's Raith Rovers, a club with a 10,000-seat stadium in place but so skint they flogged their three best players to Livingston for washers earlier in the season. There's Inverness Caledonian Thistle, currently working on a share issue to wipe out a £2 million-plus debt. Airdrie are in administration and their financial problems are so great they might not even exist soon. And Falkirk are even worse off than Raith – they have no money and because they don't have a 10,000-seat stadium they wouldn't be allowed into the SPL even if they won the league. Brockville is falling apart around their ears and so are manager Alex Totten's plans, as he is forced to let his best players leave for free. Meanwhile, an hour after the breakaway announcement was made at their very stadium, Clyde were paying off first-team coach Brian Rice because they couldn't afford him.

And these guys are claiming that the clubs further down the ladder hold them back?

Sure, it's Queen of the South's fault that Airdrie and Raith and Falkirk are all but bankrupt. Cowdenbeath are to blame for Brian Rice being on the dole. It certainly couldn't be down to financial mismanagement, could it? Face facts. These clubs are struggling because they have lived beyond their means for far too long. They only have themselves to blame for that – and now they want to dump others who *do* balance the books? It doesn't make sense. Especially when you look at the fate of the last lot who broke away. Half the SPL are in financial difficulties and being forced to trim squads and budgets. Aberdeen even had to get rid of the players' toaster! And has the new 'élite' league improved the performance of our top few in Europe as it promised it would? Of course it hasn't. The only thing the SPL has developed is the greed of wannabee chairmen. Meanwhile, what's the worst crime you can accuse the Second and Third Divisions of? Making sure they stay afloat. Is that such a bad ambition?

After training at frozen Palmerston, I am greeted at our front door by Taylor, who sings 'Happy Birthday to You'. That's right, 31 today!

Friday, 19 January 2001

Tomorrow's game with Forfar is off. More training.

Thursday, 25 January 2001

Packing for Elgin has become a real habit. It was off again on Monday, then Wednesday, which means that while the rest gear up for third-round ties on Saturday we'll hopefully be making it into the hat. I say hopefully because, fancy that, the game's still in doubt. There's another pitch inspection tomorrow, hopefully not carried out this time by Benny from *Crossroads*. We're told to make plans to down tools and meet the bus at short notice.

Well, all except JC. He's in Florida on business, only the second time in my career a manager has missed a game through his work. The other was Tommy Gemmell when I was at Albion Rovers – and funnily enough he was also away when we were playing a Highland team. We lost to Huntly that time after about ten postponements. I hope it's not an omen.

I wonder whether JC will be quietly hoping for another call-off so he doesn't need to miss a game but Scotty and Warren Pearson are in control just in case. Me? I think we really need this game played to get it off our backs.

Friday, 26 January 2001

The news came through at 1 p.m. Game on!

Now I'm running around like a blue-arsed fly to get finished in time, get home, have some pasta, get the club tracky on and meet the bus at Bothwell. By the time I get there my head's splitting and I try to sleep above the hubbub of the card school.

After dinner at the hotel, PK and I once again retire for an evening of civilised chat. While he arranges his vest drawer, I play mother with the kettle, put the milk in the cups, sort the biccies – then realise the stupid blankety-blanks hadn't given us any tea bags.

I'm down to reception like a shot to have this out with them.

'You haven't given us any tea bags.'

'Well, actually we did, sir – but your physiotherapist ordered us to remove them.'

Seconds later I'm rattling KC's door.

'Des, what can I do for you?'

'You can give me my tea bags back for a start.'

'No.'

'How no?'

'Cos no.'

'Cos no how?'

And so he tells me cos no how. It's because tea, apparently, is a diuretic and thus a factor in athletes like ourselves becoming dehydrated. It was hereby banned before games.

'I have to say,' I mused, 'that I hadn't realised I'd signed for AC Milan.'

'You haven't,' he smiled. 'You're with Queen of the South and you're getting no tea.'

Dunking the Jaffa Cakes in hot blackcurrant juice just wasn't the same.

Slept in a major cream puff.

Saturday, 27 January 2001

Woke in a better mood. Then remembered there was no tea and got grumpy again.

PK and I discuss what we think the team will be. Whatever it is, he says, he wants me to give him the ball as much as possible. He fancies himself to produce plenty of his patented swivel, half-yard and deliver routine and give Elgin much grief.

After a light breakfast – and no bloody tea – PK, Ronnie Shyness and myself walk the half-mile into town and talk some more about the line-up. We decide it's not going to be a pretty game because the result matters so much. There's no point playing well in a Cup-tie and losing. We'll take an ugly 1–0 win.

Back at the hotel, the boys are playing pool or table tennis, but PK and I decide to laze in our rooms. As ever, it is fated not to be. We're settling down to watch telly when Scotty and Wazza knock and ask for a word with PK. I make my excuses and leave. When I return, PK's face is longer than a week in Barlinnie. Before I can ask what's up, he says: 'I'm bombed.'

Instinct makes me blurt: 'You're joking.'

But he's not.

I ask him what they'd said.

'They didn't think the game would be suited to me. They reckon we'll take a pounding early on and want more aggressive players. They say they'll put me on at half-time if we're getting on top.'

By now it's 11.30 a.m. and time for our pre-match lunch but PK decides to boycott it. He's not in the mood to eat or to mix and says he needs time to calm down. Scotty takes the team talk at one and PK sits in on it. He's still miserable.

As it turns out, the pitch at Borough Briggs isn't too bad and the dressing-rooms are a decent size. We're there earlier than usual and the boys hang around before changing one by one. Some need to get stripped early, others to be reminded of the time. I keep to a strict routine week in, week out. I get my massage, pick up two pair of socks, tape up my two rings, get my tie-ups and pull on the Tubigrip bandages I need to feel comfortable under my shinpads. I also make sure I take plenty of water on board. I'd love a cup of tea but there's no point even asking.

Yet no matter how you prepare the night before, how well you sleep and eat, how focused you are, how well your warm-up goes, nothing guarantees you won't have a stinker. And, boy, do we have a stinker in the first half. We don't keep possession, we don't threaten enough and our composure's all over the shop. Yet we come in 1–0 up thanks to Pretty Boy. Funny old game, innit?

As promised, PK comes on at half-time and we pick up. Yet just as we start to look ourselves, we lose the ball in midfield and as Elgin break, The Virgin comes off his line and gives away a penalty. To the relief of all of us, he then saves it. We hang on. We've got the ugly 1–0 after all.

If we're looking forward to Airdrie in the third round, the journey home isn't so much of a treat. It'll be 11 p.m. by the time I make Cumbernauld and well gone midnight by the time the bus docks at Newcastle.

Saturday night out for the Cup heroes is a few beers, a fish supper and a hand of cards.

Sunday, 28 January 2001

The fourth-round draw is read out while I'm at the Campsie dinner – we'll be at home to Peterhead if we get past Airdrie. Not glamorous but what a chance to make the last eight.

It's a great night, with speakers Jim Leishman and George McNeill on top form and the auction raising £2,500. It pays to sponge.

Tuesday, 30 January 2001

A bleaching at training tonight, our first real going-over in ages. But probably not as much of a going-over as PK plans to give JC when he sees him on Thursday.

Meanwhile, Pretty Boy has gone through with his threat to get boots with MERRICK embossed on the tongue. I'm glad he can laugh at himself. Why should he miss out on all the fun?

Wednesday January 31

Airdrie have failed to register their foreign players in time for our Cup-tie next Tuesday. They're appealing to the SFA on Friday, but right now we could be playing their youth team for a place in the Fourth Round.

Thursday, 1 February 2001

JC's back and he's not happy. Why? Pretty Boy's getting his picture done for the *Sun* with a paper bag on his head. Fair play to the boy, he's gone through with his promise to live up to the Elephant Man tag by getting the boots done. The *Scottish Sun* love it and want to do a feature on it for Saturday. The boys think it's a great laugh too. It's only the gaffer who struggles to see the funny side. It takes a fair bit of reassurance from yours truly that having his star striker pictured in a national newspaper with his head in a bag is, in fact, the kind of PR we need. Snapper Les Gallagher fires away and Pretty Boy's revelling in his fame.

My team takes a hammering in tonight's training game but not as much of a hammering as JC's ears when PK corners him in his office. You wonder if a showdown with the boss will take away the good his second-half performance at Elgin did him – especially as we've signed another left-winger, Mark Angel, on a short-term deal.

Car Wash is also fretting over whether or not he'll start against Thistle on Saturday. I tell him not to worry, there's no way JC will leave him out after being so keen to sign him.

Saturday, 3 February 2001

Should I have stayed and fought for my place?

Would I have got back in the team at any point?

Do I regret leaving?

These questions and more are swimming round my head tonight following our 3–1 gubbing by Thistle. As I torment myself, Carolyn watches me and guesses exactly what I'm thinking. She can read me like a book.

We'd started well enough this afternoon – Queens, not me and the wife – and John O'Neill got us level after Tino Hardie had put them ahead. But the second half was one-way. Tino scored another, Trigger made it three and we were lucky not to lose more. We were totally over-run. JC puts it down to us having playing just two games in six weeks while Thistle have barely missed a beat because of their undersoil heating – and he was right in some ways because their fitness shone through in the end. More depressing was that their movement, balance, passing and finishing weren't bad either.

And so, a Saturday night spent considering my decision to leave a club undoubtedly on course to winning the league. For 14 years I've dreamed of winning something and when it eventually looks like happening, I throw it away. But you know what? I don't have a single regret about going back to Palmerston. What would be the point of hanging around Firhill with big Archie in the form he's in and JL sticking with a winning team and a successful formation? When you're part-time, you need to play – or else what's the point? I went to Queens because there was a better chance of a game and that's how it's panned out. Plus, we've not given up hopes of sneaking the second promotion place. It's not like the season's dead.

I'd feel a greater sense of achievement if I played my part in helping Queens go up than if I took a championship medal for playing a handful of games with Thistle.

It was great to see the boys again today and great to see them buzzing the way they are but I've got a new dressing-room now and it's a good one. I think my involvement with the *Scottish Sun* has helped that – guys like Pretty Boy can't believe the interest there's been in him since he started getting a few mentions. Believe me, though, he deserves it.

By the time I turn in, my head's stopped spinning. Take a day like today out of the equation and I'm enjoying my football again. I know Carolyn understands. And anyway, there was a happy side to today. Angela McPhie, my pal from the hospital visit, was my guest along with her dad Billy and it was great to see them. Angela's getting over her health worries and we've become good pals. She phones every Friday to wish me good luck for the next day. The look on her face after the game put the result well in perspective.

Tuesday, 6 February 2001

I feel physically abused. The look on every other face suggests they feel the same.

What in God's name did we do to deserve this?

The Airdrie Cup-tie was called off this morning, so we trained as normal. Well, as normal as a session can be when your gaffer's decided to take out the previous Saturday's defeat on you. He bleached us, no other word for it.

On a rain-drenched pitch at the Tech, Scotty and Wazza get their money's worth. It would have been a hard enough shift on a decent night but in gale-force wind and driving rain it's a killer. It's all timed runs and shuttles. Murder.

Never in my career have I been closer to throwing up.

To be fair to JC, it's the first time in ages he's been able to give us a stiff session and we did need it. During the on/off Elgin saga it was impossible to plan any hard work. Tonight was the night we made up for it big time.

On the way home, Car Wash and I talk to PK about how he should sort things out with JC. He wants to stay and fight for his place but wants to know how he should approach JC. We tell him that he just needs to go and explain that he's right up for winning back his shirt and knows he needs to knuckle down harder. He'll have a word on Thursday.

Thursday, 8 February 2001

Well, I didn't see that one coming. PK is no more! He rang me this morning to say that JC had phoned to say he was unhappy with his fitness and that he would be playing with the stiffs on Saturday. Oh, and not to come to training tonight.

PK, naturally, is gutted. He'd been all ready to sit down with JC and tell him he was up for knuckling down but now the wind's been taken out of his sails. He asks my advice but I have to admit I'm stumped. Surely if his fitness is a problem he should be at training?

Then he asks me to speak to the manager on his behalf to find out what the problem is. What a position that leaves me in. JC would have every reason to tell me to butt out and worry about my own position. But if I don't do what PK asks I could be letting a mate down. I decide I'll take my chances with JC.

As it turns out, I'm pulling into Palmerston just as JC's getting out of his car. I ask for a word and relay PK's call from this morning. I tell him I know it's none of my business but the boy's going off his nut worrying.

To his credit, the gaffer's totally frank. He says he's decided PK's not in his plans and that it'd be in everyone's best interests if he left the club. That was that, no room for negotiation. I thanked him for his honesty and said I'd pass the message on to PK.

'Sure,' he said, 'but he's already well aware of the situation.'

I can't help feeling there's something more involved that neither of them is letting on about.

Training on a now-frostbound Palmerston pitch is lighter than last time out. We do footwork exercises using hurdles and ropes, though the stiffs get a hammering up and down the terraces. Again, if fitness really was PK's problem, shouldn't he be slogging it out with them?

The session's barely over when the mobile goes and PK's desperate to know what the score is. I have to be honest and tell him the worst. He seems so hurt and says he can't work out why JC would want to do this to him. I feel quite sorry for the guy.

See, although PK has more front than Brighton, not far below the surface he's totally insecure, a guy who needs to be built up all the time. I've never met a footballer that needs to be appreciated so much, to be made to feel important. He's more reliant on the opinions of others than anyone I know – not because of a rampant ego but because he needs to feel accepted. I've got to know PK well over the past couple of months and I like him. He'll be a real loss to the dressing-room. He's a legend – and not only in his own lunchtime.

Friday, 9 February 2001

On business in Edinburgh today, Car Wash and I drop in at Tynecastle to blether with Craig Levein for an hour. Pretty Boy's name comes up and he's also interested in a young Arbroath centre-back called Andy Webster. We're at Gayfield tomorrow, so I suggest he comes and sees the two of them head-to-head as his own game at Dundee's been postponed, which is funny, because the two grounds are only 12 miles apart. Here's hoping there's no late call-off for us.

One definite game off for me is the one against Clydebank on 10 March. I got a call today to say I'm one of eight salesmen in the company being rewarded for business growth. The prize? Three days on an Arctic safari – igloos, snowmobiles, the lot. Elvis is on the flight as well and it'll be a once-in-a-lifetime adventure. The hardest bit will be picking my moment to tell JC.

Saturday, 10 February 2001

No late postponement today. Just an early finish.

With the score 1–1 and half-time eight minutes away, referee David Somers decided the pitch was hazardous and called a halt. To say we are highly pissed off is an understatement. We'd totally bossed the game. John O'Neill put us ahead after two minutes and we could have been two or three up before Jim Mercer's spectacular equaliser.

Sure, some puddles were gathering as rain fell on frost. Yes, the odd player was losing his footing. OK, if someone had taken a sore one we might have felt differently. But our dressing-room was still like a morgue because not only had we lost out on a possible win, we'll have to come back up here on a midweek soon. More problems for the English-based lads.

Needless to say, Arbroath seemed quite happy with the decision.

Not so chuffed was a certain Mr Levein, who'd taken up my suggestion to come on a spy mission. It turned out as big a wasted journey for him as it was for the QoS who'd driven all this way north.

Still, other results work out well for us. Thistle continue to sweep all before them and just about everyone else draws. We now have three games in hand over most of our rivals and two or three wins on the bounce would put us into a promotion free-for-all. Mind you, two or three defeats and we'll be into a relegation dogfight. Whatever happens, it looks like the rest of our season will not be meaningless.

Unless your name happens to be PK. He phoned me before the game to find out the team and as soon as I switched on again at the end of the game it rang and there he was again, desperate to know how the 37 minutes had gone. I have to tell him the truth, that Mark Angel did well on the wing in terrible conditions. It's not what he wanted to hear but why lie?

Sunday, 11 February 2001

Tomorrow night's Cup-tie with Airdrie is causing me no end of problems. I'll be in Aberdeen on business all day and driving four hours to Dumfries is hardly the ideal pre-match warm-up. I'm then meant to have meetings up there again Tuesday and Wednesday but they'll have to be hit into touch if the game goes ahead. I'll have to pack enough gear for three days – even though I may only be there one night – plus training kit in case the game's off and I need to do a session on my own. All in all, I'd rather we had another postponement and played on Wednesday so I was better prepared and in better shape. Here goes with another rain dance . . .

The house feels quiet as I get ready. Carolyn, Dani and Taylor left yesterday for a week's skiing in Andorra but it looks like I'll keep myself busy without them.

Before heading north, I've an invitation to the Old Firm game at Celtic Park with football agents Paul di Giacomo and John Lonergan, who want me to get involved with them. Celtic's win is made all the sweeter when my first-goal bet on Alan Thompson comes in at 20/1. A 150-mile drive flies by after that!

Monday, 12 February 2001

Nightmare. The game's definitely on and I'm into juggling mode.

When the news comes through, I get Ray Hardie to change a couple of appointments so I can leave Aberdeen at lunchtime. Then I ring Car Wash to pick me up at Bothwell and save my legs from a couple of hours' pedal-pushing. Business over, I hammer back to Cumbernauld, in the front door to make some pasta and out the back to hook up with my chauffeur.

Needless to say, he's not had an easy day either. He's also had to switch calls around in Glasgow but that's midweek part-time football for you. All over the country, dozens of guys have been wangling and dodging and calling in favours just like Car Wash and me to make sure we get to the dressing-room on time.

It is a good job we have a football-minded boss in Reg. He really doesn't mind these situations because he knows how much the game means to us – and that we'll pay him the time back, with compound interest on top!

We don't exactly have to fight through a media scrum to get into the Palmerston car park at the back of six but it's as near as it gets down there. With only two games on in Scotland tonight, there are more reporters and snappers than usual hanging around – we've even got a Sky telly crew setting up. Mind you, I think they might be more interested in our opponents than ourselves.

Airdrie's troubled season has run like a soap opera thanks to the never-ending feud between provisional liquidators KPMG and would-be owner Steve Archibald. Six months after I faced his hastily-put-together band of imports for Thistle in the CIS Cup, he's still in charge at New Broomfield but hasn't managed to complete his takeover. Week after week, he hints in the press about his plans being blocked. Week after week, KPMG's man Blair Nimmo warns that his patience is running thin. Now, as they come to face us in the Cup, things are coming to an ugly head.

The players have already been locked out of their stadium once when Archibald was late with weekly management fees. Then there was the business with them failing to register their overseas players in time for this tie – for a while it looked like we'd be facing their youth team but Archibald appealed to the SFA and won his case. Or, to put it another way, the SFA swept the matter under the carpet.

Ironically, we are hit by registration problems of our own. Mark Angel wasn't signed in time to play and the fact that PK's still not in the plans speaks volumes. He's so far out in the cold now he makes Dunnsy's situation back at Thistle seem tropical. Danny Patterson comes in on the left, our only change from Saturday's fiasco at Gayfield.

We get the runaround for the first 20 minutes. Airdrie, backed by a noisy band of fans (as opposed to KPMG, for they are committed to their team), give us first-hand experience of how technically gifted they are. Striker David Fernandez and midfielders Antonio Calderon and Fabrice Moreau are the pick and the latter pair combine for the opening goal. Moreau beats me to Calderon's floated free kick and heads beyond Colin Scott. The ball beat me, not the run, but I'm still raging. However, our own larger-than-usual support are soon roaring as Warren Hawke pressures their keeper Javier Sanchez Broto into a horrendous mistake and taps into an empty net.

We go in 1–1 and confident of causing an upset.

It's not to be. Five minutes after the break, Airdrie go ahead again – and after that it's a tale of three penalties and a red card in a frantic last five minutes.

First, Alan Hogg is bundled in the box and Pretty Boy steps up to try and put us level – only for Broto to dive to his right and push the shot away. Long after Airdrie booted upfield again, Peter was still grounded in the box, shattered. He was inconsolable until long after the final whistle – especially as Car Wash was then short with a pass-back, an Airdrie man went down and Jesus San Juan made it 3–1 from the spot. Our heads down, they came at us again and big Ronnie walked for handling on the line with Scotty beaten. This time, San Juan hit a post and then it was all over.

JC was delighted with our performance against a very good team, particularly because we matched them for fitness late on.

'If you show that effort and commitment for the rest of the league games,' he tells us, 'we'll have nothing to fear.'

We'll need to heed his words at Hampden on Saturday because everything Queen's Park do is based on running and organisation. It's a hell of a test on the back of this defeat.

But that's for later. Right now, I just want to get home and sleep off an exceptionally tiring day. Sometimes I wish I could swap places with Beckham or Keane to see how they'd cope.

Tuesday, 13 February 2001

The PK hotline's red-hot from early doors. First time he calls the mobile, I'm on the house phone and I tell him I'll ring back as soon as I'm free. But he's obviously used Call Back on *his* phone, because the split-second I put the receiver down it rings again. And he's off, machine-gunning me with questions about last night's game. Who played in his position? Was he any good? Did they miss him? Would he have made a difference?

It's quite obvious the cold shoulder is killing him. He's sitting at home tearing himself apart about whatever it is he's done wrong. He still can't understand why JC and the chairman pushed the boat out to sign him only to fall out of love with him so badly three months later.

He's trying to keep himself busy in the gym but I tell him he should give JL a ring and see if he can train properly at Thistle. They go back a long way together.

At night, I go to Cappielow to see JL's boys beat Clydebank 4–0. Trigger and Tino both score yet again but it's not that impressive a performance. There's a lot of huffing and puffing before, yet again, their extra fitness pays off.

In the stand, I meet Doc and Dunnsy, both of whom are still having nightmares. Doc's is injury. Dunnsy's is the manager.

Wednesday, 14 February 2001

Valentine's Day with a difference – a romantic meal in a hotel bedroom with Elvis Williams. We're down in Dumfries on business and would have eaten in the restaurant but we thought it might have looked a bit suspect in among all those loving couples. Mind you, what must the waiter have thought bringing up two meals for two blokes in a double room? Hey-ho. We hold hands and watch Man U. v Valencia in the Champions League.

The big news today is that KPMG have locked Airdrie out of New Broomfield again and this time it looks like for keeps. Archibald's contract has been terminated because of unpaid management fees and the club is on the brink of extinction. Liquidator Blair Nimmo claims that of 30-odd weekly payments so far, Archibald's been late with 19 and 4 have never been seen. He's given him until 5 p.m. tomorrow to cough up the missing £30,000. Archibald's told him to whistle for it.

The football fall-out from this is that their Scottish Cup-tie with Peterhead on Saturday is in serious jeopardy. The irony's not lost on me. Had Pretty Boy's penalty gone in on Monday night, we might have been turning up for a replay tonight to find the gates locked and the ref handing us a bye to the next round. Now, Peterhead might just be looking at making the quarter-finals without kicking a ball.

This game is one long tale of what might have been.

Thursday, 15 February 2001

Training tonight is based around JC's tactics to face Queen's Park on Saturday – they have a rigid formation and he wants our centre-back Andy Aitken to knock diagonal balls behind their full-backs and get them turning.

We finish with a game of head tennis in which us old guys hammer the weans and the mood's so good I decide the time's right to tell JC about my Arctic trip – and, for good measure, the fact that I'll probably miss the game at Berwick on 31 March because Carolyn's brother Gary's getting married that day. He takes the news well enough. Is that good or bad for me? Time will tell.

On the way home, I dread a call from PK because I'll have to tell him we've signed another left-winger. Stuart King's on loan from Preston until the end of the season. It's another right good boot in the danglies for the wee man.

Saturday, 17 February 2001

Half-time at Hampden and I'm taking a roasting. I deserve it, too.

Before kick-off, JC had told me he expected better after two mediocre performances. Then their winger Danny Ferry skinned by on the bye-line and we ended up 1–0 down. JC was spitting teeth – though I wasn't the only one getting it. He went through the lot of us for a performance that was ruining all the planning we'd put in. Funny old game, though. Forty-five minutes later he was praising us to the skies after we came back to win 2–1 through fantastic goals by Stuart King – sorry, PK – and Pretty Boy. Both strikes were well worthy of the national stadium. We'd been asked at half-time if we had the bottle to get a result and drag ourselves nearer the promotion-chasing pack. Let's hope we've proved we have.

To everyone's surprise, Thistle lose today for the first time in months, 2–0 at Stenny. It's their second defeat there this season but at least they can't blame me this time.

Carolyn and the kids will be back tomorrow night, so I decline Car Wash's offer to paint the town red and do the ironing instead.

I have to stop telling people this stuff.

Thursday, 22 February 2001

Tonight's training is mostly about set-plays. Coaches Scotty and Wazza reckon I could be an aerial threat at corners and free kicks on Saturday. I hope they mean in Stirling Albion's box and not ours.

Albion are one place below us and, while we're both uncomfortably close to relegation, a win for us would open up a decent gap and maybe even set us up for a promotion push.

I'd missed training on Tuesday night but it was worth it – I was in Manchester on business then went to watch Man U play Valencia in the Champions League. It finished 0–0 and wasn't a great game, but a terrific experience.

The downer was that Carolyn and the girls had come home from Andorra late on Sunday and with me doing a session on my own on Monday to make up for not being at Dumfries on Tuesday then going down south, I haven't had a chance to find out how their holiday went. By the time I get home tonight it's too late again. Maybe tomorrow night, eh? If they still remember who I am.

Up half the night because neighbours Jim and Anne's alarm keeps going off. I feel like I've just dozed off at last when Taylor comes in and asks if I'll switch off our alarm so she can go downstairs and watch TV. What time is it? Eight? Bollocks!

I manage to catch some shut-eye before getting up to organise myself for the game and a night out with Carolyn at the Press Ball in Glasgow's Hilton Hotel. I've had an invite through the *Scottish Sun* and we're looking forward to it – if I can get back from Palmerston in time.

Today's other big event is Angela McPhie's twenty-third birthday. She's continuing her recovery from her operations and my mum and I have both sent cards. I've also arranged for flowers to be delivered to Firhill today and Alan Archibald says he'll present them to her.

By the time she phones to say thanks I've experienced the good, the bad and the downright agonising in football.

The good? Three precious points from a 2–1 win, a wonder left-foot goal from Car Wash and a highly complimentary chat with JC about my performance.

The bad? A booking for booting the ball away in frustration.

The agonising? Chilblains on the end of my privates.

Oucharama.

We'd played Albion in bizarre conditions that swung between brilliant sunshine and sweeping blizzards. Only our game and Thistle's had survived the cold but even then the ref had to shout for an orange ball.

If only he'd done it earlier. While we were still kicking a white Mitre, I took my eye off it for a second, lost it in the lying snow, gave away a throw and took a swing that blootered it down the touchline. Yellow card. Stupid boy. By then, Car Wash had already scored that wonder goal – as in, we all wondered how he managed it with the foot he usually stands on. Shortly after, John O'Neill made it two with a deflection off my old Thistle team-mate Kevin Gaughan.

We then missed chance after chance before Stirling scored with 15 to go and we were left hanging on. JC was ecstatic. Pick of our bunch had been young Stuart King but everyone did well. It was only when I jumped in an extremely hot shower that things started going pear-shaped. The water scalded my frozen wedding tackle and . . . well, ask a doctor what happens next.

Walking like John Wayne, I went to see JC about arrangements for our midweek game at Arbroath. I'll struggle to make the pre-match meal and with Car Wash and Hawkey in the same boat we'll head straight to Gayfield if it's OK with him. He says it is, then tells me:

'You did well today.'

'Ta.'

'So how come you hadn't played that way in the last two games?'

My excuse is that I'm still trying to get some consistency. I'd gone a long time at Thistle without a regular game and I feel it's coming gradually. He accepts this reluctantly.

I like chats like these. I've always believed it can only be good for managers to discuss individual performances with players on a regular basis.

Before I shoot off for the Hilton I meet talent scout Michael Murphy. He tried to take me to Hearts when I was 17 and now works for Celtic. He's down watching Pretty Boy and asks what I think. I tell him he's worth the gamble. For, say, £150,000 Celtic would get a young man with natural ability who's desperate to improve. I hope they take it further.

Car Wash hits warp speed up the M74.

It's a great night, topped off when I win the raffle prize of a hospitality day racing sports cars round Knockhill in Fife. That'll get rid of the chilblains . . .

Tuesday, 27 February 2001

Wasn't it next week I was meant to be in the Arctic? Someone forgot to tell whoever organises the weather at home. It's been heaving snow overnight and gale-force winds have thrown it around like Julian Clary in a WWF ring. Not only will it put paid to tonight's game at Arbroath, it'll knacker just about everything today.

Transport's at a standstill. Drifts have closed the M74, M8, M77 and M73. There's little chance of getting to training. By 9 a.m. JC confirms a night off and hopes we'll be OK to get there on Thursday. Saturday's derby at Stranraer is a real biggy.

These games always mean hooking up with old friends and first in line will be Tommy Bryce – not only a former QoS team-mate but also the manager who took me to Thistle. He left Palmerston to be player-manager at Firhill during the worst of their financial troubles and it never looked like working out. The fans had expected a higher-profile name after John McVeigh was sacked and, despite good early results, they never really took to him. A run of seven straight defeats meant the knives were well and truly out and chairman Brown McMaster plunged the big one in. TB was relieved of his duties and when JL came back he was never going to fancy his predecessor being around the dressing-room as a player.

Funny – as I write this, Steve Claridge is in exactly the same position down at Portsmouth. He's being replaced as boss and is now having to decide whether or not to hang around. Just as TB went back to QoS and stuck to scoring goals, I reckon Claridge will also move on.

TB went on to have a season at Arbroath before signing for Billy McLaren just before his forty-first birthday. He may have seen better days but he can still do great things with a ball – and, as Martin O'Neill says of Lubo Moravcik, I'd loved to have seen him at 21 or even 31.

The choice TB and now Claridge had to make was also faced by Ginger Geordie Rowe at the end of last season. He spent 18 months as player-boss of QoS along with Ken Eadie and after a stressful – though successful – fight against relegation, Ginger decided he wanted to go back to just playing. Working full time as a surveyor, trying to be a good husband and father, keeping his form up on the pitch *and* running a struggling team had been just too much. He wasn't giving his best to any part of a hectic life. He could, of course, have stayed and done his stuff at the back for JC, but he too felt a clean break was better and moved to be captain of Arbroath.

I think he did the right thing, just as TB did and Claridge will. It would take an extraordinary brass neck to accept being deemed a failure, yet stay around and take a wage from the club under a different job title.

Who mentioned Bryan Robson and Middlesbrough?

NINE

Thursday, 1 March 2001

BIZARRE? The word doesn't begin to describe tonight at Palmerston.

For a start, there are only five of us at training – Car Wash, Andy Aitken, Hawkey, young Davy Milne and me. Our English contingent is stuck behind snowdrifts in Newcastle, as are JC's coaches, Scotty and Wazza. And the rest of the Glasgow boys? They're sitting on the hard shoulder of the M74 due to big Ronnie's magnificent misuse of a mate's motor.

He's not had much luck with cars lately, hasn't Ronnie. First, his bright yellow Golf GTI Banana Splitsmobile got clamped. Then it broke down. Tonight he borrowed wheels from Dundee United stopper Jim Lauchlan, stuck in £20 of your finest unleaded – then realised it was a diesel. It took another £100 to get it sorted once the AA turned up.

Stranger still, though, is the reason we've been given for Saturday's derby at Stranraer being in jeopardy. Nope, not the weather. Foot-and-mouth disease. Two farms in the Dumfries area were confirmed today as being infected and with a desperate nationwide effort on to stem the spread, it's unlikely we'll be allowed to travel to Stair Park. Maybe they're worried big Ronnie's a carrier.

Today's other big news is the imminent close of Clydebank after two creditors refused to waive debts. Administrators will decide on Tuesday whether to close the doors and only some serious negotiating can save the day now.

I'd be desperately sad if the Bankies went down the plughole – yet even as I'm thinking this a wee selfish lightbulb goes ping. If they do go out of business, it means I won't miss two of our upcoming games. I'm on my Arctic safari for one and in Manchester for the other. On the whole, though, I'd rather the games went ahead without me.

Finally, on a very strange evening, it emerges that PK has left the building. He and JC have come to an arrangement that means the legendary winger is looking for his twenty-third professional club after his seventeenth free.

PK wasn't everyone's cup of tea down here but I'm sad to see him go. He was brilliant in the dressing-room and I hope he bounces back. I'm sure it won't belong before he's dazzling another club with his footwork and his one-liners.

And I've another important reason for digging out the black armband at the big-bottomed one's departure. I'm now the oldest member of the squad. Don't it make ya feel good?

Saturday, 3 March 2001

As suspected, foot-and-mouth has claimed today's game – though I'm pretty sure the weather would have anyway.

We're now way behind in our fixtures and face midweek games pretty much until the end of the season, starting against Stenhousemuir on Tuesday, if the winter eases. Just about the only club who don't face similar problems are Thistle. Thanks to their undersoil heating, today's game with Queen's Park is one of only six in Scotland to go ahead, so Car Wash and I head for Firhill after training in Dumfries.

We find ourselves in among half the country's managers, half of whom are checking out future opposition and the other half sizing up talent. Unfortunately for any of JL's boys who fancy a move, none really stand out in a 2–1 win.

The title's all but won now, though JL plays this down as he takes the mike in the Aitken Suite afterwards. The reason for the speech? He was sixty yesterday.

I'm sure it'll be a memorable year for him.

Tuesday, 6 March 2001

What a novelty – tonight's game is on after an early-morning inspection. To be honest, I'd got it into my head that it'd be off and the news takes the wind out of my sails. It's not that I don't want to play, far from it, but I'm off to the Arctic tomorrow and still have loads to do.

On business in Glasgow this afternoon, I bump into some of the Clydebank boys coming out of administrator PKF's offices. They've just signed new one-month contracts to ensure the short-term future of the club. It's now up to the moneymen to sort out the long term.

Car Wash and I then have beans on toast 'Chez Des' before heading to Ochilview for a game that illustrates the see-saw nature of our place in this division. A win catapults us into the promotion race. Defeat and we'll be looking over our shoulders again.

Me? First and foremost I need to have a good game before being AWOL for the back-to-back Bankies games. JC's fine with the Arctic stuff but my conscience is twanging over the reason I've given him for missing the re-match. Carolyn bought me hospitality tickets to see Man U against Valencia in the Champions League but when it turned out I was already going with my work, she changed it to the Sturm Graz game instead. I don't have the heart to tell her I can't go because we've got a rearranged game, but I also didn't have the bottle to be totally straight with the gaffer, so I've told him I'm on business. To be honest, though, I'm not happy about missing the game because of our good run and I'm also faced with a dilemma over the game after the second one with Clydebank – we're at Berwick on the same day as Carolyn's brother Gary's wedding.

All the way home tonight I worried about what to do but when I got in Carolyn handed me an either-or. I could pull out of the Man U game as long as I went to the wedding. The cat is now truly among the pigeons. Having played well tonight in our 2–1 victory – Pretty Boy and goal-a-game John O'Neill did the damage – I really could do with playing in one of the Bankies games. Maybe if I was only away for one game instead of two I'd have a better chance of going straight back in the side.

I felt good tonight, first to every loose ball, strong in the tackle, excellent in the air and passing well. The noises from JC and his crew were encouraging. It was our third win on the trot and a nice way to mark my 150th game in a QoS shirt.

I tell Carolyn I'll think about Manchester but she makes a call to her friend Sharon – a big United fan – to see if she fancies going in case. She's jumping through hoops at the thought.

I finish packing and kiss the girls bye-bye for a few days.

Saturday, 10 March 2001

By kick-off time, I'm touching down at Stockholm Airport on my way home. The last three days have been one fantastic adventure, but now my mind's on the game. Now that I'm heading homeward, I really wish I was involved at Palmerston. I'll settle for a night out in Sweden instead.

So much has happened in the Arctic. I've been dog-sledding,

snowmobiling, ice fishing, slept in a hotel made of ice and spent every other spare minute keeping warm in a sauna.

My God, they told us we were going into the wilds – we just didn't realise *how* wild until they told us to fish for our dinner. We were given a cross between an old-fashioned drill and a bottle opener and had to bore down through maybe six feet of sheer ice to find a river beneath. Trouble was, the rods they gave us wouldn't dangle down that far. (Carolyn would say that's the story of my life!) Luckily our two guides, Peter and Jesper, had brought reindeer meat to cook over an open fire. It was a hell of a relief. But the whole experience was unbelievable.

We'd flown into a place called Kiruna, then driven next morning to the Ice Hotel. It's exactly that – nothing but ice. The beds, the tables, the chairs, the windows, everything's carved from it. You eat outside so you don't melt stuff. Inside, it's never above -5C and the bar only serves vodka because it's the only spirit that won't freeze. Outside? It's hard to describe the cold. If I had to guess, I'd say -20C felt like having knives plunged into you all over. Your breath hurts and, no matter how many layers you wear, the guides give you another suit to put on top.

At bedtime you had a reindeer skin to put across your ice divan, then your sleeping bag and inside that your clothes for next day – it's the only way they don't get covered in frost – then there's a sheet and finally you, naked except for a woolly hat. One of the boys went to the loo and forgot to put his boxers back on when he'd finished. Within minutes they were like a frozen pizza. And if you don't go to the loo before bed, you don't go to the loo. You just don't get back out of that bag. But it's incredibly cosy once you're inside it all.

We hit the sack after a cracking night in the Ice Bar, kilted up with the bold Elvis. The staff reckoned it was the first time any guests had been brave enough to come down in skirts and wanted to know:

> a) If we were wearing anything underneath, and
> b) If anything had fallen off in the event that we weren't.

The answers were that no, we weren't – and, incredibly, nothing had.

The get-ups went down a storm, as did the vodka. Well, what did you expect me to drink out there? Soda water?

We even ended up as part of a photo-shoot for an American magazine, glamorous jet-setters that we are. Bizarre doesn't begin to describe it.

Next morning 14 of us travelled three hours *by snowmobile* to the camp where we were made to fish for our dinner. And then we had the

night of our lives. After our reindeer burgers, seven of us hit the sauna
– in the scud, of course, because that's the way they do things over there.

To pass the time, Elvis Williams and I started up a football trivia quiz.
If I said, say, Joe Jordan, the next person had to name a player whose
surname began with the last letter of that name – so it could be Charlie
Nicholas, and so on. The forfeit for not coming up with a name was to
run out and dive starkers into the snow. Trouble was, Elvis and I did so
well we never had to go outside and ended up boiling ourselves alive –
at which point we decided we'd have to dive in the snow anyway. Just
to be different, though, we ran around the campfire once and then took
the plunge.

And that was when I realised all snow isn't the same.

The rest of them had gone into powdery, new stuff. Muggins here hit
a hard-packed drift with a sickening thud. When I tried to push myself
up, I only got stuck further in. The others got me out, then we had a
snowball fight – inside the sauna, if you will – and once we got dressed
everyone sat around drinking and singing and swapping stories. It was
as crazy as it was brilliant.

Then, about two in the morning – though as it's pitch black all the
time you can't tell the difference – we decided that before we hit the
sack we'd strip off again and walk slowly through the snow singing
'You've Lost That Loving Feeling'. And trust me, by the time we'd
finished we definitely had!

It certainly wasn't like my normal Friday night of a curry and *Friends*
with the girls.

But next day I tried to keep as close to reality as possible. While the
boys were playing Clydebank at Palmerston, I put on my Queens shirt,
got out a ball and played keepy-uppy in the snow with Elvis.

Pretty soon, though, it was time head back to Stockholm. It was
nearly the end of a magnificent adventure.

Nearly.

At our hotel, I called Saint Isabel to find out the result. We'd won 1–0
with a John O'Neill penalty to make it four in a row – and the bonus was
that Arbroath had beaten Stranraer, so we were now breathing down the
necks of the promotion pack. This called for a night on the town – as if
we needed an excuse.

Elvis and I spent the evening besieged by beautiful blondes as we
strode around the town in our kilts. They couldn't stay away from us.
Sadly, though, it wasn't our bodies they were interested in. They all
wanted to know how Henrik Larsson was doing. So we said he was so-
so. How's that for understatement?

Sunday, 11 March 2001

After a full day's travelling, it's great to see Carolyn and the girls. Spend the evening lazing and watching Dundee United knock Rangers out of the Cup.

Pressure's mounting on Dick Advocaat.

Monday, 12 March 2001

Word is that young Denis Boyle did well in my shirt on Saturday. My mind's now made up about tomorrow night.

If I don't show face at Cappielow, I could face a long spell on the sidelines – and miss out on my second promotion chase of the season. That's not why I came here.

Carolyn takes the decision very well, though she'd prefer to be sharing a double hotel bed with me rather than Sharon. Or at least I think she would.

Of course, there's still the chance Denis will get the nod to start tomorrow, but I need to at least be on the bench. JC seems quite happy when I phone to say my plans have changed.

Tuesday, 13 March 2001

Good news in the *Scottish Sun* – PK's going for his sixth promotion in a row after signing for Third Division title-chasers Brechin and his old Dunfermline gaffer Dick Campbell, the only man I know who could eat an apple through a tennis racket. I wish them every success together.

As I arrive at Cappielow tonight, JC and Scotty ask me for a word. Here it comes. Sorry, baldy, but you're not playing.

Wrong.

In fact, they want to know if I've just driven up from Manchester and, if so, how my legs are feeling. They reckon my performance dipped in the Cup-tie against Airdrie after I came straight from Aberdeen. I tell them I've been working from home and feel fresh. That settles it, I'm in – but with the warning that Denis has played well on Saturday and that there's competition for the shirt now. The consolation for the kid from Donegal is that he's starting in left-midfield.

In the dressing-room, the boys are winding me up about having been away at camp with the cubs. It's great to be back.

The laughter tails off as JC comes in and tells us to get our game heads on. He's preaching concentration, movement, shape and tempo. We take it all in then go behind in two minutes.

My old Thistle team-mate Eric Paton bursts into our box, is dumped on his derriere by Andy Aitken, dusts himself down and plants the spot-kick in the bottom corner. JC will be raging. It takes another 73 minutes of Davie the Virgin being almost a spectator in goals before we equalise and – would you Adam 'n' Eve it – it's Car Wash who drills one in from 25 yards. Five minutes later we're ahead when who else but John O'Neill nets from the spot after Stephen Pickering is fouled. Davie's wonder save in the dying minutes sees us home – and the reaction at the end speaks volumes.

The players go mental, the fans go mental. Even the directors are hanging over the edge of the stand to applaud us into the tunnel. Inside, JC and his men go mental as well, praising us to the skies for our efforts. We now have a real chance of going up with Thistle – it's up to us to take it.

I'm relatively happy with my performance and the gaffers seem to be as well. My sharpness is finally up to scratch and that means my tackling's more solid. Long may it continue.

Thursday, 15 March 2001

Foot-and-mouth claims our trip to Forfar on Saturday because Station Park backs onto farmland – but the game's switched to Palmerston, which seems to me to defeat the purpose of trying to isolate the disease. Maybe they think we'd take more punters up there than they'll bring down here, but what do numbers matter? Surely one person travelling could spread infection?

Training tonight is nothing more than a loosen-off after a rush of games. In fact, we only work for half an hour before JC gives us a huge treat. We're led into his office to find it set up like a cinema and are given Pot Noodles, muesli bars and high-carbohydrate drinks while we watch a video of our boss in his playing days. And there was me thinking movies hadn't been invented then. To be fair, he looked not a bad player, good enough to score for fun against the likes of Peter Shilton. Pity about the Amos Brearly sideburns and lack of teeth!

Show over, it's up the road and in for an early night after the exertions of Cappielow and Stockholm. I intend to sleep until my name changes to Rip Van McKeown.

Sunday, 18 March 2001

Yesterday was a sore one. Last night was absolute agony. Not only did we lose 3–2 at home to Forfar, but my shoulder also popped yet again and did me out of another night's sleep.

We were 2–1 up when I went to clear a corner, took a dunt, slipped and felt the bugger go. By the time I'd come out of shock, I realised they'd equalised in the confusion. Not the best painkiller in the world, believe me. KC and I waggled it back in and I was able to finish the game, but only to see Davie Beaton curl a world-class free kick into Davie's top corner for the winner in injury time – injury time caused, of course, by me and my bloody shoulder.

What a sickener. We'd led first through Pretty Boy and then again through Il Prolifico O'Neill but threw it away and, with Arbroath and Berwick both winning, it's a massive blow.

JC missed no one at half-time or full-time. He questioned our application, knew we could have been two or three down by the break and told us that, while Forfar deserved their victory, we really beat ourselves.

He was dead right. We got exactly what we deserved – nothing. Il Prolifico wasn't happy with me for saying so. He reckoned we should all have been pulling together and not bringing the place down. Voices end up raised but it was all just down to frustration.

Most pissed off of all, though, was big Ronnie. He got the hook at half-time and felt things had got no better without him. It wasn't a happy camp.

Before heading home, I was presented with a memento of my 150th game. Andy Aitken got the same and Davie the Virgin picked up a trophy for his 165th appearance. Then it was up the M74 with a trophy and a dodgy shoulder to pop my head in at Carolyn's brother Gary's stag night. After that it was a long night.

Still, things brightened up the following day. Celtic beat Killie 3–0 in the CIS Cup final with a hat-trick from a man whose application can never be doubted, Henrik Larsson. We're lucky to have him in our game and should cherish both his skill and workrate. Plus, I had a fiver on him to score the first goal in a 3–0 win. It won me and my shoulder £200. Truly, the man is a genius.

Tuesday, 20 March 2001

Battered, abused, bullied, over-ran, bossed, outplayed, destroyed, humped and pissed on.

Just some of the words to describe how we feel after what Arbroath did to us tonight. We've lost 5–2 and we're lucky it wasn't worse.

It all started well enough, Mark Angel rattling a wonder goal from 30 yards just a couple of minutes in. Yet the next thing we had to celebrate was a consolation goal right on the final whistle and, to be honest, we weren't doing too many cartwheels.

In between, we were taken apart by teenage winger Kevin Heenan – the latest in a long line to have built a career out of 90 minutes against me – and good old Ginger Geordie Rowe. Ginger rattled the bar to set up their equaliser, then slung in a cross which led to our sub Phil Nixon heading an o.g., although ex-Queens man Stevie Mallan tried to claim it to add to the genuine one he'd scored earlier. Manager's son Paul Brownlie got the other two but, to be honest, his *dad* could have given us a hard time at the back.

JC refused to make any excuses, even though his plans took a knock from way before kick-off. We were halfway through dinner at a Perth hotel when Stuart King started feeling unwell and next thing his face made me look bronzed. I shout the club doc, Stuart tells him he's been feeling fluish all day and is now on the verge of collapsing. Then I go and badger the hotel manager to give the boy a room to lie down in and he obliges. See? I might not be much like Roberto Carlos but I could give Florence Nightingale a run for her money. Unless she's playing outside-right. Anyway, Stuart stays behind for a kip and gets picked up after the game. Turns out he was the lucky one.

JC, though, simply put our defeat down to a bad night at the office and gave Arbroath credit for their performance in gale-force winds. Well, they've had plenty of practice.

Our promotion hopes are now well and truly dented and Arbroath must be favourites to go up. But everyone still has everyone else to play, so who knows? We need to get back on the rails at Berwick on Sunday, the same day Arbroath go to Stranraer. As Elvis once sang: 'It's now or never.'

Wednesday, 21 March 2001

If Daddy's report card from last night read 'Must do better', little Danielle has no such worries. Her teacher waxes lyrical about her at parents' night tonight.

At least one D. McKeown is producing the goods.

Thursday, 22 March 2001

JC's reaction to Tuesday's defeat seems mild in hindsight and, as we head for training tonight, Car Wash and I wonder if there might be a full-scale inquest awaiting. It often used to happen this way at Thistle – JL would be cool after a bad result but once he'd had a couple of days to stew he'd let rip. Videoing every bloody game didn't help. He'd sit and pore over tapes then call in guilty men for 'chats' on their performances.

But we needn't have worried. JC's watching the stiffs play Tarff Rovers, so Wazza's left coaching nine men – ironic, as we were as good as two men short at Gayfield. We do some running then have some fun with the ball before going back to Palmerston to catch the last ten minutes of the game.

We're taking cars to Berwick on Sunday and I offer to drive one load. It's not the ideal way to travel but we're heading from such different directions a bus makes no sense.

My last duty tonight is to remind the gaffer that I'll miss next Saturday's game – Berwick again, this time at home – because of Carolyn's brother Gary's wedding.

The worrying thing is, JC doesn't seem too distraught.

Friday, 23 March 2001

A busy day in the transfer market for my old club Airdrie. Administrators KPMG have given preferred-bidder status to a consortium of businessmen who've put ex-Morton and Clydebank boss Ian McCall in charge. Ian's a good guy but he's been unlucky in his choice of clubs as a manager. Not the man to stand next to in a thunderstorm! Still, if you can get results like he did at two clubs in such a mess, you can get them anywhere and maybe that's how the new Airdrie board see it.

His first problem is signing a team to face Falkirk tomorrow. Steve Archibald took all his foreigners with him when his bid collapsed and McCall was left with just *one* signed senior player. His name is Eddie Forrest – and he's injured. So McCall hits the blower and snaps up whoever he can get. I'm delighted that one of the first was Dunnsy – at last the wee man can escape from the place he's nicknamed Firhell and get a game of football. We've spoken regularly since I left and whenever he's asked I've told him straight that he had to get out. It's taken him longer than he thought it would, though, and the rumours were he was so down they didn't let him wear shoelaces or shave unaccompanied. Now you can only hope his mood picks up.

Whether Carolyn's ever will is another matter. Me disappearing early to Berwick on Mother's Day is the straw that appears to have broken the back of every camel in captivity. Not only that, but at night I'm down to go to ex-Rangers star John Brown's testimonial dinner in Glasgow. She's none too chuffed and it's time for our quarterly discussion about my lack of involvement in her and the kids' lives. My defence is that there just aren't enough hours in the day in which to do everything I have to do but she says that whenever it comes down to a straight choice I satisfy my own timetable and not the family's. As ever, we reach no conclusion and find no way forward bar me promising to make more of an effort on the home front. Maybe if I went without sleep . . .

Sunday, 25 March 2001

So that was Mother's Day. A kiss on the cheek for Carolyn as I got up, the girls and I bringing her tea and toast in bed and two phone calls later in the day. So much for her getting pampered – though she'd say it was no different from any other day, except that I don't usually play on Sundays.

The game itself mirrored yesterday's Scotland–Belgium thriller at Hampden. Like Scotland, Berwick were 2–0 up and coasting before throwing it away in the last 20 minutes. Yet again, Pretty Boy and Il Prolifico scored to rescue a poor performance but at least we never let our heads go down after a terrible week. We've ground out an important result.

JC was delighted with our performances but not with referee Alan Gemmill, who's taken charge of our last three games and had a stinker each time. Surely it can't be clever to have the same ref handling the same team three times in a week? What chance does a player who's crossed him have of a fair hearing a few days later? It's not good for us or the whistler himself.

Another thing that's not good for us is Ginger Geordie's goal which gives Arbroath a 1–0 win at Stranraer and leaves us nine points off second place with eight games to go.

That night, I'm among 980 who turn out to honour John Brown at a dinner in Glasgow's Thistle Hotel – and while I'm very much a Celtic man, I'm as fervent as any in my praise of the guy. Bomber worked his socks off to win honours way beyond his natural ability. That's no

186 DON'T GIVE UP THE DAY JOB

disrespect, just plain fact. He gave 100 per cent for every club he played for and eventually earned himself the move to Rangers he'd always dreamed of. There, he lived out the fantasies of every punter in the Ibrox stands. He was their man out on the turf. He deserves everything he got from the game.

In a game now full of mercenaries and prima donnas, guys like Bomber are few and far between – imagine his effort transplanted into talents like shiftless Stephane Guivarc'h, narky Marco Negri or even £12 million new man Tore Andre Flo? They'd be untouchable! It's guys like John Brown who deserve testimonials and who deserve our applause, no matter who we support.

Late on, I return home to find Carolyn asleep. I decide not to wake her to ask how her day's been.

Monday, 26 March 2001

On business in Edinburgh, I grab a lunchtime curry with Craig Levein. He's working away quietly at Hearts, building his own team brick by brick and doing it the right way – he's already told those he doesn't fancy that they can look for a new club.

Unfortunately for the boys at Firhill, JL has not done likewise. They still haven't been spoken to and there's no sign of any announcements. I'm sure the writing's on the wall for one or two, probably including Moorie, who's been no nearer a game lately than the odd run as a sub. However, the longer JL leaves off speaking to those he *does* rate the more chance of them having been tied up elsewhere. It's a dangerous game of poker.

Later, I get a phone call from the legend that is PK. He's right on course for that sixth successive promotion after 5–1 and 3–0 wins in their last two games propel Brechin to the top of the Third Division. He's struck gold again!

Tuesday, 27 March 2001

No trip to Dumfries tonight. I'm laid low with a migraine. JC's fine about it but reminds me that, as I've asked for Thursday off, I better be working out on my own in between times. I tell him not to worry. Some Nurofen and a lie down will sort me out soon enough.

Whether that would work for wee Dunnsy's another matter. After a narrow defeat by Falkirk on Saturday, he and his new Airdrie mates have been gubbed 6–0 at Alloa tonight.

Alongside him in the firing line has been Ian Cameron, who's also finally taken the plunge to get out of Firhill and be unhappy at a different club – though both may be reviewing their choice of route after this. However, when the sting of such a hiding fades, I'm sure both will decide that it's still better than sitting in the stand. What use is a footballer who doesn't get to kick a ball?

Wednesday, 28 March 2001

What a beautiful relief – my head feels much better and I'm able to keep my word to JC by working out before watching Scotland play San Marino on the telly.

Carolyn's given me a new training route that she and her running partner Karen use. My lungs and legs feel fine through eight miles but my back's breaking. The base is agony but like the true hero/idiot I am I plough on and by the end my hammies are screaming as well.

By the time the game starts I feel like I've run 28 miles but the pain eases when Colin Hendry slams the first goal at 25/1. I'm getting good at this betting game. Pity I only have a fiver on him!

However, it wasn't that strike or even his magnificent second that would make all the headlines. Hendry ended the game – and possibly his international career if FIFA get involved – with an elbow in the throat of young San Marinese sub Nicola Albani.

Albani came straight off the bench and over to mark the big man at a Scotland free kick. And mark him he did, holding his shirt so tight Hendry lashed out once, twice, then a third time to free himself. Third time, he laid the boy out. Within 30 seconds of coming in, he was going back off strapped down on a stretcher after swallowing his tongue.

Neither the referee nor his assistants took any action and Hendry then went on TV to claim Albani had been play-acting. My immediate thought was that a quick look at the action replays before he shot his mouth off would have changed his tack.

It may well be that he would still have claimed to have been doing nothing more sinister than shrugging off an annoying opponent. But he would surely have realised how hard he'd hit the guy and that he most certainly was not play-acting. I've got no doubt that this matter is not over by a long chalk.

Thursday, 29 March 2001

No training on a night which belongs to Danielle. She makes her First Confession at church and it's such a big occasion that I need to be there. Although religion can be the source of so many problems, Danielle is very demonstrative about her thoughts and credit for this must go to her late Granda Dan, Carolyn's dad, who died a couple of years ago. His faith was incredible and he passed a great deal on to all his grandchildren.

Friday, 30 March 2001

Once again, the last working day of the month brings a frantic search for sales. We're not far from reaching our highest target ever and it's all hands to the pump to make up the deficit.

No game tomorrow, so for once I can take up the offer of a Friday night out. During the season I say no so often that eventually people stop asking but this evening I'm delighted to go to a leaving do for a girl called Louise Morrison who works for MacRoberts Solicitors.

After a great night with the young scamps, I left them to dance the night away and, although I'd missed my usual Friday night *Friends*, I found the traditional curry waiting. And although I'm not playing tomorrow because of the wedding, I'd also stuck to my normal day-before-game routine of a bowl of pasta for lunch. Old habits die hard, I suppose.

Saturday, 31 March 2001

Not a bad start to the day as Stephen Gerrard arrows a 30-yarder beyond Fabien Barthez to put Liverpool 1–0 up in this morning's big TV clash with Man U. That would be the same Stephen Gerrard I had a fiver on at 16/1. Told you I was getting good at this!

The rest of the day is about Gary and Gillian's wedding, where Carolyn and I marvel at Dani and Taylor in their roles as flower girls, though I have to admit my mind occasionally strayed to what was happening down at Palmerston. However, had Gillian not been as late as a Vinnie Jones tackle, I'd have been out of church long before my Queens mates were doing their warm-up. She's 35 minutes behind schedule and even the usually-cool Gary's starting to panic. Eventually a call to her home reveals that she's not had trouble with cold feet but her headgear.

So too Thistle, who secure promotion with a Peter Lindau treble at Stirling then try to see who can wear the silliest hat for the cameras. Why players subject themselves to this humiliation I'll never know – probably because I've never won anything – and I'm sure when they see the Sunday papers they'll be cringing. If any of them are conscious by then!

By the time the wedding snapper's done his bit, I've been in touch with Palmerston. My pal Sandra Brown had promised to keep her mobile switched on and at half-time she tells me Pretty Boy's equaliser has sent us in at 1–1. Paddy Atkinson's taken my place with new signing Stephen Walklate replacing him on the right. Our other deadline-day signing, keeper Jamie Campbell from Clydebank, is also in. Jamie's arrival seems to mean Davie Mathieson has played his last game for the club. He's been told he can leave on a free at the end of the season, with current number two Colin Scott kept on, possibly as coach. Davie won't be happy. He's been a good servant and I rate him highly. What will anger him most is that JC waited until after the deadline to tell him where he stands, so it'll be next season before he can play for anyone else.

Had I called Sandra back at half past four she'd have told me we were cruising thanks to goals from Il Prolifico and debutant Graeme Armstrong. But by the time I escaped the reception the game was over and she'd left a voice message saying it had finished 3–3 and we'd been lucky to hang on.

Elsewhere, Ginger Geordie has struck in the last minute at Stenny – his second late winner in six days – to almost certainly give Arbroath the second promotion place.

And, to the delight of almost everyone at the wedding, Rangers have lost at home to Dundee United and Celtic will be champions if they win three games in six days. If so, it will heap further embarrassment on the SPL, who have created the six-and-six split to ensure an exciting end to the season. The split comes next Saturday, so it looks like know-all Roger Mitchell didn't bank on the Midas touch of Martin O'Neill – or the total collapse of Rangers. Back to the drawing board, Rog!

And back to the reception for me, where everyone has a great night, especially Dani and Taylor, who, like their dad, are never off the dance floor. I may not have been flying up and down the wing today but I've probably sweated twice as much jiving about in a kilt. Don't tell JC, though – he'll introduce the Dashing White Sergeant at training . . .

TEN

ALTHOUGH I MISSED yesterday's game, I've still been on club duty this weekend after JC asked me to go on this afternoon's *Daily Record* march against drugs in Glasgow.

Every club in Scotland was meant to be represented but there were very few players on show. Apart from myself, I only saw Ronald de Boer of Rangers. That's the first and only time *we'll* ever be mentioned in the same breath.

I took Dani with me and it's a shame she was oblivious to some of the adults she was mixing with. When I tried to explain who the Lisbon Lions were, that they were heroes of her papa and grandad, she couldn't work out how such old men could be such good footballers. All she could ask was: 'Are they better than Henrik Larsson?'

The day itself belonged to thousands of ordinary people who demonstrated their anger at the drug culture now evident in our society. I hope this is something else both Dani and Taylor remain oblivious to for a long time.

What I've been oblivious to is the fact that I was meant to call JC tonight to find out the arrangements for Tuesday's game at Stranraer. I don't realise until ten o'clock when I'm soaking in a bath. By the time I get out it'll be too late. Shit!

I'm not sure why I'm so bothered because Car Wash has already told me when we've to be there. Maybe it's just the fact that in football it's always better to double-check, that you take nothing for granted. Or maybe missing another game's made me more aware of how hard it might be to get back in. This hobby of mine's worrying me a lot more than it used to.

Dani's eight today but Daddy's not there to wake her with a kiss. It's also our monthly sales meeting, so she's still sound asleep by the time I'm leaving for work. I call her about 8.15 a.m. to sing 'Happy Birthday' and tell her Mum will take her out later to get a new bike. She set off for school older and wiser.

Next call, JC. He wants to know how my Saturday went but I'm more interested in his. He says he was relieved with a point after being under the cosh for the last half-hour. He also tells me to be at Stair Park for quarter past six tomorrow night. He doesn't hint at what his team will be but my hunch is I'll start on the bench at best.

Good news from today's meeting is that we've had a record month. The news sends me home happy to see my girls – Carolyn, Dani, Taylor, Saint Isabel and mum-in-law Margaret. We're eating at Guidi's tonight and Carolyn's taking Dani and her pals to a movie on Saturday.

I'll miss that outing as well. I'll be back at Firhill, hopefully trying to stop Thistle winning the very title I started this season hoping to get my mitts on. Back in August, I'd dreamed of a day like this, the emotion of the crowd. Now I'm expecting what you'd call a warm welcome. Or, to put it another way, a slaughtering.

Tuesday, 3 April 2001

Bench it is. McKeown is named No. 12 and it's no surprise. All day I'd felt I wouldn't start and I can't argue with the decision. While I'm getting changed, though, JC sidles over.

'Make sure you get a good warm-up, Des.'

'Aye?'

'Yeah, I've only left you out because you missed training all last week as well as the game on Saturday. Be ready.'

Sure enough, just after half-time, on I go for Stuart King. Just call me wide and tricky. We're 1–0 down to Ian Harty's first-minute goal, we've come back into it, but haven't made any real chances. Would I make the difference?

Sorry.

We keep on dominating but the goal won't come, we get exposed at the back and Harty cashes in with his second of the night.

JC's happy with everything except the scoreline. He can't question our possession, commitment or attitude. It's just a shame about our defending of the two goals and our lack of luck up front. It's our first blank of the season.

On the way out, I see Billy McLaren and congratulate him on their win. He looks at me, looks at the Celica, and says: 'Nice car, Des – I'll need to check that your tax records are in order.'

It's a long two hours home.

Wednesday, 4 April 2001

Celtic beat Dundee tonight and now a win against St Mirren on Saturday will clinch the SPL title before the infamous split. Ian Harte also scores the first goal for Leeds against Deportivo La Coruna at 12/1.

Two lovely bits of news, especially with me having a fiver on Harte. If I was having as much joy on the pitch as I am at the bookies I'd be playing for Real Madrid.

Thursday, 5 April 2001

Saturday's game isn't just on my mind. Everyone I meet seems to want to talk about it – or, more accurately, how I feel about being on the wrong side of it. They all want to know how I feel about missing out on a championship medal and assume I regret leaving Firhill.

But no matter the irony looming up at me, I still feel the same as I did back in November. Playing still matters more than just being a part of a successful club. I know I wouldn't have forced myself back in at Thistle. Big Archie's been outstanding, hasn't been injured and has missed one game through suspension since I left. In fact, the whole team has been pretty much the same as last week for months now. I'm delighted for Archie, for all of them.

I did the right thing getting out when I did and nothing that happens on Saturday will change my mind.

But I can't say I'm buzzing right now. If I'm honest, I'm longing for the summer. It's not that I'm not enjoying my football, more that I can't wait for next season. I want Queens to finish as high as possible, get a good break and have a real crack at it next time round. I've struggled to get my fitness right ever since I was first left out at Firhill in October. You can't keep your standards up if you're not playing, all the good of pre-season is lost. All those postponements we had soon after I moved to Palmerston didn't help either. It's all been a bit of a damp squib. Now

I just want it to be the end of June so I can start all over again.

Mind you, that's where I came in on Page One. The uncertainty. The not knowing. The desperation to prove yourself at the end of one season to win a place come the next. I need a good run-in to show JC what I can offer the club. It's just odd that I'm hoping to start doing it at Firhill.

After training tonight it appears I might start but in an unusual position. We shaped up in a 3-5-2, with me in centre-midfield and Car Wash at the back. Car Wash? A libero? Gimme a break!

Of course, JC might just be toying with a few ideas. It might mean nothing come Saturday. I certainly hope the quality of the session isn't a pointer either – it's dreadful. The squad seems less motivated than usual and the whole thing feels slack. Is a long season taking its toll?

We can only hope attitudes and performances are better on Saturday as we try to keep Thistle's champagne on ice. If they beat us and Arbroath drop points at home to Stirling, my old team wins the title.

If I'd written it as a chapter in a novel the publishers would have laughed at me.

Saturday, 7 April 2001

Champagne corks popped all over Glasgow today. But not at Firhill.

Two hours after Celtic secured their 37th championship with a 1–0 win over St Mirren, we silenced the Jags fans by beating them 2–0. It was their first home defeat and the first time they'd failed to score on their own patch. The fact that Arbroath drew with Stirling only rubbed in their disappointment and disbelief.

I'd like to say I masterminded their downfall from my new central-midfield berth. I can't, though. We did go 3-5-2 but Car Wash was in his usual place and I was at left wing-back. Still, at least JC picked me.

Before the game I went round all the Thistle boys plus JL, GC, Walter the Vet, Ricky, Chico and Disco Dave to congratulate them on promotion. I wanted to get it out of the way before concentrating on my own job.

JC had obviously put a lot of thought into stopping them and his plans worked perfectly. We got at them for the first 20 minutes and on 23 we got a double break. First, Stevie Doc handled on the line and was sent off. Then, Il Prolifico stuck away the penalty. I couldn't believe Doc's bad luck – he was only just back in the side after missing most of the season with his dodgy ankle. Still, that's what he gets for being gorgeous.

Thistle were rattled and we never let them off the hook. We closed them down, took the game to them and but for an unbelievable miss by Hawkey – straight in front of goal, nobody to beat, screws it wide – we'd have gone in two up.

We've always got Il Prolifico, though. Ten minutes after the break he dived to head the second and by then we might have been four or five up.

The contest was over just after the hour when Nally was red-carded for a second booking and Tino Hardie followed him for mumping at ref Brian Cassidy, who spent the rest of the game getting pelters from the punters while we played keep-ball.

We could have scored more but two was enough. We went off bouncing and I was delighted with my own performance. It was a sweeter victory than most. No gloating message on the dressing-room mirror from Ricky and Chico this time.

The Aitken Suite was subdued and I took great delight in trying to liven it up. To be fair, most of them took it well considering they'd not only been beaten but had found out Arbroath had done their best to hand the league over. Most were big enough to congratulate me on our win and wish me luck for the future.

It had hit me that with Thistle going up it might well be my last visit on football business, so I made sure I said my farewells to the usual suspects – Aitken Suite dollies Laura, Jessie, Marie, Carol, Jean and Bernie, plus my pal Angela McPhie and her dad Billy. I think I'm turning her into a closet QoS fan. Secretly, she seemed chuffed with the result.

Afterwards, I gave Moorie a lift home and a counselling session. He's demented at how things have panned out and is at a seriously low ebb. This summer will be crunch time for him – I think he's resigned to going part-time and getting a real job.

No teetotal nonsense tonight. Carolyn and I have a glass of champagne to celebrate a good day at the office and Celtic winning the league.

Tuesday, 10 April 2001

It seemed like the right thing to do at the time. But now, 300 miles later, I wish I hadn't bothered. All the way from Aberdeen to Dundee to Dumfries – and for what? The worst training session yet, that's what.

On Saturday I'd told JC I'd either be late down tonight or missing altogether because of business commitments in the north-east. I drove to Aberdeen on Sunday night after a day with the girls then went on a few appointments with Ray Hardie yesterday. I nipped into Pittodrie to see if my old QoS team-mates Jamie McAllister or David Lilley were around, but no joy. However, I did meet an old pal of Ray's in Jim White.

Jim works in the commercial department, but it also turns out he and Carolyn's uncle Tom Morrison signed as players with Aberdeen on the same day in the late 60s. He showed me round then told me Lills was playing in an Under-21 game at night, so I went back to watch. Today I headed down to Dundee knowing I'd have to put in a hell of a shift to get finished and make it to training. But, good pro that I am, I decided to put the foot down and get there.

Now, as I write this shortly before midnight, it all seems a hell of a waste of time and energy.

It wasn't the travelling that sickened me. It was the training. It was a shambles – and I'm not the only one who thought so. Almost everyone reckoned it was poor stuff and were moaning that the nights when everything was short and sharp seem to have disappeared. Everything feels drawn-out and laborious these days. JC had said after Saturday that if that was how we played after a session as poor as Thursday's, he'd have to give us a shocker every night. I piped up that if that was the case we'd have tied up the league long ago.

Sadly, it's getting no better. As I looked around me, the words 'demob' and 'happy' sprung to mind.

Thursday, 12 April 2001

Who knows, maybe the season's also taking its toll on JC and Scotty, but they seem to have run out of ideas. Maybe they're looking forward to a break and a fresh start as much as I am.

Whatever the reasons, the boys are demented. With five games to go, there's little or nothing to be gained by bleaching us or hammering tactics into us. This is the time you look forward to small-sided games to keep up your sharpness and, just as important, your enjoyment. Sadly, the staff don't seem to share this view. Things were marginally better tonight but that's not saying a hell of a lot.

Many of the boys aren't helped by having contracts on their minds. Those about to become free agents want to talk turkey, but JC's not going out of his way to put minds at ease. The only guy he's spoken to is Il Prolifico and even then discussions only started tonight. The rest need to wait and see.

Thankfully, I have a contract for next season. But if I didn't I'd be pushing hard to find out where I was in the plans. I like to have things discussed, agreed and signed well before the summer so I can prepare properly for the next campaign.

Before all that, though, we have Arbroath down here on Saturday. It's a big one for me after their teenage winger Kevin Heenan played so well when they beat us 5–2 the other midweek. I'll have my work cut out but I'm up for it.

Saturday, 14 April 2001

A 1–0 victory and Heenan anonymous? Sounds like I had a good day.
Wrong.

Unfortunately I had hee-haw to do with keeping the boy wonder quiet.

I was on the bench.

Around half-one, as we watched the final minutes of Man U. v Coventry, Wazza shouted that the gaffer wanted a word. Now, to the short of confidence it's the worst thing you can hear before a game because it usually means you're not playing. To me, however, it meant JC was probably going to bounce some tactical idea or other around. And in a way I was right. His tactical idea was that, although I had played brilliantly – his word – at Firhill last week, he wanted someone with a bit more pace against Heenan.

What a boot in the gonads.

OK, so I'm no Linford Christie, but speed's not everything. I argued that last week's performance entitled me to pit my wits against a boy who was good but no Luis Figo. He's 18, just starting out, and although he's got promise he can't be called exceptional yet. If I'm not good enough to even get the *chance* to shackle him, what does that say about me? JC simply came back saying he felt that Heenan gave me 'one or two problems' in the 5–2 game. I agreed, but said we were playing a different system now and it'd counter their style of play better.

It didn't matter. The decision had been made.

Paddy Atkinson switched wing-back roles to take my position, with Stephen Walklate coming in on the right. It was the only change to a team which last week had gained its best result of the season.

JC started his team talk by explaining his decision and also said that from now on if anybody was unhappy with any of his decisions they would be free to leave the club. From this he was suggesting I hadn't taken the decision well and had caused him problems. I wasn't happy with this inference and resolved to speak to him later.

As soon as the staff had gone, the guys wanted to know what had happened. I told them it was no big deal but Il Prolifico immediately declared I was to be on 24-hour suicide watch. I suggested it should be 24-hour murder patrol.

I've never felt less emotion during the warm-up for any game. I was absolutely gutted. It was the biggest slap in the face of my career and it had demoralised me. For the first time, I wondered if all the sacrifices were worth it, if I'd really miss the game that much if I chucked it. Or, worse, if it would miss me.

After 14 years of giving my all to whoever I'd played for, I was going through the motions. It was a desperately unhappy time. The game seemed to go around me in a blur.

My head was still mince when JC shouted me five minutes from half-time.

'Think you can do a job for me at right wing-back?'

'Course.'

'Right, I want you to match Mercer and challenge him in the air. Try to get him working back the way as well.'

'OK, when?'

'Half-time.'

Now I got down to serious business, a proper warm-up. I was part of it again and my mind was back on the job. Chuck it? Forget it! We had a game to win. And I had a manager to prove wrong.

Walklate had struggled against Mercer, who's the tallest winger in the world at about 6 ft 14in. and, although it meant we'd now have a right-footer at left-back and vice-versa, I was better suited than Paddy to take him on for high balls. So, at least I was good for something.

The second half flew by and Arbroath had the better chances but in the last minute Dean Muir volleyed in to win us the game and hand Thistle the league a week after we'd denied them it. They'd only drawn at Forfar but Arbroath had needed to win and now at last JL and the boys could open the bubbly.

JC made a big play of how well I'd done and that it had underlined his squad philosophy. Players, though, don't want squad philosophies. They want to play. I want to play. His words of encouragement were lost on me. I was still haunted by what he'd said pre-match. I went and saw him, asked him what he'd meant by implying I'd caused problems after being dropped. He apologised and said it wasn't what he'd meant, that he'd only wanted it known that anyone who's unhappy with his decisions can come and discuss them or ask away. Maybe. But it sure as hell didn't sound like it.

Down in the Houliston Lounge, fans wanted to know why I'd been left out. I said it was a tactical decision and it won us the game. It was the truth but they weren't convinced.

Car Wash and I were joined on the journey home by The Silhouette. He hinted that he might be coming back to Palmerston in the summer when his contract's up at Arbroath. He'd be a good signing and the fans would be happy but it might mean me needing a divorce lawyer. Big Jimmy likes the odd night out or fifty.

Meanwhile, I have a week to wonder whether or not I'll get a start next week. Suppose it depends how quick Stenhousemuir's right-winger is.

Monday, 16 April 2001

Played golf today, then bought a mountain bike.

I've never felt closer to the end of my playing career.

OK, so it was only 18 holes with my brother Gerry, brother-in-law Bryce and their pal Paul McLaren, but the walk and the relaxation gave me time to think about the future.

See, I've always reckoned that when I stop playing, the natural progression would be to move into coaching or management. At 28, I was probably one of the youngest guys to get the full set of SFA badges. I was laying down markers for when my legs gave up, teeing up the chance to carry on in the game I love. Now, just three years on, I'm asking myself if I still want the same things.

This book has been a confession of how, for 14 years, my life has been dedicated to football. For 12 of those years, Carolyn has played second fiddle to a hobby – and no matter how well she takes things, it isn't fair on her, nor does it create a healthy family life for Dani and Taylor. I've missed out on seeing their little personalities develop because when I'm not working I'm training and when I'm not training I'm playing. It's not right.

There's a few years left in the old legs yet but all of a sudden I'm stuck with the dilemma over what to do when it all ends. Management or coaching seemed natural before but now I see it would only prolong my time away from the girls. Do I want to put myself and them through that?

And what about other stuff I'd like to do? How would football affect that? When would I get time for days like this on the golf course, to see Dani and Taylor ski, to drop everything and go on holiday simply because I fancied? I've always wanted to run the London and New York marathons. Would it ever happen? Would anything ever change? I'd love to play golf more often. I might actually be a decent player if I got in more than five or six rounds a year. But if I had the time, would I spend more and more of it hitting a smaller ball than before? Would that be any fairer on Carolyn and the kids? Probably. At least I wouldn't be two hours away at the same time every second night.

As for the mountain bike, that's a significant symbol of my current thoughts. It'll keep me fit, sure, but that pales in comparison to the other reason for having it. Taylor can now ride a two-wheeler and she and Dani are always asking when we can go on a family bike run. That's when it hits me that I don't do what normal dads do and that I need to change. I need to involve myself more in their lives as they grow up. Because it won't be long before they've grown up and left me.

Do I sound old before my time? Perhaps. But it's just how I'm feeling. Football has limited my family life so much that decisions need to be made before I *am* past it.

Easier said than done, eh?

It's all right having good thoughts on the golf course but when push comes to shove I'm not sure if I can give it all up. There has to be a compromise.

And you might be reading it.

My fortnightly column for the *Scottish Sun*, coupled with writing this book, has added journalism as a way to stay involved in the game. I'm loving it and hope sports editor Steve Wolstencroft will let me have another crack next season. Who knows what might be next?

One way or another, I just can't see myself being out of the game.

The fire always burns for your first love.

Tuesday, 17 April 2001

Bugger. Migraine.

I'm at an appointment in Glasgow when my vision goes blurred and then the headache bites. It can only be described as like having your head locked in a vice that's tightened every time you see a light or try to move.

My first thought is that it'll clear up in time for me to make training.

Then I get real and realise there's no chance. I call JC and tell him I'm phoning for a doc, then go home to bed.

I'm getting headaches – usually these bloody migraines – more and more frequently ever since a serious concussion last season. The concerns I had after collapsing in the street back in June have returned and I need to find out what's up once and for all.

By the time I'm home the pain is unbearable and I lie down in blissful darkness. Carolyn phones for a doctor's appointment. Can you believe it, the first they've got is 4 May. You wouldn't need to be ill, would you?

The only lift at the end of a rotten day is the news that Berwick beat Arbroath 1–0 tonight to open up the promotion race once again. Both of them plus Stranraer and ourselves are now in the frame to go up with Thistle – and with the other three all still to play each other and Thistle, we must have a chance.

Wednesday, 18 April 2001

Feeling much better today, so I went for a half-hour's run on the bike. Good exercise, except for your jacksie. It feels like the boot up the bot JC gave me on Saturday!

Still, my arse hasn't been skelped as hard as Sir Alex Ferguson's was tonight. Man U were beaten in Munich and are out of the Champions League. My one comfort from the game is that even at the top level some of the mistakes are unbelievable. Sometimes seeing the top players struggle helps you deal with your own poor performances.

Arsenal are also out but Leeds are in the semis. It's been a good year for the English teams and Celtic and Rangers need to go some to get anywhere near their standards next season.

Thursday, 19 April 2001

The shortlists for the SPFA Player of the Year Awards are out today. I'm delighted that my two nominations – Trigger and Tino – are both up for the Second Division prize – along with an old Firhill mate, Isaac English. Last but not least is Pretty Boy, a fantastic achievement for a guy in his first senior season.

My Young Player of the Year vote, which covers all the leagues, went to Celtic's Stilian Petrov. His contribution to Celtic's season before his horrific leg break was sensational considering a miserable first season in Scottish football. I'm sure he'll lift the trophy.

As for *the* Player of the Year? No contest. If Henrik Larsson doesn't win it after the season he's had I'll run naked from Glasgow to London.

A scary thought? Maybe, but not as scary as training tonight.

Yet again the content was poor and performances matched it. The pitches down at the Tech are drying out quickly and the bobbles this creates don't help anyone. Neither does the thought that these are the conditions we'll play the rest of our games in.

Fans don't appreciate just how tough it can be to get the ball down and play on solid surfaces – a pretty solid reason for forgetting the idea of summer football. Few clubs could afford the sprinkler systems they'd need to keep pitches lush enough to knock it about on.

About the only thing that makes the night worthwhile is the crack in the car going down – Car Wash, keeper Colin Scott and I going down memory lane on the M74, talking about what happened to the guys we grew up playing alongside.

Colin and I are the same age and names flew fast and furious. Sadly, most schoolboy superstars didn't fulfil the potential of their teenage years and this took up most of the conversation.

Best of our lot was Deano Connolly. He signed for Arsenal and should have been a megastar but, like so many boys, he never cracked it. John Bishop, Mark MacAdam and Scott Kopel at Dundee United could tell the same story. So too Jim Frith and Jim Milligan of Rangers, John Dickson of Aberdeen, Raymond McStay, Stevie Duff, Stevie Brennan, Dugald McCarrison, Martin Melvin and Jamie McEwan at Celtic, my old pal Tid at Villa, Motherwell's Stevie Cadden and Stevie Bryce and Clyde's John Devlin, Stevie Quinn and Paul McLaughlin.

None of these guys are still playing senior football. It'd be easier to list my peers who *are*, the lucky few like Motherwell's Scott Leitch, Wigan's Stuart Balmer, Livingston's Gerry Britton, Gary McSwegan and Stevie Fulton at Hearts, Nally at Thistle and St Johnstone pair Stevie Frail and Paddy Connolly.

I suppose the only guy who lived out all our dreams was Paul Lambert. He's worked his way up from the groundstaff at St Mirren to Motherwell to that incredible Champions League triumph with Borussia Dortmund to being indispensable for Celtic and Scotland. Not bad for a boy from Linwood.

And so the names kept coming, the ones who could and should have made it, until Colin and I realised we were doing all right still to be involved into our thirties. We may not be superstars but at least we're alive and kicking. I don't know whether to feel happy for myself or sad for football.

Saturday, 21 April 2001

Did I say alive and kicking? Today, my career may as well be dead and buried.

Humped 3–1 by Stenhousemuir on a Palmerston pitch that made the Tech look like a bowling green, we came off to find Berwick, Stranraer and Arbroath had all won and our promotion hopes were knackered with a capital F. I was back on the left side and did myself no favours, though who did? The lucky ones were Car Wash and Pretty Boy, who realised through suspension how much they're needed.

There was no spark, no threat, no appetite and no complaints at the result. Stenny were first to most loose balls and Isaac English punished our slackness with two goals. Il Prolifico got one back but we didn't deserve to be in the game.

JC and Scotty didn't miss us and hit the wall. They were truly disappointed in our effort and application, but no one needed to be told – especially after the reaction from our fans at the end. I've never heard a reaction as negative and angry in either of my spells at Palmerston and you couldn't blame a single one of them for taking the hump.

More than a few lads went home wondering where they now fit into JC's plans for next season and knowing they only had three games left to regain some Brownie points.

I was one of them.

I'm starting to wonder if the gaffer is regretting his decision to sign me and whether my future's as secure as I'd want it to be. Paranoia? Who said paranoia?

Tuesday, 24 April 2001

Aberdeen to Dumfries again today. I could have seen it far enough. Another 300-mile trek with as much excitement at the other end as a trip to a piles specialist. Except that our training's a bigger pain in the arse right now.

I'm not a negative guy. Some guys could start a fight in an empty house: I could start a party. I just can't see light at the end of our long, black tunnel of shambolic sessions. As I start south, I'd bet my house on us all going through the motions again, muttering under our breath about how crap it all is.

I'd have lost my house, as it happens.

Tonight we have a full-scale practice match on Palmerston, the perfect pick-me-up for any player and especially one who's just done a day's work. Ask any footballer if they'd rather play a game or train and they'll all tell you the same. Games, please, sir!

Scotty picks teams and hands out bibs. It looks like he and JC have shaped up Saturday's team and I'm in it. A notable absentee is big Ronnie. That's ominous.

We play three half-hour sessions and, despite a stunning headed goal in the second, I'm rested from the third while most of the others stay on. What does that mean? I'm starting to second-guess everything they're doing with me.

After training, JC wants to speak to a few of the boys about next season. Dean Muir comes back out with the news that his contract's not being renewed. Others are saying nothing, but I have my fears for them. We'll maybe find out more come Thursday.

When JC's free I corner him for a word.

'Stevie Docherty's been on the blower to me. Asked me to drop his name in with you.'

'Really? I'd be interested, but why'd he want to leave Firhill?'

'He hates it. Says he'll only stay as a last option.'

He's one of a growing number who can't face another season's training under JL and GC, First Division or not. He'll have choices but he says he likes how we play and likes the guys. I've filled him in on the good atmosphere in the dressing-room and the refreshing training sessions. I'll keep the recent blips from him. No point putting the boy off. And neither will I discourage him even though his arrival would ease me out as best-looking player at the club.

JC asks me to have a word with him at the PFA dinner on Sunday night. It's always a great night for whispers in ears as wanted men are nobbled by managers and their spies. I wonder who'll tap me up? Barcelona would be nice but I've heard bad things about Juve.

The promotion scramble takes a new twist tonight with Forfar getting a 1–1 home draw with Arbroath, who now face a massive game at home to Berwick on Saturday. If they win, they're up. If they lose, Berwick can go up on the final day at home to Stranraer. Sadly, my mate Geordie Rowe was sent off tonight and will miss the biggest game of his season – maybe even his career. Guys like us don't get chances like these too often. Then again, Scottish football has no place for hammer-throwers. Especially ginger ones.

As for Forfar, they're second-bottom and go to third-bottom Queen's Park on Saturday needing to win to retain a chance of survival. We will relegate bottom club Stirling Albion if we get a point at Forthbank.

Thursday, 26 April 2001

Another afternoon spent behind the wheel – but this time I loved every minute. Carolyn and I went to Knockhill Racetrack in Fife to use up the prize I won in the raffle at the Press Ball a few weeks ago. We race single-seaters, rally cars, sports cars and get some time spinning around the treacherous skid pan.

And yet none of it prepared me for my experience on the M74 after training tonight.

I'm driving home with Car Wash, Il Prolifico and Martin 'Gattuso' Hughes when Norman Bates appears in my rear-view.

Near Moffat we passed a guy sitting in the middle lane in a white Peugeot. He pulls out behind us and flashes his lights at us. Straight off I reckon it must be someone who knew me, so I let him pass and had a look. He stares ahead, no wave. He pulls in, so I'm behind him again. Ten miles on, he slows, I pull out, go past. He pulls out behind and flashes. Then on goes his full beam, right in my rear-view. I pull in but this time he sits tight in the fast lane.

About Abington, where it's pitch black, he goes back to his sidelights. Then, suddenly, he's going at 100 mph with no lights on at all. He can obviously still see me but we can't see where he is. By this time I've gone across to the inside lane and am coming up behind an artic lorry. I indicate to move out but the Peugeot suddenly flicks his lights on and is level with me, two lanes across. When I overtake the lorry, I'm now behind the guy. He puts his hazards on. I call the cops and thankfully get off to drop the guys at Strathclyde Park.

The guy was off his trolley and it's just as well we'd had our best session in months or he might have really upset us.

The full night was five-a-sides, exactly what we'd been crying out for. Even better, my team – including Il Prolifico and three kids – won all three games. It was knackering but a hell of a lot of fun.

Then it all got serious for some of the lads.

After Dean's free, Gattuso and big Ronnie have been released. Ronnie didn't even show face tonight. I'm sure JC still hasn't made up his mind about some others and that the last three games might be their last chance saloon.

I don't want it to become my local.

Friday, 27 April 2001

At the other end of the football scale, a career is also being ended.

Colin Hendry looks to have played his last international after FIFA banned him for six games for the San Marino elbowing incident. I still believe if he'd admitted the offence straight after the game, he'd have got off more lightly. At the same time, though, I feel sorry for Colin. What he did happens all the time and very few players can honestly say they've never lashed out in frustration, whether at having their shirt tugged or simply being booted up in the air. Hendry clearly hurt the boy badly, though, and for him to suggest otherwise and for Craig Brown to then try to deflect attention from the incident by attacking San Marino for fouls *they* had committed was an act of folly. A simple sorry from both men would have defused the situation. Hendry might still have been banned – rightly – but I believe he'd have been given the sentence his offence deserved. Had the referee taken action, he'd have got one game, two at most. Instead, FIFA gave a wholehearted player the punishment they felt Scotland's attitude deserved.

As my old boss Billy McLaren often said, what goes around comes around.

Saturday, 28 April 2001

Ten to five and JC's much happier, even if few others around Forthbank share his feelings. We've just ground out a 1–1 draw that sent Stirling down to Division Three. Pretty Boy came back from suspension to put us ahead with an unbelievable volley – and then spoiled it by getting together with Andy Aitken for the most ridiculous dance routine since *Saturday Night Fever*. Except that no drunk at a wedding will ever, ever copy it.

The second half belonged to Stirling, desperate men bombarding our goal and Craig Feroz finally breaking through. It wasn't enough. We held on and JC praised us for burying them.

I was much happier today, sharper and fitter for 90 minutes, my heading and passing back to their best and my tackling as crisp as the onslaught required. Hopefully it's enough to show the gaffer I should be part of his plans. I'm sure I'm not the only one.

At the death, there was a strange hush from the home fans, as if gathering their thoughts on their fate, before they broke into applause for players who had given their lot. Though maybe if they'd gone at it as hard all season they wouldn't be relegated.

Forfar, meanwhile, have given themselves a real chance of escaping by winning 2–0 at Hampden. We now play both in the next week and if I could hand-pick a survivor it'd be Queen's – they're closer to home and you get to play at the national stadium. Then again, if these things were decided on locality, we'd be playing derbies against Newcastle, Sunderland and Middlesbrough.

You can but dream. And occasionally, as Arbroath found out this afternoon, they come true.

Ginger Geordie, The Silhouette and Marvellous Stevie Mallan will be giving it pelters at the annual Supporters' Club Dance tonight after they beat Berwick 2–0 at Gayfield. I'm chuffed to bits for my old pals.

Livingston's boys will be celebrating too after they tied up the First Division with a win at Inverness and started preparing for life with the millionaires. Joining us in the poor house, though, are Alloa and Morton – if, of course, Morton survive long enough to take their place in the Second Division.

The only championship still to be decided is the Third Division, with Cowdenbeath, Hamilton and PK's Brechin all still in the hunt. Hamilton are favourites – they have a game in hand and the other two meet at Central Park next Saturday – but it gives PK the chance of his sixth successive promotion party.

The SFL computer has played a blinder this season. You couldn't have scripted some of the fixtures over the last couple of weeks. Meaningless games? Forget it!

Sunday, 29 April 2001

Kilt pressed and ready for the biggest night out of the season. It's the annual Scottish Professional Footballers' Association dinner and award ceremony. A glitzy Who's Who of our national game, a star-studded tribute to the men who thrill the masses with their breathtaking skills and heart-felt commitment.

OK, so it's actually an unholy bunfight that turns into the kind of vomit-splattered piss-up George Best would tut-tut at. But none of us would miss it for the world.

The day will go something like this. Teamloads will descend on Glasgow at lunchtime to watch the Old Firm game on telly and drink a lot. Then they'll have a bag of crisps and watch the Premiership game of the day and drink a lot.

Then they'll drink a lot more, stagger along to the Thistle Hotel, drink some more, pick at their dinner, make a lot of noise during the speeches, boo colleagues as they're presented with trophies, drink a lot, fight, go to the dancing in their tuxes and fall over.

Athletes, every one.

Anyway, I'd like to take a few moments before the carnage to pay tribute to a few prize-winning pals of my own. Guys who might never win PFA gongs but who deserve recognition for many different reasons.

Some are great players. Some might have been but for circumstances. Others would never have been great even under the circumstance that they were the only player left on earth after a hydrogen bomb dropped. Others are unforgettable for social reasons, some for anti-social reasons – but every one, and many more not mentioned here, help make the world of part-time Scottish football a wonderful place, win, lose or draw.

So without further ado, may I present my all-time Favourite Team-Mates XI . . .

1. Davie Mathieson, aka the Virgin – a tremendous goalkeeper who should have played at a much higher level than the Second Division. Possibly jinxed by involvement at Scotland Under-21 level. Still young enough to make it despite being freed by JC.

2. George Rowe, aka The Ginger God – every team needs a ginge as his mates at Clydebank, QoS and Arbroath will testify. It takes the pressure off us baldy guys. Also worth his weight in copper for a few goals from the back each season.

3. Andy MacFarlane, aka The Chippendale – a mate from my first spell at QoS and a George Michael lookalike despite being 4 ft 10 in. Fancied himself as a ladies' man until fiancée Gillian told him he wasn't. I only picked him so he could finally get a game at left-back.

4. Tom Callaghan, aka Tid – on his day, a tough, ball-winning central midfielder who could pass a ball and score goals. Unfortunately, that day was ten years and three stones ago. My only regret is not becoming a close pal years before I did. A gem, the life and soul of any party.

5. Jim Thomson, aka The Silhouette – the thinnest man in Scottish football and also owner of its tightest perm. With his all-year-round tan and white teeth, he'll tell you he's a ladies' man, but when he gets the odd look-in his patter's as sophisticated as his clearances. My room-mate first time at Queens and we drove to training together. Boring? My engine used to go to sleep on the M74.

6. Alan Archibald, aka (strangely enough) Archie – an Adonis who can also play a bit. The perfect foil in central defence for JT, as they are complete opposites . . . Archie's good-looking, talented, quiet and well-built. Main reason for me leaving Thistle. Once he had my shirt there was no way back.

7. John McLaren, aka Lazy Arse – brother of Killie's Andy and a sensational talent who could have done anything had he worked for it. Unfortunately, he ran as if the hairs in his arse were tied together and most of the time he didn't bother running at all. Juggling ability wouldn't have been out of place in a circus. Had he been Brazilian I probably wouldn't have known him.

8. Tommy Bryce, aka Twinkletoes – still going strong at 41 and 8. a guy I'd loved to have watched when he was 21. One of the most gifted players I've had the honour of playing alongside and it's a travesty he spent most of his career in the lower leagues. Also had enough faith to make me Thistle captain when he was manager and I have to thank him for that. A model pro, a genuine guy and a moaning-faced bastard!

9. Scott McLean, aka Trigger – my vote as PFA Player of the Year and the most complete striker I've ever played alongside. A great finisher, deceptively quick, strong as an ox and thick as a rhino sandwich. Does great justice to his nickname after the *Only Fools and Horses* dunce. If he believes how good he is and works hard he could play for Scotland.

10. Peter Weatherson, aka Pretty Boy – if Trigger is my complete striker, PB is next in line. An exceptional talent who desperately wants to reach the top and could get there. Sadly, makes Quasimodo look like Richard Gere.

11. Tommy Burns, aka TB – The perfect role model for any young player and a guy who certainly influenced me. Him playing in front of me in a trial game was the reason Celtic signed me. A tremendous ambassador for the game whose

karaoke party piece is 'Mack the Knife'. That and being left-footed are the only things we have in common.

Manager? Billy McLaren, aka Psycho – rescued my career by signing me for QoS from Albion Rovers. Knows when to kick you up the arse and when to pat you on the back. I really enjoyed my time under him and have the deepest respect for him. Also handy to know if you need back up in a fight.

And now the awards for The Worst Of Everything . . .

Worst patter? Jimmy Thomson – always have two Nurofen handy.

Worst hairdo? George Rowe – not so much the style as the colour. The ginge's ginge.

Worst dress sense? Ian McAuley of Stirling Albion – he used to have a Versace jacket that could have doubled for Clint Eastwood's poncho.

Worst breath? Trigger after a night out – you could get steaming when he talks to you.

Worst ability? Jimmy Thomson again – it's a miracle he made it senior. Looks like the Straw Man from *The Wizard of Oz* when he plays.

Worst taste in music? JT continues to sweep the boards – buys whatever is deemed to be trendy, no matter how pish. But actually listens to Classic FM on his way to games.

Worst night-out companion? Who else but JT – constantly opens his shirt to show off his 'build' to the lay-deez. Will one day realise they do not find stick insects attractive.

Worst room-mate? Jamie Smith at Thistle – two nights in Belfast and he never said a word, but did hog the TV remote.

Worst language? Allan 'Taxi Doors' Moore – quite happily splits up words by putting a swear word in the middle of it. Unbe-fucking-lievably crude!

Worst excuse for a goal? The Ginge for QoS v Stranraer a few years ago with a punch Lennox Lewis would have been proud of.

Worst six-pack? Tid has a keg.

Worst attitude? Johnny McLaren – so laid-back he was horizontal. Couldn't have cared if the team bus was heading for New Kilbowie or New Delhi.

Worst with money? The Ginge – tighter than two coats of paint.

About to move house again, so he's got Maureen taking the drawing pins out of the wallpaper for the flit. No wonder the guy's got more dosh than the Beatles.

Worst with women? Trigger – yes, even worse than JT. They stampede out of the room like frightened wildebeest.

Worst memory? PK – survives from terrible amnesia. Apparently he's never had a bad game.

Worst driver? Graham 'Car Wash' Connell – drives his ladymobile like a sports coupe. Fools absolutely no one.

Worst drinker? JT – two pints and he's Richard Gere, Charles Atlas, Rivaldo and Elvis rolled into one! Three and he's sleeping.

Biggest womaniser? Ronnie McQuilter – *if* you believe his tales. Comes across as Scotland's answer to Hugh Hefner, except richer. Thankfully now settling down as a one-man woman.

Most shameless groupie? Tid Callaghan's best mate Anthony Sermanni has been with him every step of the way from Aston Villa to Thistle. Most chairmen think they've actually signed two new players because within five minutes of Tid arriving Sermanni's in the lounge with the rest of the squad. Renowned throughout Scottish football for his devotion, he is a million-carat diamond and all-round good guy.

Worst moaner? Gus MacPherson of Killie is without peer – has been on at me all season about getting a mention in *Des's Diary*. An out-and-out egomaniac who would get that mention if the column was about players with less hair than me!

Worst personal hygiene? John Lambie always appears very well presented but that's solely down to his players. Never has shampoo, deodorant or aftershave yet smells like a Paris brothel and has hair like Lionel Blair. Once he's out of football he'll ming.

Worst habit? JT never used to wear pants under his shorts, which must have been lovely for the laundry ladies.

Worst singer? How will he get all these trophies home – JT quite literally murdered John Denver. Two nights after the thin man destroyed 'Take Me Home Country Road' at our house, we learned Denver was dead in a plane crash. He must have heard the rumours.

Anyway, with the official bit out of the road, it's back to the bunfight. You have to the say clubs get the players they deserve at their next training session after the SPFA do because most chip into the beer kitty and fuel an incredible bonding exercise. It's a great chance to spend proper time with your team-mates – especially for us part-timers – and with guys you usually only see over the trenches.

I hook up with the likes of big Derek Townsley, my old QoS buddy who's now at Motherwell but is being linked with a summer move to Hibs. Then there's my former Albion Rovers coach, the ex-Hibs and England striker Joe Baker, who receives a special achievement award. Davie McDonald, another ex-Rover and now a financial adviser, is there. So's Martin McBride, my old San Siro di Coatbridge pal who is now out of the game. His brother Michael is now physio at Livingston and may well be required tonight the way their players are still going at the drink.

The SPFA always have the awards before the dinner – probably because more people are still conscious that way – and there are no real surprises. Larsson is main man on the day he scored his fiftieth of the season, although I'd have thrown in a special prize for Lubo Moravcik, who scored the first goal in a 3–0 win at Ibrox at 14/1. Petrov won the Young Player award to a standing ovation, Livvy's David Bingham added the First Division gong to those from the Second and Third he'd won in previous years and East Stirling's young striker Stevie Hislop gets the Third Division honour.

Our division's award goes to Trigger, as expected, but I'm still delighted that our own Pretty Boy was there on the night as a nominee. His day will come, I'm sure of that.

JC's asked me to have a word with one of the other contenders, Stenny frontman Isaac English, to see if he fancies joining us. I'm also in the ears of Stranraer midfielder Billy McDonald and Berwick striker Paul Ronald. I'm fairly sure that by entrusting me with these confidences, the gaffer sees me as part of things for the future. Meanwhile, another JC signing target behaves in his customary style. The Silhouette is drunk before the awards are handed out. What am I talking about? He's been drunk since the final whistle yesterday. He spends most of the night foghorning 'Dessie Boooooy' across the hall. Maybe if I keep ignoring him he'll go away, although I've tried it for years and it hasn't worked.

After the ceremony, the food fights and the crack at the bar, it all shifts to Victoria's Nightclub for civilised conversation, backgammon – and the best story of the night, if not the century.

Livvy's Barry Wilson, an old pal from battles down many a wing, is telling anyone who'll listen about his ten minutes in the Scotland squad for the previous week's friendly in Poland. A couple of days later it made massive headlines in the *Scottish Sun* and the whole world was in on it. But hearing it from the extremely drunken horse's mouth was magnificent.

So. He's at home, upstairs with his wee girl Cara, when the mobile rings. His wife Alison picks up and shouts to him: 'Barry, Craig Brown's on the phone for you.'

And Barry shouts back: 'Aye, right!'

We'll let the man himself take it up from here . . .

'I thought the boy's were winding me up – well, you would, wouldn't you? – but took the call anyway and the voice says: "Barry, it's Craig Brown here, how's things?" I said I was fine but I think the way I said it he knew I thought it was a wind-up, so he says: "Listen, Barry, this is Craig Brown – I'm on to see if you can play against Poland on Wednesday."'

'So what did you say?' we all asked at once.

'Well, my first thought was that we had Airdrie at home on the Tuesday, right, and surely he would have known that. That made me surer it was a wind-up. He goes: "I'd like you to play wide-right if that suits" and I think, "That'd suit me just fine if you really *were* Craig Brown." Then he says: "I got your number from the physio Pip Yates and Jimmy Calderwood's okayed it."'

'But Jimmy Calderwood's not your . . .'

'I know. That's when I told him: "Craig, I don't play for Dunfermline. I play for Livingston."'

'And what did he say?'

'Nothing – the phone went dead. So right away I ring big Leish and ask if he's heard that Scotland want me. He says no and reckons someone's having me on. He was pissing himself. But I've just come off the phone to him when the mobile goes again – and it's Craig back on. He was mortified – he said he'd made a terrible mistake and was really sorry.'

'So what had happened?'

'He'd been trying to get hold of Barry *Nicholson*, hadn't he? So he's called Stevie Crawford to tell him *he's* in the squad and asks for Barry's number. But Stevie's not got it, so he says he'll phone Jason Dair for it. Trouble is, Jason's a pal of both of us, so when he goes into his mobile phone book, he's got two Barrys and . . .'

'He gives Stevie the wrong one?'

'Correct! So he goes back on to Craig with what he thinks is Barry

Nick's number and Craig ends up phoning me. I tell you, the ten minutes between his two calls were the most terrifying of my life – I was shitting myself.'

'But you must have been excited?'

'Aye – but I thought: "Look, Scotland are struggling for players, but surely not *that* badly. Why's he wanting me?" I said to Aileen: "I've been playing OK, but this is unbelievable!" I think she was even more shocked than I was. Anyway, when he told me what had really happened I was a bit disappointed but I had to be realistic. Me? Play for Scotland?'

'And was Broon OK about it?'

'Superb – we had a laugh but I think he was pretty embarrassed. If it was the best ten minutes of my life, it must have been the worst of his.'

Marvellous. I wonder how many times he'll re-tell that story before he's old and grey?

Monday, 30 April 2001

While the rest of Scottish football sleeps it off, I'm at work as normal.

It's a long, long day. I can't wait to get to bed, especially with a game as important as tomorrow night's at Forfar coming up.

Tuesday, 1 May 2001

After our monthly sales meeting, Car Wash and I hit hyper speed to Forfar, braking only to pick up Il Prolifico at Cumbernauld. We hit sunlit Station Park before the team bus.

When JC arrives I tell him I'm on the case with his signing targets. He seems happy, or at least he hasn't dropped me. I'm in at left-back.

By half-time we haven't given them a sniff and Pretty Boy has thundered us into the lead. We're in control.

Oh no we're not.

Forfar storm back to win 3–1 and leave Queen's Park all but down. Their coach John McCormack will be sick – as am I. Literally.

For the first time in my life, I vomit while I'm playing. I'd just told Stevie Pickering that I felt ropy as we came back out after the interval and he said he felt the same, when up it came. Everything. There I was, crouching down while the play raged on, everyone else looking at me like I was an alien. So nothing new there, then.

I can no more explain it than I can our collapse. JC wasn't down about the effort we put in but the mistakes at the back – and luckily none were down to me – were another story.

Scotty is heard to say: 'This won't happen next season . . .'

Saturday, 5 May 2001

Thursday was our last training session. Today the season will end.

One more ride on the roller-coaster that has been non-stop since June last year.

One more game in a season that has seen championship parties put on ice and relegation worries become a reality.

The final chapter in a campaign that never got started for me and was everything I feared it might be. It never got started because it was March before there was any pattern to the games I played in. Early on with Thistle I was left kicking my heels on the bench or in the stand. Then the weather bit hard just when I joined QoS. And since then my form hasn't been anywhere near what I'd have wanted. I need a good pre-season to put it all right.

I told JC this on Thursday before training when I asked him where I stood for next year. He said he'd be happy to have me here but that nobody was guaranteed a game. I asked if anybody had been guaranteed a game this season. He said no. From where I stood that meant no change and meant the only person who could guarantee I was playing every week was me. He agreed.

I tried to start proving it this afternoon on the right side of defence.

Which is, of course, the wrong side.

When he told me where I was playing, it could only mean one thing – Queen's Park had someone quick down our left and he didn't think my legs could cope. Instead, Paddy Atkinson was given the job of tailing young Kevin Finlayson. Wherever the boy went, Paddy went and I'd switch sides accordingly.

I suppose I was happy just to be playing but it seemed an odd set-up to have two full-backs playing on their weaker foot to accommodate the fact that one wasn't quick enough in the eyes of the gaffer. As it turned out, when the ball came near me it was usually at head height. Not that anything I did made much difference to a low-key performance. We lost 1–0, although the win was no use to Cowboy's team in the end. Forfar beat Stirling 3–0, so we witnessed our second relegation wake in a week.

I felt sorry for Cowboy, a coach who knows he'll lose his best players at the end of each season because they're amateur and can walk away. He can't even replace like for like by offering wages. He pays £4 a night expenses. The attraction for players is the chance to call Hampden home and the way Queen's look after their squad. The only amateur club in the business puts many professional outfits to shame.

There would be tears, too, in Brechin's dressing-room after a 2–1 defeat at Cowdenbeath kept them in the Third Division. No sixth promotion on the trot for PK, then. But joy for Hamilton, champions a year after being relegated thanks to that 15-point league punishment for their unpaid players going on strike.

My only reason to be happy on the season's final day is that it didn't all end in the same embarrassment as last year. No hook, no long walk to sulk alone in the dressing-room, no finding solace in Phil Collins' music.

But the defeat confirmed how much work needs to be done here over the summer. I am now totally focused on what I need to do. I must get supremely fit and put JC in a position where he simply can't leave me out.

It's been a bizarre season. So close to glory for the first time in my career, yet so far. I'm glad I left Thistle and played games rather than hang onto the coat-tails of a title-winning side. I've played 32 games, slogged through 109 training sessions, crunched 110,000 sit ups, pumped 18,000 press ups and put 20,000 miles on the car. Who knows how different it all might have been if fate had played another hand?

But no matter what, the sacrifices would all have been the same. I'd have still missed Carolyn and Taylor's birthdays. I'd have still been training on my wedding anniversary. I'd still have spent Mother's Day in Berwick. I'd have still missed the family skiing holiday to Andorra and had to give up my Christmas present from Carolyn, a trip to see Man U at Old Trafford in the Champions League. No matter what, there would still have been all the old uncertainties, the insecurities, the fall-outs with the missus, the buzzing highs and the numbing lows. No matter what, the commitment would still have far outweighed the financial reward. But you know what? I wouldn't change a thing. Next season's roller-coaster can't clank to a stop in front of me quick enough. I can't wait to strap myself in for the fifteenth time.

And I'll tell you something else. More and more players are ready to do it my way. Sadly, some will find themselves forced to, but I'd rather see them jump before they're pushed. It's simple economics – middle-of-the-road full-time football won't set you up for life.

They shouldn't feel ashamed of taking the plunge. I hope I've proved in this book that part-time *doesn't* mean second-rate. I believe guys like Moorie will soon be wondering why they didn't do it years ago.

Our own Il Prolifico has been with Queen's Park, Celtic and Bournemouth but has now decided, at 28, to earn an honest living. He's moved into advertising sales and, along with his wages at Palmerston, will do quite nicely. He's looking to the future. Football doesn't do that for you.

Hopefully more young guys with big ambitions and average ability will, like I did as a starstruck Celtic teenager, realise their limitations and think twice before signing full-time. The journeyman pro can either stumble from contract to contract and find himself 34 with nothing to fall back on. Or he can be like me and have his cake and eat it. A career, a pension *and* a game of football for money on a Saturday?

There's no debate. Don't give up the day job.

ELEVEN

Tuesday, 8 May 2001

THIS IS WHERE WE CAME IN. The end of season weigh-in.

A year ago tonight, I was on the scales at Thistle before facing an uncertain summer. And here we go again, this time at Dumfries.

To be honest, you could e-mail the club with your holiday dates and how heavy you are. There seems no need to make a 170-mile round trip for such formalities but obviously managers have their reasons for calling their squad together one last time. In JC's case, it was a chance to read us all a sermon. Trouble was, we sat down expecting it to leave us motivated. Instead, we went away totally demoralised.

This was the gospel according to a man who demanded better next time out. There was no room for negotiation. Take it or leave.

He told us all that for too many years at Queen of the South the players had been on easy street. He brought up the bonus paid to last season's team who avoided relegation by default when the league docked Hamilton 15 points. He vowed that whoever played for him would no longer benefit from failure. From next season, PFA dinner tickets would come out of the squad's own pockets. He told us there and then what the bonuses for promotion and even the title would be next season. Again, no room for negotiation. He wanted everyone to know before a ball was kicked what they could earn from success. He said he would speak to one person and one person only on any dressing-room concerns and that would be his club captain. Who that would be he did not say. The thing that hit all of us as we listened was that the squad might not be the same come July, so he'd have to go over all this again. So was this the best time to make the speech?

No matter, on he went. As he laid down the law, it became clear he was not a man who liked confrontation. His office door would not be open. Or rather, it would be open one last time at the end of the sermon – for anyone who didn't like his style to come and ask away.

It all begged the question: if this is what he was like handling a bunch of Second Division part-timers, what would he be like if he was managing highly-paid superstars? Would he have wielded the big stick to millionaires, or given them room for manoeuvre? I'd like to think if this was his style, it would remain his style. I wish him all the best with it as he moves up the ladder.

Me? I didn't go knocking at his door to ask for a move. But he told me I could have one if I wanted.

In actual fact, I only went in to chin him about the PFA business. My argument was that the club picking up the tab was a bit of goodwill that was appreciated by the lads. JC's argument back was that other clubs didn't do it. I told him that's why players at some other clubs weren't as happy to be there.

Then he hit me with it.

'Listen, Des, while you're here. If I'm being honest . . .'

Which worries me, because it makes me think that at other times he's not been honest.

'. . . I'm looking to sign another left-back. I don't see you as my first choice.'

I can't say I was shocked. I'd felt it coming, even if last Thursday he hadn't spelled it out when I'd asked him where I stood.

'I understand, Des, that at your age you want to be playing football every week. I can't guarantee you that, so if you want to look at moving, feel free.'

For the second time in a matter of days, I told him it wasn't his problem. I still knew the only person who could guarantee me a game was me. And that I'd be battering my guts out from tomorrow to do it.

But then again, didn't I promise myself that at Thistle?

THANKS . . .

To all the players and staff at PTFC and QoS for their co-operation with
this project.

To everybody at Oyez who have supported me through the last year and
in particular Reg, Ray, Stevie, Car Wash, Elvis and Dunky.

To Steve Wolstencroft for giving me the chance to write for the *Scottish
Sun* – and to Susan McLaughlin, sorry for being a pest.

To John Kirkby for the cover photo and to Tommy 'Really, Really Big
Club' Taylor for help with other pictures.

To all my clients for their motivation and especially to Susan Ross at
Arthur Andersen who planted the seed in my head to write this book.

To Pamela Gray, who typed the first 45,000 words of this book before I
learned to use a computer.

To my family for their support in everything I do. Thanks Vincent,
Helen, Claire, Gerry, Margaret, Kevin, Emma, Aidan, Veronica,
Bryce, Sean, David, Anne Marie, Stuart, Mary, Martin, Tony, Emma,
Tom, Jackie, Gary, Gillian, Gran, Annie, Twin and Papa Bear (Big
John).

To Saint Isabel and Saint Margaret, without whom I couldn't devote as
much time to football.

To Bill Leckie, who may be small in height but is enormous in talent,
huge in generosity and a giant of a friend. Thanks, wee man – without
you this would not have been possible.

To Melanie and little Georgia for letting Bill away with spending so
much time on all of this.

And most of all to Carolyn, Danielle and Taylor for putting up with me.
I love you all!